# A Life Worth Knowing

## A Chronological Harmony
## of the Four Gospels

# A Life Worth Knowing

## A Chronological Harmony
## of the Four Gospels

Compiled by

David R. Barrett

Fresh Ink Media

# A Life Worth Knowing:
# A Chronological Harmony of the Four Gospels
## by David R. Barrett

Published by Fresh Ink Media

ISBN: 978-0-9880768-5-3

~ ~ ~

This harmony was created using the **World English Bible (WEB)** translation which is in the Public Domain.

Cover design by Katharine Barrett, St. Catharines, ON

## DEDICATION

For Katharine, my beautiful wife and best friend, who walks hand in hand with me on this "big adventure" of finding His life in the words of the text and the musings of each other's heart.

For Meaghan, Hannah, Emily and Evan: May you continue to discover how the story of your life is meant to be a retelling of His.

And for Russ Moulds, who first taught me to love "the book," and who showed me that if you are willing to approach them without traditions or preconceptions, the scriptures will lead you to wonderful places where you are not supposed to go.

# CONTENTS

# Introduction

After reading the Bible for 35 years, I realized that I had a bizarre perception of the life of Jesus. I saw his life like a scrapbook. The Gospels were full of all these wonderful stories that sort of hung there by themselves, not really connected to a bigger picture or story. For me, the Parable of the Rich Man and Lazarus could stand on its own. It did not matter who Jesus was addressing. It did not matter when he spoke this parable. It did not matter where Jesus had just been or where he was going after he told this parable. All his teachings and miracles were this collection of independent, unrelated treasures.

Although I knew the Gospel stories, I did not know the story of the Gospels. This was particularly true for the time period from his baptism to the beginning of "passion week." Everything that he taught and did was just a vague string of disconnected events. *A Life Worth Knowing* is the result of my own shift from a scrapbook view of the Gospel to seeing Jesus' life as a beautiful, chronological story.

When I understand the flow of his life and story, he becomes much more real to me. There is the danger with all historical figures, that they become these plastic, unrealistic non-persons. When we separate historical figures from the drama of their life and story, they can be transformed into something that never actually existed. We encounter the power and uniqueness of Jesus as we watch him storm around the Galilee and Judea, confronting the oppressors, opposing the religious, healing the sick and demonized and reaching out with kindness to the marginalized. It is the story, not our church traditions, that brings us face to face with our passionate, untamed and glorious Savior.

I have put together this volume for three main reasons. First, I want to create a big picture backdrop that will provide a context for digging into the details of his life. There *is* value in just spending time with the Parable of the Rich Man and Lazarus, but it will be much more meaningful if we realize that Jesus spoke this parable when he was on the run for his life. And shortly after teaching this parable, he intentionally put himself into even greater danger in order to raise his friend Lazarus from the grave.

The reader will quickly realize that *A Life Worth Knowing* assumes that Jesus' public ministry lasted just a little over one year. This is not the traditional view. The most common opinion is that his public ministry lasted for 3 ½ years, although scholarly opinions can vary from a one year ministry to a twelve year ministry. I am not going to argue or try to defend my position except to say that after all of my reading and research (which certainly has NOT been exhaustive), I believe that the one year ministry makes the most sense, fits best with the Gospel accounts and creates a beautiful narrative for the life of Jesus. My main misgiving with the one year ministry theory has to do with John 6.4, which I address in the footnote for that portion of the text. Although I feel confident about the context that I have created, I also realize that I could be wrong.

The second reason for putting this volume together is to provide a chronological harmony of the gospels that will be enjoyable to read. I have a number of harmonies on my bookshelf and kindle which, in my opinion, have some very serious practical flaws. Many of the paper harmonies have formatting issues that make them less than inviting. Some are not offered in an e-book format. Those that are available as an e-book have very few options for navigating around the text in a way that enable the reader to stay grounded in the context of the story. Although placing the contents of Jesus' public ministry in a calendar format was a bit of an afterthought on my part, I would not be surprised if it winds up being one of the features of the book that the reader finds most valuable.

Lastly, I have put together this volume with the hope that it might help the church to know Him better. We need caution when it comes to how we approach the scriptures. The scriptures are not a reservoir of eternal life. They are a sign post that is meant to point and lead us to Jesus, the one who has and is eternal life. The scriptures are an invitation to relationship. Ultimately, the earthly life that Jesus lived is worth knowing because it can help us embrace the present reality of His life. That life is certainly worth knowing.

David Barrett
St. Catharines, Ontario
December, 2014

# A Short Note
# on the Jewishness of Jesus

One of the challenges of reading something that was written 1900 years ago is understanding and appreciating the cultural context of that original time and place. It is very easy and quite common to take a 21st century understanding of a word or concept (e.g. farming, garden, pastor, etc.) and read it back into the text of the New Testament. The more that we know about the history and culture of first century Israel, the less likely we are to "misread" the text.

Jesus was a first century Jewish rabbi. He grew up among a people who had a rich heritage and a unique religious worldview. They believed that YHWH had broken into their history, to set them apart as a people who would eventually bless the entire world. The first century Jewish mindset was radically different from our own. The more that we can understand the cultural and historical soil that Jesus flourished in, the less likely we are to create him and those of his day in our own image.

Although it is far beyond the scope and purpose of this present volume to delve into the culture and history of first century Israel, I do want to at least give a quick overview of the seven Feasts of the Lord. These feasts provided Jesus and the Jewish nation with their rhythm for life as they walked through each calendar year.

The seven Feasts of the Lord as recorded in Leviticus 23 are:

1.    Peshach (Passover)

2.    Unleavened Bread

3.    Firstfruits

4.    Shavuot (Pentecost)

5.    Yom Teruah (Day of Trumpets)

6.    Yom Kippur (Day of Atonement)

7.    Sukkot (Tabernacles)

According to Deuteronomy 16.16, there were three times during the year when every Jewish male was expected to appear before YHWH in Jerusalem. These "pilgrimage feasts" were Unleavened Bread (which included Passover and Firstfruits) in the early spring, Shavuot in the late spring, and Sukkot in the fall.

Not only did Jesus attend these feasts as any Jewish rabbi would, but his life and ministry are a fulfillment of the spring and fall feasts. When we learn the details and specifics of the Feasts of the Lord, we discover that they are a beautiful picture and foreshadowing of the One who was to come. The graphic on the cover of this book is an attempt to represent this awesome mystery. In the center is Yeshua, the Lion of the tribe of Judah. Surrounding him are symbols for the three pilgrimage feasts:

- a lamb and barley for Peshach

- the Torah and a wheat loaf for Shavuot, and

- a tent and grapes for Sukkot

Although the Feasts are only one aspect of Jewish culture and history that brings the story of Jesus to life, they are a good place to start if the reader wants to delve deeper into this subject. I am, by no means, an expert in this area. I can, however, point you to a few sources that I have found incredibly valuable.

• There is a wealth of excellent (and free) information (audio and print) by Ray Vander Laan at his **Follow the Rabbi** website: http://www.followtherabbi.com/

• For a more formal and scholarly look at the Jewishness of Jesus, read **Jesus the Jewish Theologian** by Brad H. Young.

# Part 1:
# The Beginning, Birth and Childhood

ישוע

# (4 BCE - 11 CE)

The beginning of the Good News of Jesus Christ, the Son of God.

*(Mark 1.1)*

## Introduction

Since many have undertaken to set in order a narrative concerning those matters which have been fulfilled among us, even as those who from the beginning were eyewitnesses and servants of the word delivered them to us, it seemed good to me also, having traced the course of all things accurately from the first, to write to you in order, most excellent Theophilus; that you might know the certainty concerning the things in which you were instructed.

*(Luke 1.1-4)*

## Prologue

In the beginning was the Word, and the Word was with God, and the Word was God. The same was in the beginning with God. All things were made through him. Without him was not anything made that has been made. In him was life, and the life was the light of men. The light shines in the darkness, and the darkness hasn't overcome it.

There came a man, sent from God, whose name was John. The same came as a witness, that he might testify about the light, that all might believe through him. He was not the light, but was sent that he might testify about the

1

light.   The true light that enlightens everyone was coming into the world.

He was in the world, and the world was made through him, and the world didn't recognize him.   He came to his own, and those who were his own didn't receive him.   But as many as received him, to them he gave the right to become God's children, to those who believe in his name: who were born not of blood, nor of the will of the flesh, nor of the will of man, but of God.

The Word became flesh, and lived among us. We saw his glory, such glory as of the one and only Son of the Father, full of grace and truth.   John testified about him. He cried out, saying, "This was he of whom I said, 'He who comes after me has surpassed me, for he was before me.'"   From his fullness we all received grace upon grace.   For the law was given through Moses. Grace and truth were realized through Jesus Christ.   No one has seen God at any time. The one and only Son, who is in the bosom of the Father, he has declared him.

*(John 1.1-18)*

## Gabriel Visits Zacharias

There was in the days of Herod, the king of Judea, a certain priest named Zacharias, of the priestly division of Abijah. He had a wife of the daughters of Aaron, and her name was Elizabeth.   They were both righteous before God, walking blamelessly in all the commandments and ordinances of the Lord.   But they had no child, because Elizabeth was barren, and they both were well advanced in years.   Now while he executed the priest's office before God in the order of his division, according to the custom of the priest's office, his lot was to enter into the temple of the Lord and burn incense.   The whole multitude of the people were praying outside at the hour of incense.

An angel of the Lord appeared to him, standing on the right side of the altar of incense.   Zacharias was troubled when he saw him, and fear fell upon him.   But the angel said to him, "Don't be afraid, Zacharias, because your request has

2

been heard, and your wife, Elizabeth, will bear you a son, and you shall call his name John. You will have joy and gladness; and many will rejoice at his birth. For he will be great in the sight of the Lord, and he will drink no wine nor strong drink. He will be filled with the Holy Spirit, even from his mother's womb. He will turn many of the children of Israel to the Lord, their God. He will go before him in the spirit and power of Elijah, 'to turn the hearts of the fathers to the children,' and the disobedient to the wisdom of the just; to prepare a people prepared for the Lord."

Zacharias said to the angel, "How can I be sure of this? For I am an old man, and my wife is well advanced in years."

The angel answered him, "I am Gabriel, who stands in the presence of God. I was sent to speak to you, and to bring you this good news. Behold, you will be silent and not able to speak, until the day that these things will happen, because you didn't believe my words, which will be fulfilled in their proper time."

The people were waiting for Zacharias, and they marveled that he delayed in the temple. When he came out, he could not speak to them, and they perceived that he had seen a vision in the temple. He continued making signs to them, and remained mute. When the days of his service were fulfilled, he departed to his house.

After these days Elizabeth, his wife, conceived, and she hid herself five months, saying, "Thus has the Lord done to me in the days in which he looked at me, to take away my reproach among men."

*(Luke 1.5-25)*

### Gabriel Visits Mary

Now in the sixth month, the angel Gabriel was sent from God to a city of Galilee, named Nazareth, to a virgin pledged to be married to a man whose name was Joseph, of David's house. The virgin's name was Mary. Having come in, the angel said to her, "Rejoice, you highly favored one! The Lord is with you. Blessed are you among women!"

3

But when she saw him, she was greatly troubled at the saying, and considered what kind of salutation this might be. The angel said to her, "Don't be afraid, Mary, for you have found favor with God. Behold, you will conceive in your womb, and give birth to a son, and will call his name 'Jesus.' He will be great, and will be called the Son of the Most High. The Lord God will give him the throne of his father, David, and he will reign over the house of Jacob forever. There will be no end to his Kingdom."

Mary said to the angel, "How can this be, seeing I am a virgin?"

The angel answered her, "The Holy Spirit will come on you, and the power of the Most High will overshadow you. Therefore also the holy one who is born from you will be called the Son of God. Behold, Elizabeth, your relative, also has conceived a son in her old age; and this is the sixth month with her who was called barren. For nothing spoken by God is impossible."

Mary said, "Behold, the servant of the Lord; let it be done to me according to your word."

The angel departed from her.

*(Luke 1. 26-28)*

## *An Angel in Joseph's Dream*

Now the birth of Jesus Christ was like this; for after his mother, Mary, was engaged to Joseph, before they came together, she was found pregnant by the Holy Spirit. Joseph, her husband, being a righteous man, and not willing to make her a public example, intended to put her away secretly.

But when he thought about these things, behold, an angel of the Lord appeared to him in a dream, saying, "Joseph, son of David, don't be afraid to take to yourself Mary, your wife, for that which is conceived in her is of the Holy Spirit. She shall give birth to a son. You shall call his name Jesus, for it is he who shall save his people from their sins."

4

Now all this has happened, that it might be fulfilled which was spoken by the Lord through the prophet, saying:

"Behold, the virgin shall be with child,
and shall give birth to a son.
They shall call his name 'Immanuel';
which is, being interpreted, 'God with us.'"
(Isaiah 7.14)

Joseph arose from his sleep, and did as the angel of the Lord commanded him, and took his wife to himself; and didn't know her sexually until she had given birth to her firstborn son. He named him Jesus.

*(Matthew 1.18-25)*

## Mary Visits Elizabeth

Mary arose in those days and went into the hill country with haste, into a city of Judah, and entered into the house of Zacharias and greeted Elizabeth. When Elizabeth heard Mary's greeting, the baby leaped in her womb, and Elizabeth was filled with the Holy Spirit. She called out with a loud voice, and said, "Blessed are you among women, and blessed is the fruit of your womb! Why am I so favored, that the mother of my Lord should come to me? For behold, when the voice of your greeting came into my ears, the baby leaped in my womb for joy! Blessed is she who believed, for there will be a fulfillment of the things which have been spoken to her from the Lord!"

Mary said:

*"My soul magnifies the Lord.*
*My spirit has rejoiced in God my Savior,*
*for he has looked at the humble state of his servant.*
*For behold, from now on, all generations will*
*call me blessed.*
*For he who is mighty has done great things for me.*
*Holy is his name.*
*His mercy is for generations of generations*
*on those who fear him.*
*He has shown strength with his arm.*

5

*He has scattered the proud in the imagination*
*of their hearts.*
*He has put down princes from their thrones.*
*And has exalted the lowly.*
*He has filled the hungry with good things.*
*He has sent the rich away empty.*
*He has given help to Israel, his servant,*
*that he might remember mercy,*
*as he spoke to our fathers, to Abraham*
*and his offspring forever."*

Mary stayed with her about three months, and then returned to her house.

*(Luke 1.39-56)*

## John's Birth

Now the time that Elizabeth should give birth was fulfilled, and she gave birth to a son. Her neighbors and her relatives heard that the Lord had magnified his mercy towards her, and they rejoiced with her.

On the eighth day, they came to circumcise the child; and they would have called him Zacharias, after the name of the father. His mother answered, "Not so; but he will be called John."

They said to her, "There is no one among your relatives who is called by this name." They made signs to his father, what he would have him called. He asked for a writing tablet, and wrote, "His name is John." They all marveled.

His mouth was opened immediately, and his tongue freed, and he spoke, blessing God. Fear came on all who lived around them, and all these sayings were talked about throughout all the hill country of Judea. All who heard them laid them up in their heart, saying, "What then will this child be?" The hand of the Lord was with him.

His father, Zacharias, was filled with the Holy Spirit, and prophesied, saying:

6

*"Blessed be the Lord, the God of Israel,*
*for he has visited and redeemed his people;*
*and has raised up a horn of salvation for us*
*in the house of his servant David*
*(as he spoke by the mouth of his holy prophets*
*who have been from of old),*
*salvation from our enemies,*
*and from the hand of all who hate us;*
*to show mercy towards our fathers,*
*to remember his holy covenant,*
*the oath which he spoke to Abraham, our father,*
*to grant to us that we, being delivered*
*out of the hand of our enemies,*
*should serve him without fear,*
*in holiness and righteousness before him*
*all the days of our life.*
*And you, child, will be called a prophet*
*of the Most High,*
*for you will go before the face of the Lord*
*to prepare his ways,*
*to give knowledge of salvation to his people*
*by the remission of their sins,*
*because of the tender mercy of our God,*
*whereby the dawn from on high will visit us,*
*to shine on those who sit in darkness*
*and the shadow of death;*
*to guide our feet into the way of peace."*

The child was growing, and becoming strong in spirit, and was in the desert until the day of his public appearance to Israel.

*(Luke 1.57-80)*

## Jesus' Birth

Now in those days, a decree went out from Caesar Augustus that all the world should be enrolled. This was the first enrollment made when Quirinius was governor of Syria. All went to enroll themselves, everyone to his own city.

7

Joseph also went up from Galilee, out of the city of Nazareth, into Judea, to David's city, which is called Bethlehem, because he was of the house and family of David; to enroll himself with Mary, who was pledged to be married to him as wife, being pregnant.

While they were there, the day had come for her to give birth. She gave birth to her firstborn son. She wrapped him in bands of cloth, and laid him in a feeding trough, because there was no room for them in the inn.

There were shepherds in the same country staying in the field, and keeping watch by night over their flock. Behold, an angel of the Lord stood by them, and the glory of the Lord shone around them, and they were terrified. The angel said to them, "Don't be afraid, for behold, I bring you good news of great joy which will be to all the people. For there is born to you today, in David's city, a Savior, who is Christ the Lord. This is the sign to you: you will find a baby wrapped in strips of cloth, lying in a feeding trough."

Suddenly, there was with the angel a multitude of the heavenly army praising God, and saying:

*"Glory to God in the highest,*
*on earth peace, good will toward men."*

When the angels went away from them into the sky, the shepherds said to one another, "Let's go to Bethlehem, now, and see this thing that has happened, which the Lord has made known to us." They came with haste, and found both Mary and Joseph, and the baby was lying in the feeding trough.

When they saw it, they publicized widely the saying which was spoken to them about this child. All who heard it wondered at the things which were spoken to them by the shepherds. But Mary kept all these sayings, pondering them in her heart. The shepherds returned, glorifying and praising God for all the things that they had heard and seen, just as it was told them.

*(Luke 2.1-20)*

8

## Jesus is Circumcised

When eight days were fulfilled for the circumcision of the child, his name was called Jesus, which was given by the angel before he was conceived in the womb.

*(Luke 2.21)*

## Jesus is Redeemed

When the days of their purification according to the law of Moses were fulfilled, they brought him up to Jerusalem, to present him to the Lord (as it is written in the law of the Lord, "Every male who opens the womb shall be called holy to the Lord"), and to offer a sacrifice according to that which is said in the law of the Lord, "A pair of turtledoves, or two young pigeons."

Behold, there was a man in Jerusalem whose name was Simeon. This man was righteous and devout, looking for the consolation of Israel, and the Holy Spirit was on him. It had been revealed to him by the Holy Spirit that he should not see death before he had seen the Lord's Christ. He came in the Spirit into the temple. When the parents brought in the child, Jesus, that they might do concerning him according to the custom of the law, then he received him into his arms, and blessed God, and said,

*"Now you are releasing your servant, Master,*
*according to your word, in peace:*
*for my eyes have seen your salvation,*
*which you have prepared before the face of all peoples;*
*a light for revelation to the nations,*
*and the glory of your people Israel."*

Joseph and his mother were marveling at the things which were spoken concerning him, and Simeon blessed them, and said to Mary, his mother, "Behold, this child is set for the falling and the rising of many in Israel, and for a sign which is spoken against. Yes, a sword will pierce through your own soul, that the thoughts of many hearts may be revealed."

There was one Anna, a prophetess, the daughter of Phanuel, of the tribe of Asher (she was of a great age, having lived with a husband seven years from her virginity, and she had been a widow for about eighty-four years), who didn't depart from the temple, worshiping with fastings and petitions night and day. Coming up at that very hour, she gave thanks to the Lord, and spoke of him to all those who were looking for redemption in Jerusalem.

When they had accomplished all things that were according to the law of the Lord, they returned into Galilee, to their own city, Nazareth. The child was growing, and was becoming strong in spirit, being filled with wisdom, and the grace of God was upon him.

*(Luke 2.22-40)*

## The Magi Visit Jesus

Now when Jesus was born in Bethlehem of Judea in the days of King Herod, behold, wise men from the east came to Jerusalem, saying, "Where is he who is born King of the Jews? For we saw his star in the east, and have come to worship him." When King Herod heard it, he was troubled, and all Jerusalem with him. Gathering together all the chief priests and scribes of the people, he asked them where the Christ would be born. They said to him, "In Bethlehem of Judea, for this is written through the prophet:

> 'You Bethlehem, land of Judah,
> are in no way least among the princes of Judah:
> for out of you shall come a governor,
> who shall shepherd my people, Israel.'" *(Micah 5.2)*

Then Herod secretly called the wise men, and learned from them exactly what time the star appeared. He sent them to Bethlehem, and said, "Go and search diligently for the young child. When you have found him, bring me word, so that I also may come and worship him."

10

They, having heard the king, went their way; and behold, the star, which they saw in the east, went before them, until it came and stood over where the young child was. When they saw the star, they rejoiced with exceedingly great joy. They came into the house and saw the young child with Mary, his mother, and they fell down and worshiped him. Opening their treasures, they offered to him gifts: gold, frankincense, and myrrh. Being warned in a dream that they shouldn't return to Herod, they went back to their own country another way.

*(Matthew 2.1-12)*

## *Jesus' Family Flees to Egypt*

Now when they had departed, behold, an angel of the Lord appeared to Joseph in a dream, saying, "Arise and take the young child and his mother, and flee into Egypt, and stay there until I tell you, for Herod will seek the young child to destroy him." He arose and took the young child and his mother by night, and departed into Egypt, and was there until the death of Herod; that it might be fulfilled which was spoken by the Lord through the prophet, saying, "Out of Egypt I called my son." (Hosea 11.1)

Then Herod, when he saw that he was mocked by the wise men, was exceedingly angry, and sent out, and killed all the male children who were in Bethlehem and in all the surrounding countryside, from two years old and under, according to the exact time which he had learned from the wise men. Then that which was spoken by Jeremiah the prophet was fulfilled, saying:

> *"A voice was heard in Ramah,*
> *lamentation, weeping and great mourning,*
> *Rachel weeping for her children:*
> *she wouldn't be comforted,*
> *because they are no more." (Jeremiah 31.15)*

But when Herod was dead, behold, an angel of the Lord appeared in a dream to Joseph in Egypt, saying, "Arise and take the young child and his mother, and go into the

11

land of Israel, for those who sought the young child's life are dead."

He arose and took the young child and his mother, and came into the land of Israel. But when he heard that Archelaus was reigning over Judea in the place of his father, Herod, he was afraid to go there. Being warned in a dream, he withdrew into the region of Galilee, and came and lived in a city called Nazareth; that it might be fulfilled which was spoken through the prophets: "He will be called a Nazarene."

*(Matthew 2.13-23)*

## Twelve Year Old Jesus Visits the Temple

His parents went every year to Jerusalem at the feast of the Passover.

When he was twelve years old, they went up to Jerusalem according to the custom of the feast, and when they had fulfilled the days, as they were returning, the boy Jesus stayed behind in Jerusalem. Joseph and his mother didn't know it, but supposing him to be in the company, they went a day's journey, and they looked for him among their relatives and acquaintances. When they didn't find him, they returned to Jerusalem, looking for him.

After three days they found him in the temple, sitting in the middle of the teachers, both listening to them, and asking them questions. All who heard him were amazed at his understanding and his answers. When they saw him, they were astonished, and his mother said to him, "Son, why have you treated us this way? Behold, your father and I were anxiously looking for you."

He said to them, "Why were you looking for me? Didn't you know that I must be in my Father's house?" They didn't understand the saying which he spoke to them. And he went down with them, and came to Nazareth. He was subject to them, and his mother kept all these sayings in her heart. And Jesus increased in wisdom and stature, and in favor with God and men.

*(Luke 2.41-52)*

## *The Genealogy of Jesus Through His Mother*

The book of the genealogy of Jesus Christ, the son of David, the son of Abraham.

*Abraham became the father of Isaac.*
*Isaac became the father of Jacob.*
*Jacob became the father of Judah and his brothers.*
*Judah became the father of Perez and Zerah by Tamar.*
*Perez became the father of Hezron.*
*Hezron became the father of Ram.*
*Ram became the father of Amminadab.*
*Amminadab became the father of Nahshon.*
*Nahshon became the father of Salmon.*
*Salmon became the father of Boaz by Rahab.*
*Boaz became the father of Obed by Ruth.*
*Obed became the father of Jesse.*
*Jesse became the father of King David.*
*David became the father of Solomon*
*by her who had been Uriah's wife.*

*Solomon became the father of Rehoboam.*
*Rehoboam became the father of Abijah.*
*Abijah became the father of Asa.*
*Asa became the father of Jehoshaphat.*
*Jehoshaphat became the father of Joram.*
*Joram became the father of Uzziah.*
*Uzziah became the father of Jotham.*
*Jotham became the father of Ahaz.*
*Ahaz became the father of Hezekiah.*
*Hezekiah became the father of Manasseh.*
*Manasseh became the father of Amon.*
*Amon became the father of Josiah.*
*Josiah became the father of Jechoniah*
*and his brothers, at the time of the exile to Babylon.*

After the exile to Babylon, Jechoniah became the father of Shealtiel.

*Shealtiel became the father of Zerubbabel.*
*Zerubbabel became the father of Abiud.*
*Abiud became the father of Eliakim.*

13

*Eliakim became the father of Azor.*
*Azor became the father of Zadok.*
*Zadok became the father of Achim.*
*Achim became the father of Eliud.*
*Eliud became the father of Eleazar.*
*Eleazar became the father of Matthan.*
*Matthan became the father of Jacob.*
*Jacob became the father of Joseph,*
*the husband of Mary, from whom was born Jesus,*
*who is called Christ.*

So all the generations from Abraham to David are fourteen generations; from David to the exile to Babylon fourteen generations; and from the carrying away to Babylon to the Christ, fourteen generations.

*(Matthew 1.1-17)*

### The Genealogy of Jesus Through His Father

Jesus, being the son (as was supposed) of Joseph, the son of Heli, the son of Matthat, the son of Levi, the son of Melchi, the son of Jannai, the son of Joseph, the son of Mattathias, the son of Amos, the son of Nahum, the son of Esli, the son of Naggai, the son of Maath, the son of Mattathias, the son of Semein, the son of Joseph, the son of Judah, the son of Joanan, the son of Rhesa, the son of Zerubbabel, the son of Shealtiel, the son of Neri, the son of Melchi, the son of Addi, the son of Cosam, the son of Elmodam, the son of Er, the son of Jose, the son of Eliezer, the son of Jorim, the son of Matthat, the son of Levi, the son of Simeon, the son of Judah, the son of Joseph, the son of Jonan, the son of Eliakim, the son of Melea, the son of Menan, the son of Mattatha, the son of Nathan, the son of David, the son of Jesse, the son of Obed, the son of Boaz, the son of Salmon, the son of Nahshon, the son of Amminadab, the son of Aram, the son of Hezron, the son of Perez, the son of Judah, the son of Jacob, the son of Isaac, the son of Abraham, the son of Terah, the son of Nahor, the son of Serug, the son of Reu, the son of Peleg, the son of Eber, the son of Shelah, the son of Cainan, the son of Arphaxad, the son of Shem, the son of Noah, the son of Lamech, the son of Methuselah, the son of Enoch, the son of Jared, the son of Mahalaleel, the son of Cainan, the son of Enos, the son of Seth, the son of Adam, the son of God.

*(Luke 3.23b-38)*

# Part 2:

# Baptism Until the End of Passover

## (Winter, 26 CE - April, 27 CE)

## *The Ministry of John, Son of Zacharias*

Now in the fifteenth year of the reign of Tiberius Caesar, Pontius Pilate being governor of Judea, and Herod being tetrarch of Galilee, and his brother Philip tetrarch of the region of Ituraea and Trachonitis, and Lysanias tetrarch of Abilene, in the high priesthood of Annas and Caiaphas, the word of God came to John, the Baptizer, the son of Zacharias, in the wilderness of Judea. He came into all the region around the Jordan, preaching the baptism of repentance for remission of sins, saying, "Repent, for the Kingdom of Heaven is at hand!". As it is written in the book of the words of Isaiah the prophet:

> *"The voice of one crying in the wilderness,*
> *'Make ready the way of the Lord.*
> *Make his paths straight.*
> *Every valley will be filled.*
> *Every mountain and hill will be brought low.*
> *The crooked will become straight,*
> *and the rough ways smooth.*
> *All flesh will see God's salvation.'" (Isaiah 40.3-5)*

Now John himself wore clothing made of camel's hair, with a leather belt around his waist. His food was locusts and wild honey. All the country of Judea and all those of Jerusalem went out to him. They were baptized by him in the Jordan river, confessing their sins.

But when he saw many of the Pharisees and Sadducees coming for his baptism, he said to the multitudes who went out to be baptized by him, "You offspring of vipers! Who warned you to flee from the wrath to come? Therefore produce fruits worthy of repentance, and don't begin to say among yourselves, 'We have Abraham for our father;' for I tell you that God is able to raise up children to Abraham from these stones! Even now the ax also lies at the root of the trees. Every tree therefore that doesn't produce good fruit is cut down, and thrown into the fire."

The multitudes asked him, "What then must we do?"

He answered them, "He who has two coats, let him give to him who has none. He who has food, let him do likewise."

Tax collectors also came to be baptized, and they said to him, "Teacher, what must we do?"

He said to them, "Collect no more than that which is appointed to you."

Soldiers also asked him, saying, "What about us? What must we do?"

He said to them, "Extort from no one by violence, neither accuse anyone wrongfully. Be content with your wages."

As the people were in expectation, and all men reasoned in their hearts concerning John, whether perhaps he was the Christ, John answered them all, "I indeed baptize you with water, but he comes who is mightier than I, the strap of whose sandals I am not worthy to loosen. He will baptize you in the Holy Spirit and fire, whose winnowing fork (fan) is in his hand, and he will thoroughly cleanse his threshing floor, and will gather the wheat into his barn; but he will burn up the chaff with unquenchable fire."

*(Matthew 3.1-12; Mark 1.2-8;*
*Luke 3.1-17)*

# FEBRUARY & MARCH
## 27 CE

## The Baptism of Jesus

Then Jesus came from Galilee to the Jordan to John, to be baptized by him. But John would have hindered him, saying, "I need to be baptized by you, and you come to me?"

But Jesus, answering, said to him, "Allow it now, for this is the fitting way for us to fulfill all righteousness." Then he allowed him.

Jesus, when he was baptized, went up directly from the water. Now when all the people were baptized, Jesus also had been baptized, and was praying. And behold, the heavens were opened to him. He saw the Spirit of God descending in a bodily form like a dove, and coming on him. Behold, a voice out of the heavens said, "This is my beloved Son, with whom I am well pleased."

*(Matthew 3.13-17; Mark 1.9-11;*
*Luke 3.21, 22)*

## Jesus is Tempted by Satan

Then Jesus was led up by the Spirit into the wilderness to be tempted by Satan, the devil. Afterward, when he had fasted forty days and forty nights with the wild animals, and when they were completed, he was hungry. The tempter came and said to him, "If you are the Son of God, command that these stones become bread."

But he answered, "It is written, *'Man shall not live by bread alone, but by every word that proceeds out of the mouth of God.'"* *(Deuteronomy 8.3)*

Then the devil took him into the holy city. He set him on the pinnacle of the temple, and said to him, "If you are the Son of God, throw yourself down, for it is written:

> *'He will put his angels in charge of you.' and,*
> *'On their hands they will bear you up,*
> *so that you don't dash your foot against a stone.'"*
> *(Psalm 91.11,12)*

Jesus said to him, "Again, it is written, *'You shall not test the Lord, your God.'"* *(Deuteronomy 6.16)*

Again, the devil took him to an exceedingly high mountain, and showed him all the kingdoms of the world, and their glory, in a moment of time. The devil said to him, "I will give you all this authority, and their glory, for it has been delivered to me; and I give it to whomever I want. If you therefore will worship before me, it will all be yours."

Then Jesus said to him, "Get behind me, Satan! For it is written, *'You shall worship the Lord your God, and you shall serve him only.'"* *(Deuteronomy 6.13)*

When the devil had completed every temptation, he departed from him until another time. And behold, angels came and served him.

*(Matthew 4.1-11; Mark 1.12,13;*
*Luke 4.1-13)*

# MARCH
# 27 CE

## John Testifies about Jesus

This is John's testimony, when the Jews sent priests and Levites from Jerusalem to ask him, "Who are you?" He declared, and didn't deny, but he declared, "I am not the Christ."

They asked him, "What then? Are you Elijah?"

He said, "I am not."

"Are you the prophet?"

He answered, "No."

They said therefore to him, "Who are you? Give us an answer to take back to those who sent us. What do you say about yourself?"

He said, "I am the voice of one crying in the wilderness, 'Make straight the way of the Lord,' as Isaiah the prophet said."

The ones who had been sent were from the Pharisees. They asked him, "Why then do you baptize, if you are not the Christ, nor Elijah, nor the prophet?"

John answered them, "I baptize in water, but among you stands one whom you don't know. He is the one who comes after me, who is preferred before me, whose sandal strap I'm not worthy to loosen." These things were done in Bethany beyond the Jordan, where John was baptizing.

The next day, he saw Jesus coming to him, and said, "Behold, the Lamb of God, who takes away the sin of the world! This is he of whom I said, 'After me comes a man who is preferred before me, for he was before me.' I didn't know him, but for this reason I came baptizing in water: that he would be revealed to Israel."

John testified, saying, "I have seen the Spirit descending like a dove out of heaven, and it remained on him. I didn't recognize him, but he who sent me to baptize in water, he said to me, 'On whomever you will see the Spirit descending, and remaining on him, the same is he who baptizes in the Holy Spirit.' I have seen, and have testified that this is the Son of God."

Jesus himself, when he began to teach, was about thirty years old.

*(Luke 3.23a; John 1.19-34)*

## Jesus' First Disciples

Again, the next day, John was standing with two of his disciples, and he looked at Jesus as he walked, and said, "Behold, the Lamb of God!" The two disciples heard him speak, and they followed Jesus. Jesus turned, and saw them following, and said to them, "What are you looking for?"

They said to him, "Rabbi" (which is to say, being interpreted, Teacher), "where are you staying?"

He said to them, "Come, and see."

They came and saw where he was staying, and they stayed with him that day. It was about the tenth hour. One of the two who heard John, and followed him, was Andrew, Simon Peter's brother. He first found his own brother, Simon, and said to him, "We have found the Messiah!" (which is, being interpreted, Christ). He brought him to Jesus. Jesus looked at him, and said, "You are Simon the son of Jonah. You shall be called Cephas" (which is by interpretation, Peter).

*(John 1.35-42)*

28

## *Into Galilee and More Disciples*

On the next day, he was determined to go out into Galilee, and he found Philip. Jesus said to him, "Follow me." Now Philip was from Bethsaida, of the city of Andrew and Peter. Philip found Nathanael, and said to him, "We have found him, of whom Moses in the law, and the prophets, wrote: Jesus of Nazareth, the son of Joseph."

Nathanael said to him, "Can any good thing come out of Nazareth?"

Philip said to him, "Come and see."

Jesus saw Nathanael coming to him, and said about him, "Behold, an Israelite indeed, in whom is no deceit!"

Nathanael said to him, "How do you know me?"

Jesus answered him, "Before Philip called you, when you were under the fig tree, I saw you."

Nathanael answered him, "Rabbi, you are the Son of God! You are King of Israel!"

Jesus answered him, "Because I told you, 'I saw you underneath the fig tree,' do you believe? You will see greater things than these!" He said to him, "Most certainly, I tell you, hereafter you will see heaven opened, and the angels of God ascending and descending on the Son of Man."

*(John 1.43-51)*

29

# APRIL
## 27 CE

## *The Wedding at Cana*

The third day, there was a marriage in Cana of Galilee. Jesus' mother was there. Jesus also was invited, with his disciples, to the marriage. When the wine ran out, Jesus' mother said to him, "They have no wine."

Jesus said to her, "Woman, what does that have to do with you and me? My hour has not yet come."

His mother said to the servants, "Whatever he says to you, do it." Now there were six water pots of stone set there after the Jews' way of purifying, containing two or three metretes (76-114 litres) apiece. Jesus said to them, "Fill the water pots with water." They filled them up to the brim. He said to them, "Now draw some out, and take it to the ruler of the feast." So they took it.

When the ruler of the feast tasted the water now become wine, and didn't know where it came from (but the servants who had drawn the water knew), the ruler of the feast called the bridegroom, and said to him, "Everyone serves the good wine first, and when the guests have drunk freely, then that which is worse. You have kept the good wine until now!"

This beginning of his signs Jesus did in Cana of Galilee, and revealed his glory; and his disciples believed in him. After this, he went down to Capernaum, he, and his mother, his brothers, and his disciples; and they stayed there a few days.

*(John 2.1-12)*

## Jesus Cleanses the Temple

The Passover of the Jews was at hand, and Jesus went up to Jerusalem. He found in the temple those who sold oxen, sheep, and doves, and the changers of money sitting. He made a whip of cords, and threw all out of the temple, both the sheep and the oxen; and he poured out the changers' money, and overthrew their tables.

To those who sold the doves, he said, "Take these things out of here! Don't make my Father's house a marketplace!" His disciples remembered that it was written, *"Zeal for your house will eat me up." (Psalm 69.9)*

The Jews therefore answered him, "What sign do you show us, seeing that you do these things?"

Jesus answered them, "Destroy this temple, and in three days I will raise it up."

The Jews therefore said, "It took forty-six years to build this temple! Will you raise it up in three days?" But he spoke of the temple of his body. When therefore he was raised from the dead, his disciples remembered that he said this, and they believed the Scripture, and the word which Jesus had said.

Now when he was in Jerusalem at the Passover, during the feast, many believed in his name, observing his signs which he did. But Jesus didn't trust himself to them, because he knew everyone, and because he didn't need for anyone to testify concerning man; for he himself knew what was in man.

*(John 2.13-25)*

## *Jesus Talks with Nicodemus*

Now there was a man of the Pharisees named Nicodemus, a ruler of the Jews. The same came to him by night, and said to him, "Rabbi, we know that you are a teacher come from God, for no one can do these signs that you do, unless God is with him."

Jesus answered him, "Most certainly, I tell you, unless one is born anew, he can't see God's Kingdom."

Nicodemus said to him, "How can a man be born when he is old? Can he enter a second time into his mother's womb, and be born?"

Jesus answered, "Most certainly I tell you, unless one is born of water and spirit, he can't enter into God's Kingdom! That which is born of the flesh is flesh. That which is born of the Spirit is spirit. Don't marvel that I said to you, 'You must be born anew.' The wind blows where it wants to, and you hear its sound, but don't know where it comes from and where it is going. So is everyone who is born of the Spirit."

Nicodemus answered him, "How can these things be?"

Jesus answered him, "Are you the teacher of Israel, and don't understand these things? Most certainly I tell you, we speak that which we know, and testify of that which we have seen, and you don't receive our witness. If I told you earthly things and you don't believe, how will you believe if I tell you heavenly things?

"No one has ascended into heaven, but he who descended out of heaven, the Son of Man, who is in heaven. As Moses lifted up the serpent in the wilderness, even so must the Son of Man be lifted up, that whoever believes in him should not perish, but have eternal life. For God so loved the world, that he gave his one and only Son, that whoever believes in him should not perish, but have eternal life. For God didn't send his Son into the world to judge the world, but that the world should be saved through him. He who believes in him is not judged. He who doesn't believe has been judged already, because he has not believed in the name of the one and only Son of God.

"This is the judgment, that the light has come into the world, and men loved the darkness rather than the light; for their works were evil. For everyone who does evil hates the light, and doesn't come to the light, lest his works would be exposed. But he who does the truth comes to the light, that his works may be revealed, that they have been done in God."

*(John 3.1-21)*

# Part 3:

# The End of Passover Until the End of Shavuot

# (April - June, 27 CE)

# APRIL & MAY
## 27 CE

## John's Final Testimony about Jesus

After these things, Jesus came with his disciples into the land of Judea. He stayed there with them, and baptized. John also was baptizing in Enon near Salim, because there was much water there. They came, and were baptized. For John was not yet thrown into prison.

There arose therefore a questioning on the part of John's disciples with some Jews about purification. They came to John, and said to him, "Rabbi, he who was with you beyond the Jordan, to whom you have testified, behold, the same baptizes, and everyone is coming to him."

John answered, "A man can receive nothing, unless it has been given him from heaven. You yourselves testify that I said, 'I am not the Christ,' but, 'I have been sent before him.' He who has the bride is the bridegroom; but the friend of the bridegroom, who stands and hears him, rejoices greatly because of the bridegroom's voice. This, my joy, therefore is made full. He must increase, but I must decrease.

"He who comes from above is above all. He who is from the earth belongs to the earth, and speaks of the earth. He who comes from heaven is above all. What he has seen and heard, of that he testifies; and no one receives his witness. He who has received his witness has set his seal to this, that God is true. For he whom God has sent speaks the words of God; for God gives the Spirit without measure. The Father loves the Son, and has given all things into his hand. One who believes in the Son has eternal life, but one who

41

disobeys the Son won't see life, but the wrath of God remains on him."

*(John 3.22-36)*

## *Jesus Visits Samaria*

Therefore when the Lord knew that the Pharisees had heard that Jesus was making and baptizing more disciples than John (although Jesus himself didn't baptize, but his disciples), he left Judea, and departed for Galilee.

He needed to pass through Samaria. So he came to a city of Samaria, called Sychar, near the parcel of ground that Jacob gave to his son, Joseph. Jacob's well was there. Jesus therefore, being tired from his journey, sat down by the well. It was about the sixth hour (noon). A woman of Samaria came to draw water. Jesus said to her, "Give me a drink." For his disciples had gone away into the city to buy food.

The Samaritan woman therefore said to him, "How is it that you, being a Jew, ask for a drink from me, a Samaritan woman?" (For Jews have no dealings with Samaritans.)

Jesus answered her, "If you knew the gift of God, and who it is who says to you, 'Give me a drink,' you would have asked him, and he would have given you living water."

The woman said to him, "Sir, you have nothing to draw with, and the well is deep. So where do you get that living water? Are you greater than our father, Jacob, who gave us the well, and drank of it himself, as did his children, and his livestock?"

Jesus answered her, "Everyone who drinks of this water will thirst again, but whoever drinks of the water that I will give him will never thirst again; but the water that I will give him will become in him a well of water springing up to eternal life."

The woman said to him, "Sir, give me this water, so that I don't get thirsty, neither come all the way here to draw."

42

Jesus said to her, "Go, call your husband, and come here."

The woman answered, "I have no husband."

Jesus said to her, "You said well, 'I have no husband,' for you have had five husbands; and he whom you now have is not your husband. This you have said truly."

The woman said to him, "Sir, I perceive that you are a prophet. Our fathers worshiped in this mountain, and you Jews say that in Jerusalem is the place where people ought to worship."

Jesus said to her, "Woman, believe me, the hour comes, when neither in this mountain, nor in Jerusalem, will you worship the Father. You worship that which you don't know. We worship that which we know; for salvation is from the Jews. But the hour comes, and now is, when the true worshipers will worship the Father in spirit and truth, for the Father seeks such to be his worshipers. God is spirit, and those who worship him must worship in spirit and truth."

The woman said to him, "I know that Messiah comes, he who is called Christ. When he has come, he will declare to us all things."

Jesus said to her, "I am he, the one who speaks to you."

At this, his disciples came. They marveled that he was speaking with a woman; yet no one said, "What are you looking for?" or, "Why do you speak with her?" So the woman left her water pot, and went away into the city, and said to the people, "Come, see a man who told me everything that I did. Can this be the Christ?" They went out of the city, and were coming to him.

In the meanwhile, the disciples urged him, saying, "Rabbi, eat."

But he said to them, "I have food to eat that you don't know about."

The disciples therefore said to one another, "Has anyone brought him something to eat?"

43

Jesus said to them, "My food is to do the will of him who sent me, and to accomplish his work. Don't you say, 'There are yet four months until the harvest?' Behold, I tell you, lift up your eyes, and look at the fields, that they are white for harvest already. He who reaps receives wages, and gathers fruit to eternal life; that both he who sows and he who reaps may rejoice together. For in this the saying is true, 'One sows, and another reaps.' I sent you to reap that for which you haven't labored. Others have labored, and you have entered into their labor."

From that city many of the Samaritans believed in him because of the word of the woman, who testified, "He told me everything that I did." So when the Samaritans came to him, they begged him to stay with them. He stayed there two days. Many more believed because of his word. They said to the woman, "Now we believe, not because of your speaking; for we have heard for ourselves, and know that this is indeed the Christ, the Savior of the world."

*(John 4.1-42)*

## Jesus Heals a Nobleman's Son

After the two days he went out from there and went into Galilee. For Jesus himself testified that a prophet has no honor in his own country. So when he came into Galilee, the Galileans received him, having seen all the things that he did in Jerusalem at the feast, for they also went to the feast.

Jesus came therefore again to Cana of Galilee, where he made the water into wine. There was a certain nobleman whose son was sick at Capernaum. When he heard that Jesus had come out of Judea into Galilee, he went to him, and begged him that he would come down and heal his son, for he was at the point of death.

Jesus therefore said to him, "Unless you see signs and wonders, you will in no way believe."

The nobleman said to him, "Sir, come down before my child dies."

Jesus said to him, "Go your way. Your son lives."

The man believed the word that Jesus spoke to him, and he went his way. As he was now going down, his servants met him and reported, saying "Your child lives!" So he inquired of them the hour when he began to get better. They said therefore to him, "Yesterday at the seventh hour (1:00 p.m.), the fever left him." So the father knew that it was at that hour in which Jesus said to him, "Your son lives." He believed, as did his whole house.

This is again the second sign that Jesus did, having come out of Judea into Galilee.

*(John 4.43-54)*

## John, Son of Zacharias, is Imprisoned

Then with many other exhortations John preached good news to the people, but Herod the tetrarch, being reproved by him for Herodias, his brother's wife, and for all the evil things which Herod had done, added this also to them all, that he shut up John in prison.

*(Luke 3.18-20)*

## Jesus Heals the Man at the Pool of Bethesda

After these things, there was a feast of the Jews, and Jesus went up to Jerusalem. Now in Jerusalem by the sheep gate, there is a pool, which is called in Hebrew, "Bethesda", having five porches. In these lay a great multitude of those who were sick, blind, lame, or paralyzed, waiting for the moving of the water; for an angel went down at certain times into the pool, and stirred up the water. Whoever stepped in first after the stirring of the water was healed of whatever disease he had.

A certain man was there, who had been sick for thirty-eight years. When Jesus saw him lying there, and knew that he had been sick for a long time, he asked him, "Do you want to be made well?"

The sick man answered him, "Sir, I have no one to put me into the pool when the water is stirred up, but while I'm coming, another steps down before me."

Jesus said to him, "Arise, take up your mat, and walk." Immediately, the man was made well, and took up his mat and walked.

Now it was the Sabbath on that day. So the Jews said to him who was cured, "It is the Sabbath. It is not lawful for you to carry the mat."

He answered them, "He who made me well, the same said to me, 'Take up your mat, and walk.'"

Then they asked him, "Who is the man who said to you, 'Take up your mat, and walk'?" But he who was healed didn't know who it was, for Jesus had withdrawn, a crowd being in the place.

Afterward Jesus found him in the temple, and said to him, "Behold, you are made well. Sin no more, so that nothing worse happens to you."

The man went away, and told the Jews that it was Jesus who had made him well. For this cause the Jews persecuted Jesus, and sought to kill him, because he did these things on the Sabbath. But Jesus answered them, "My Father is still working, so I am working, too." For this cause therefore the Jews sought all the more to kill him, because he not only broke the Sabbath, but also called God his own Father, making himself equal with God.

Jesus therefore answered them, "Most certainly, I tell you, the Son can do nothing of himself, but what he sees the Father doing. For whatever things he does, these the Son also does likewise. For the Father has affection for the Son, and shows him all things that he himself does. He will show him greater works than these, that you may marvel. For as the Father raises the dead and gives them life, even so the Son also gives life to whom he desires. For the Father judges no one, but he has given all judgment to the Son, that all may honor the Son, even as they honor the Father. He who doesn't honor the Son doesn't honor the Father who sent him.

"Most certainly I tell you, he who hears my word, and believes him who sent me, has eternal life, and doesn't come into judgment, but has passed out of death into life. Most

46

certainly, I tell you, the hour comes, and now is, when the dead will hear the Son of God's voice; and those who hear will live. For as the Father has life in himself, even so he gave to the Son also to have life in himself. He also gave him authority to execute judgment, because he is a son of man.

"Don't marvel at this, for the hour comes, in which all that are in the tombs will hear his voice, and will come out; those who have done good, to the resurrection of life; and those who have done evil, to the resurrection of judgment. I can of myself do nothing. As I hear, I judge, and my judgment is righteous; because I don't seek my own will, but the will of my Father who sent me.

"If I testify about myself, my witness is not valid. It is another who testifies about me. I know that the testimony which he testifies about me is true. You have sent to John, and he has testified to the truth. But the testimony which I receive is not from man. However, I say these things that you may be saved. He was the burning and shining lamp, and you were willing to rejoice for a while in his light. But the testimony which I have is greater than that of John, for the works which the Father gave me to accomplish, the very works that I do, testify about me, that the Father has sent me. The Father himself, who sent me, has testified about me. You have neither heard his voice at any time, nor seen his form. You don't have his word living in you; because you don't believe him whom he sent.

"You search the Scriptures, because you think that in them you have eternal life; and these are they which testify about me. Yet you will not come to me, that you may have life. I don't receive glory from men. But I know you, that you don't have God's love in yourselves. I have come in my Father's name, and you don't receive me. If another comes in his own name, you will receive him. How can you believe, who receive glory from one another, and you don't seek the glory that comes from the only God?

"Don't think that I will accuse you to the Father.

There is one who accuses you, even Moses, on whom you have set your hope.  For if you believed Moses, you would believe me; for he wrote about me.  But if you don't believe his writings, how will you believe my words?"

*(John 5.1-47)*

# Part 4:

# The End of Shavuot Until the Beginning of Sukkot

(June - October, 27 CE)

# JUNE
# 27 CE

## Jesus is Rejected in Nazareth

Now when Jesus heard that John was delivered up into custody, he withdrew and returned in the power of the Spirit into Galilee. News about him spread through all the surrounding area. He taught in their synagogues, being glorified by all.

He came to Nazareth, where he had been brought up. He entered, as was his custom, into the synagogue on the Sabbath day, and stood up to read. The book of the prophet Isaiah was handed to him. He opened the book, and found the place where it was written:

> *"The Spirit of the Lord is on me,*
> *because he has anointed me to preach*
> *good news to the poor.*
> *He has sent me to heal the broken-hearted,*
> *to proclaim release to the captives,*
> *recovering of sight to the blind,*
> *to deliver those who are crushed,*
> *and to proclaim the acceptable year*
> *of the Lord." (Isaiah 61.1-2)*

He closed the book, gave it back to the attendant, and sat down. The eyes of all in the synagogue were fastened on him. He began to tell them, "Today, this Scripture has been fulfilled in your hearing."

All testified about him, and wondered at the gracious words which proceeded out of his mouth, and they said, "Isn't this Joseph's son?"

He said to them, "Doubtless you will tell me this parable, 'Physician, heal yourself! Whatever we have heard done at Capernaum, do also here in your hometown.'" He said, "Most certainly I tell you, no prophet is acceptable in his hometown. But truly I tell you, there were many widows in Israel in the days of Elijah, when the sky was shut up three years and six months, when a great famine came over all the land. Elijah was sent to none of them, except to Zarephath, in the land of Sidon, to a woman who was a widow. There were many lepers in Israel in the time of Elisha the prophet, yet not one of them was cleansed, except Naaman, the Syrian."

They were all filled with wrath in the synagogue, as they heard these things. They rose up, threw him out of the city, and led him to the brow of the hill that their city was built on, that they might throw him off the cliff. But he, passing through the middle of them, went his way.

*(Matthew 4.12; Mark 1.14a;*
*Luke 4.14-30)*

## Jesus Goes to Capernaum

Leaving Nazareth, he came and lived in Capernaum, a city in Galilee, which is by the sea, in the region of Zebulun and Naphtali, that it might be fulfilled which was spoken through Isaiah the prophet, saying:

> *"The land of Zebulun and the land of Naphtali,*
> *toward the sea, beyond the Jordan,*
> *Galilee of the Gentiles,*
> *the people who sat in darkness saw a great light,*
> *to those who sat in the region and shadow of death,*
> *to them light has dawned." (Isaiah 9.1-2)*

From that time, Jesus began to preach the Good News of God's Kingdom, saying, "Repent! For the Kingdom of

Heaven is at hand. The time is fulfilled, and God's Kingdom is at hand! Repent, and believe in the Good News."

*(Matthew 4.13-17; Mark 1.14b)*

## Jesus Calls Four Fishermen

Walking by the sea of Galilee, Jesus saw two brothers: Simon, who is called Peter, and Andrew, his brother, casting a net into the sea; for they were fishermen. He said to them, "Come after me, and I will make you fishers for men."

They immediately left their nets and followed him. Going on from there, he saw two other brothers, James the son of Zebedee, and John his brother, in the boat with Zebedee their father, mending their nets. Immediately he called them, and they left their father, Zebedee, in the boat with the hired servants and they went after him.

*(Matthew 4.18-22; Mark 1.16-20)*

## The Man with the Unclean Spirit

They went into Capernaum, and immediately on the Sabbath day he entered into the synagogue and taught. They were astonished at his teaching, for he taught them as having authority, and not as the scribes. Immediately there was in their synagogue a man with an unclean spirit, and he cried out, saying, "Ha! What do we have to do with you, Jesus, you Nazarene? Have you come to destroy us? I know you who you are: the Holy One of God!"

Jesus rebuked him, saying, "Be quiet, and come out of him!"

The unclean spirit/demon, convulsing and throwing him down in the middle of them, crying with a loud voice, came out of him, having done him no harm. They were all amazed, so that they questioned among themselves, saying, "What is this word? A new teaching? For with authority and power he commands even the unclean spirits, and they obey him and come out!" The report of him went out immediately everywhere into all the region of Galilee and its surrounding area.

*(Mark 1.21-28; Luke 4.31-37)*

## Jesus Heals Peter's Mother-in-Law

Immediately, when they had come out of the synagogue, they came into the house of Simon and Andrew, with James and John. Now Simon's wife's mother lay sick with a great fever, and immediately they told/begged him about her. He came, stood over her and rebuked the fever. He took her by the hand, and raised her up. The fever left her, and immediately she rose up and served them.

At evening, when the sun had set, they brought to him all who were sick, and those who were demonized *(1)*. All the city was gathered together at the door. Jesus laid his hands on every one of them, and healed them. Demons also came out of many, crying out, and saying, "You are the Christ, the Son of God!" Rebuking them, he didn't allow them to speak, because they knew that he was the Christ. He cast out the spirits with a word, and healed all who were sick; that it might be fulfilled which was spoken through Isaiah the prophet, saying:

*"He took our infirmities, and bore our diseases."* (Isaiah 53.4)

Early in the morning, while it was still dark, he rose up and went out, and departed into a deserted, uninhabited place, and prayed there. Simon and those who were with him followed after him; and they found him, and told him, "Everyone is looking for you."

He said to them, "Let's go elsewhere into the next towns, that I may preach there also, because I came out for this reason."

The multitudes came to him, and held on to him, so that he wouldn't go away from them. But he said to them, "I must preach the good news of God's Kingdom to the other cities also. For this reason I have been sent."

*(Matthew 8.14-17; Mark 1.29-38;*
*Luke 4.38-43)*

## *Jesus Travels Throughout Galilee*

Jesus went about in all Galilee, teaching in their synagogues, preaching the Good News of the Kingdom, and healing every disease and every sickness among the people. The report about him went out into all Syria. They brought to him all who were sick, afflicted with various diseases and torments, demonized, epileptics, and paralytics; and he healed them. Great multitudes from Galilee, Decapolis, Jerusalem, Judea and from beyond the Jordan followed him.

*(Matthew 4.23-25; Mark 1.39;*
*Luke 4.44)*

# JULY
## 27 CE

## The Call by the Sea

Now while the multitude pressed on him and heard the word of God, he was standing by the lake of Gennesaret. He saw two boats standing by the lake, but the fishermen had gone out of them, and were washing their nets. He entered into one of the boats, which was Simon's, and asked him to put out a little from the land. He sat down and taught the multitudes from the boat.

When he had finished speaking, he said to Simon, "Put out into the deep, and let down your nets for a catch."

Simon answered him, "Master, we worked all night, and took nothing; but at your word I will let down the net."

When they had done this, they caught a great multitude of fish, and their net was breaking. They beckoned to their partners in the other boat, that they should come and help them. They came, and filled both boats, so that they began to sink. But Simon Peter, when he saw it, fell down at Jesus' knees, saying, "Depart from me, for I am a sinful man, Lord." For he was amazed, and all who were with him, at the catch of fish which they had caught; and so also were James and John, sons of Zebedee, who were partners with Simon.

Jesus said to Simon, "Don't be afraid. From now on you will be catching people alive." When they had brought their boats to land, they left everything, and followed him.

*(Luke 5.1-11)*

61

## *The Teaching on the Mountain*

Seeing the multitudes, he went up onto the mountain. When he had sat down, his disciples came to him. He opened his mouth and taught them, saying,

> "Blessed are the poor in spirit,
> for theirs is the Kingdom of Heaven.
> Blessed are those who mourn,
> for they shall be comforted.
> Blessed are the gentle, for they shall inherit the earth.
> Blessed are those who hunger
> and thirst after righteousness,
> for they shall be filled.
> Blessed are the merciful, for they shall obtain mercy.
> Blessed are the pure in heart, for they shall see God.
> Blessed are the peacemakers,
> for they shall be called children of God.

Blessed are those who have been persecuted for righteousness' sake, for theirs is the Kingdom of Heaven.

"Blessed are you when people reproach you, persecute you, and say all kinds of evil against you falsely, for my sake. Rejoice, and be exceedingly glad, for great is your reward in heaven. For that is how they persecuted the prophets who were before you.

"You are the salt of the earth, but if the salt has lost its flavor, with what will it be salted? It is then good for nothing, but to be cast out and trodden under the feet of men. You are the light of the world. A city located on a hill can't be hidden. Neither do you light a lamp, and put it under a measuring basket, but on a stand; and it shines to all who are in the house. Even so, let your light shine before men; that they may see your good works, and glorify your Father who is in heaven.

"Don't think that I came to destroy the law or the prophets. I didn't come to destroy, but to fulfill. For most certainly, I tell you, until heaven and earth pass away, not even the smallest letter or one tiny pen stroke shall in any way pass away from the law, until all things are accomplished. Whoever, therefore, shall break one of these

62

least commandments, and teach others to do so, shall be called least in the Kingdom of Heaven; but whoever shall do and teach them shall be called great in the Kingdom of Heaven.   For I tell you that unless your righteousness exceeds that of the scribes and Pharisees, there is no way you will enter into the Kingdom of Heaven.

"You have heard that it was said to the ancient ones, 'You shall not murder;' and 'Whoever murders will be in danger of the judgment.'   But I tell you, that everyone who is angry with his brother without a cause will be in danger of the judgment; and whoever says to his brother, 'Raca!' will be in danger of the council; and whoever says, 'You fool!' will be in danger of the fire of Gehenna.

"If therefore you are offering your gift at the altar, and there remember that your brother has anything against you, leave your gift there before the altar, and go your way. First be reconciled to your brother, and then come and offer your gift. Agree with your adversary quickly, while you are with him on the way; lest perhaps the prosecutor deliver you to the judge, and the judge deliver you to the officer, and you be cast into prison.   Most certainly I tell you, you shall by no means get out of there, until you have paid the last penny.

"You have heard that it was said, 'You shall not commit adultery;' but I tell you that everyone who gazes at a woman to lust after her has committed adultery with her already in his heart.  If your right eye causes you to stumble, pluck it out and throw it away from you. For it is more profitable for you that one of your members should perish, than for your whole body to be cast into Gehenna.  If your right hand causes you to stumble, cut it off, and throw it away from you. For it is more profitable for you that one of your members should perish, than for your whole body to be cast into Gehenna.

"It was also said, 'Whoever shall put away his wife, let him give her a writing of divorce,' but I tell you that whoever puts away his wife, except for the cause of sexual immorality, makes her an adulteress; and whoever marries her when she is put away commits adultery.

"Again you have heard that it was said to them of old time, 'You shall not make false vows, but shall perform to the Lord your vows,' but I tell you, don't swear at all: neither by heaven, for it is the throne of God; nor by the earth, for it is the footstool of his feet; nor by Jerusalem, for it is the city of the great King. Neither shall you swear by your head, for you can't make one hair white or black. But let your 'Yes' be 'Yes' and your 'No' be 'No.' Whatever is more than these is of the evil one.

"You have heard that it was said, 'An eye for an eye, and a tooth for a tooth.' But I tell you, don't resist him who is evil; but whoever strikes you on your right cheek, turn to him the other also. If anyone sues you to take away your coat, let him have your cloak also. Whoever compels you to go one mile, go with him two. Give to him who asks you, and don't turn away him who desires to borrow from you.

"You have heard that it was said, 'You shall love your neighbor and hate your enemy.' But I tell you, love your enemies, bless those who curse you, do good to those who hate you, and pray for those who mistreat you and persecute you, that you may be children of your Father who is in heaven. For he makes his sun to rise on the evil and the good, and sends rain on the just and the unjust. For if you love those who love you, what reward do you have? Don't even the tax collectors do the same? If you only greet your friends, what more do you do than others? Don't even the tax collectors do the same? Therefore you shall be perfect, just as your Father in heaven is perfect.

"Be careful that you don't do your charitable giving before men, to be seen by them, or else you have no reward from your Father who is in heaven. Therefore when you do merciful deeds, don't sound a trumpet before yourself, as the hypocrites do in the synagogues and in the streets, that they may get glory from men. Most certainly I tell you, they have received their reward. But when you do merciful deeds, don't let your left hand know what your right hand does, so that your merciful deeds may be in secret; then your Father who sees in secret will reward you openly.

"When you pray, you shall not be as the hypocrites, for they love to stand and pray in the synagogues and in the corners of the streets, that they may be seen by men. Most certainly, I tell you, they have received their reward. But you, when you pray, enter into your inner room, and having shut your door, pray to your Father who is in secret, and your Father who sees in secret will reward you openly. In praying, don't use vain repetitions, as the Gentiles do; for they think that they will be heard for their much speaking. Therefore don't be like them, for your Father knows what things you need, before you ask him.

"Pray like this: 'Our Father in heaven, may your name be kept holy. Let your Kingdom come. Let your will be done, as in heaven, so on earth. Give us today our daily bread. Forgive us our debts, as we also forgive our debtors. Bring us not into temptation, but deliver us from the evil one. For yours is the Kingdom, the power, and the glory forever. Amen.'

"For if you forgive men their trespasses, your heavenly Father will also forgive you. But if you don't forgive men their trespasses, neither will your Father forgive your trespasses.

"Moreover when you fast, don't be like the hypocrites, with sad faces. For they disfigure their faces, that they may be seen by men to be fasting. Most certainly I tell you, they have received their reward. But you, when you fast, anoint your head, and wash your face; so that you are not seen by men to be fasting, but by your Father who is in secret, and your Father, who sees in secret, will reward you.

"Don't lay up treasures for yourselves on the earth, where moth and rust consume, and where thieves break through and steal; but lay up for yourselves treasures in heaven, where neither moth nor rust consume, and where thieves don't break through and steal; for where your treasure is, there your heart will be also.

"The lamp of the body is the eye. If therefore your eye is sound, your whole body will be full of light. But if your eye is evil, your whole body will be full of darkness. If therefore the light that is in you is darkness, how great is the darkness!

"No one can serve two masters, for either he will hate the one and love the other; or else he will be devoted to one

65

and despise the other. You can't serve both God and Mammon. Therefore I tell you, don't be anxious for your life: what you will eat, or what you will drink; nor yet for your body, what you will wear. Isn't life more than food, and the body more than clothing? See the birds of the sky, that they don't sow, neither do they reap, nor gather into barns. Your heavenly Father feeds them. Aren't you of much more value than they?

"Which of you, by being anxious, can add one moment to his lifespan? Why are you anxious about clothing? Consider the lilies of the field, how they grow. They don't toil, neither do they spin, yet I tell you that even Solomon in all his glory was not dressed like one of these. But if God so clothes the grass of the field, which today exists, and tomorrow is thrown into the oven, won't he much more clothe you, you of little faith?

"Therefore don't be anxious, saying, 'What will we eat?', 'What will we drink?' or, 'With what will we be clothed?' For the Gentiles seek after all these things; for your heavenly Father knows that you need all these things. But seek first God's Kingdom, and his righteousness; and all these things will be given to you as well. Therefore don't be anxious for tomorrow, for tomorrow will be anxious for itself. Each day's own evil is sufficient.

"Don't judge, so that you won't be judged. For with whatever judgment you judge, you will be judged; and with whatever measure you measure, it will be measured to you. Why do you see the speck that is in your brother's eye, but don't consider the beam that is in your own eye? Or how will you tell your brother, 'Let me remove the speck from your eye;' and behold, the beam is in your own eye? You hypocrite! First remove the beam out of your own eye, and then you can see clearly to remove the speck out of your brother's eye.

"Don't give that which is holy to the dogs, neither throw your pearls before the pigs, lest perhaps they trample them under their feet, and turn and tear you to pieces.

"Ask, and it will be given you. Seek, and you will find. Knock, and it will be opened for you. For everyone who asks receives. He who seeks finds. To him who knocks it will be opened. Or who is there among you, who, if his son asks him for bread, will give him a stone? Or if he asks for a fish, who will give him a serpent? If you then, being evil, know how to give good gifts to your children, how much more will your Father who is in heaven give good things to those who ask him! Therefore whatever you desire for men to do to you, you shall also do to them; for this is the law and the prophets.

"Enter in by the narrow gate; for wide is the gate and broad is the way that leads to destruction, and many are those who enter in by it. How narrow is the gate, and restricted is the way that leads to life! Few are those who find it.

"Beware of false prophets, who come to you in sheep's clothing, but inwardly are ravening wolves. By their fruits you will know them. Do you gather grapes from thorns, or figs from thistles? Even so, every good tree produces good fruit; but the corrupt tree produces evil fruit. A good tree can't produce evil fruit, neither can a corrupt tree produce good fruit. Every tree that doesn't grow good fruit is cut down, and thrown into the fire. Therefore by their fruits you will know them. Not everyone who says to me, 'Lord, Lord,' will enter into the Kingdom of Heaven; but he who does the will of my Father who is in heaven. Many will tell me in that day, 'Lord, Lord, didn't we prophesy in your name, in your name cast out demons, and in your name do many mighty works?' Then I will tell them, 'I never knew you. Depart from me, you who work iniquity.'

"Everyone therefore who hears these words of mine, and does them, I will liken him to a wise man, who built his house on a rock. The rain came down, the floods came, and the winds blew, and beat on that house; and it didn't fall, for it was founded on the rock. Everyone who hears these words of mine, and doesn't do them will be like a foolish man, who built his house on the sand. The rain came down, the floods came, and the winds blew, and beat on that house; and it fell—and great was its fall."

When Jesus had finished saying these things, the

multitudes were astonished at his teaching, for he taught them with authority, and not like the scribes.

*(Matthew 5.1-7.29)*

## Jesus Heals a Leper

When he came down from the mountain, great multitudes followed him. While he was in one of the cities, behold, there was a man full of leprosy. When he saw Jesus, he came to him, fell on his face, worshipped and begged him, saying, "Lord, if you want to, you can make me clean."

Jesus, being moved with compassion, stretched out his hand, and touched him, saying, "I want to. Be made clean." When he had said this, immediately his leprosy departed from him, and he was made clean. Jesus strictly warned him, and sent him out, and said to him, "See that you tell nobody, but go, show yourself to the priest, and offer for your cleansing the gift/things that Moses commanded, as a testimony to them."

But he went out, and began to proclaim it much, and to spread about the matter, so that Jesus could no more openly enter into a city, but was outside in desert places: and they came to him from everywhere. The report concerning him spread much more, and great multitudes came together to hear, and to be healed by him of their infirmities. But he withdrew himself into the desert, and prayed.

*(Matthew 8.1-4; Mark 1.40-45;*
*Luke 5.12-16)*

## A Paralytic and Four Friends

When he entered again into Capernaum, his own city, after some days, it was heard that he was in the house. Immediately many were gathered together, so that there was no more room, not even around the door; and he spoke the word to them. He was teaching; and there were Pharisees and teachers of the law sitting by, who had come out of every village of Galilee, Judea, and Jerusalem. The power of the Lord was with him to heal them.

68

Behold, four men brought a paralyzed man on a cot, and they sought to bring him in to lay before Jesus. When they could not come near to him for the crowd, they went up to the housetop and they removed the roof where he was. When they had broken it up, they let him down through the tiles with his cot into the middle before Jesus. Seeing their faith, Jesus said to the paralytic, "Son, cheer up! Your sins are forgiven you."

But there were some of the scribes and Pharisees sitting there, and reasoning in their hearts, "This man blasphemes! Why does this man speak blasphemies like that? Who can forgive sins but God alone?"

Immediately Jesus, perceiving their thoughts in his spirit and that they so reasoned within themselves, said to them, "Why do you reason these evil things in your hearts? Which is easier, to tell the paralytic, 'Your sins are forgiven;' or to say, 'Arise, and take up your bed, and walk?' But that you may know that the Son of Man has authority on earth to forgive sins"—he said to the paralytic—"I tell you, arise, take up your mat, and go to your house."

Immediately he rose up before them, and took up that which he was laying on, and departed to his house, glorifying God in front of them all. Amazement took hold on all, and they glorified God who had given such authority to men. They were filled with fear, saying, "We have seen strange things today. We have never seen anything like this!"

*(Matthew 9.1-7; Mark 2.1-12;*
*Luke 5.17-26)*

### Jesus Calls Matthew (Levi)

After these things he went out again by the seaside. All the multitude came to him and he taught them.

As he passed by, he saw a tax collector named Levi (Matthew), the son of Alphaeus, sitting at the tax office. Jesus said to him, "Follow me!" He left everything, and rose up and followed him. Levi made a great feast for him in his house. Jesus was reclining at the table in Levi's house, and many tax collectors and sinners sat down with Jesus and his disciples, for there were many, and they followed him. Their scribes and Pharisees, when they saw that he was eating with the sinners and tax collectors, murmured against his disciples and said, "Why do you and your teacher eat and drink with tax collectors and sinners?"

When Jesus heard it, he answered them, "Those who are healthy have no need for a physician, but those who are sick do. But you go and learn what this means: 'I desire mercy, and not sacrifice,' (Hosea 6.6), for I have not come to call the righteous, but sinners to repentance."

*(Matthew 9.9-13; Mark 2.13-17;*
*Luke 5.27-32)*

### Old Garments and New Wine

John's disciples and the Pharisees were fasting. Then John's disciples came to Jesus, saying, "Why do we and the Pharisees fast and pray often, but your disciples don't fast but rather eat and drink?"

He said to them, "Can you make the friends of the bridegroom, the groomsmen, mourn and fast while the bridegroom is with them? As long as they have the bridegroom with them, they can't fast. But the days will come when the bridegroom will be taken away from them. Then they will fast in those days."

He also told a parable to them. "No one sews a piece of unshrunken cloth from a new garment on an old garment, or else the patch shrinks and the new tears away from the old, and a worse hole is made, and also the piece from the new will not match the old. No one puts new wine into old wine skins, or else the new wine will burst the skins, and it will be spilled, and the skins will be destroyed. But new wine must be put into fresh wine skins, and both are preserved. No man having drunk old wine immediately desires new, for he says, 'The old is better.'"

*(Matthew 9.14-17; Mark 2.18-22;*
*Luke 5.33-39)*

# AUGUST
# 27 CE

## Jesus is Lord of the Sabbath

Now on the second Sabbath after the first, he was going through the grain fields. His disciples plucked the heads of grain and ate, rubbing them in their hands. But some of the Pharisees said to them, "Why do you and your disciples do that which is not lawful to do on the Sabbath day?"

Jesus, answering them, said, "Haven't you read what David did when he had need and was hungry-- he and those who were with him? How he entered into God's house when Abiathar was high priest, and took and ate the show bread, and gave also to those who were with him, which was not lawful for him to eat, neither for those who were with him, but only for the priests?

Or have you not read in the law, that on the Sabbath day, the priests in the temple profane the Sabbath, and are guiltless? But I tell you that one greater than the temple is here. But if you had known what this means, 'I desire mercy, and not sacrifice,' (Hosea 6.6) you would not have condemned the guiltless. Jesus said to them, "The Sabbath was made for man, not man for the Sabbath. The Son of Man is lord even of the Sabbath."

*(Matthew 12.1-8; Mark 2.23-28;*
*Luke 6.1-5)*

## Jesus Heals a Man's Withered Hand

It also happened on another Sabbath that he entered into the synagogue and taught. There was a man there, and his right hand was withered. The scribes and the Pharisees watched him, to see whether he would heal on the Sabbath, that they might find an accusation against him. But he knew their thoughts; and he said to the man who had the withered hand, "Rise up, and stand in the middle." He arose and stood. They asked him, "Is it lawful to heal on the Sabbath day?" that they might accuse him.

Then Jesus said to them, "I will ask you something: Is it lawful on the Sabbath to do good, or to do harm? To save a life, or to kill? What man is there among you, who has one sheep, and if this one falls into a pit on the Sabbath day, won't he grab on to it, and lift it out? Of how much more value then is a man than a sheep! Therefore it is lawful to do good on the Sabbath day." But they were silent.

When he had looked around at them with anger, being grieved at the hardening of their hearts, Jesus said to the man, "Stretch out your hand." He stretched it out, and his hand was restored as sound, whole and healthy as the other. But they were filled with rage, and talked with one another about what they might do to Jesus. The Pharisees went out, and immediately conspired with the Herodians against him, how they might destroy him.

*(Matthew 12.9-14; Mark 3.1-6;*
*Luke 6.6-11)*

## Crowds Come to Jesus

Jesus, perceiving that, withdrew to the sea with his disciples, and a great multitude followed him from Galilee, from Judea, from Jerusalem, from Idumaea, beyond the Jordan, and those from around Tyre and Sidon. A great multitude, hearing what great things he did, came to him. He spoke to his disciples that a little boat should stay near him because of the crowd, so that they wouldn't press on him. For he had healed many, so that as many as had diseases pressed on him that they might touch him. The unclean spirits, whenever they saw him, fell down before him, and cried, "You are the Son of God!" He sternly warned them that they should not make him known.

Great multitudes followed him; and he healed them all, and commanded them that they should not make him known: that it might be fulfilled which was spoken through Isaiah the prophet, saying:

> *"Behold, my servant whom I have chosen;*
> *my beloved in whom my soul is well pleased:*
> *I will put my Spirit on him.*
> *He will proclaim justice to the nations.*
> *He will not strive, nor shout;*
> *neither will anyone hear his voice in the streets.*
> *He won't break a bruised reed.*
> *He won't quench a smoking flax,*
> *until he leads justice to victory.*
> *In his name, the nations will hope."* *(Isaiah 42.1-4)*

*(Matthew 12.15-21; Mark 3.7-12)*

## *Jesus Chooses the Twelve*

In these days, he went out to the mountain to pray, and he continued all night in prayer to God. When it was day, he called his disciples, and from them he chose twelve, that they might be with him, and that he might send them out to preach, and to have authority to heal sicknesses and to cast out demons  These twelve he also named apostles and their names are:

> The first, Simon, whom he also named Peter;
> Andrew, his brother;
> James, the son of Zebedee;
> John, the brother of James; and he called them
> Boanerges, which means, Sons of Thunder;
> Philip;
> Bartholomew;
> Matthew, the tax collector;
> Thomas;
> James, the son of Alphaeus;

Simon the Canaanite, who was called the Zealot;
Judas (Lebbaeus) who was also called Thaddaeus,
the son of James;
and Judas Iscariot, who also betrayed him
and became a traitor.

He came down with them, and stood on a level place,
with a crowd of his disciples, and a great number of the
people from all Judea and Jerusalem, and the sea coast of
Tyre and Sidon, who came to hear him and to be healed of
their diseases; as well as those who were troubled by unclean
spirits, and they were being healed. All the multitude sought
to touch him, for power came out of him and healed them all.

*(Matthew 10.2-4; Mark 3.13-19;*
*Luke 6.12-19)*

### The Teaching on the Plain

Jesus lifted up his eyes to his disciples, and said,

"Blessed are you who are poor,
God's Kingdom is yours.
Blessed are you who hunger now,
for you will be filled.
Blessed are you who weep now, for you will laugh.

"Blessed are you when men shall hate you, and when
they shall exclude and mock you, and throw out your name
as evil, for the Son of Man's sake. Rejoice in that day, and
leap for joy, for behold, your reward is great in heaven, for
their fathers did the same thing to the prophets.

"But woe to you who are rich!
For you have received your consolation.
Woe to you, you who are full now,
for you will be hungry.
Woe to you who laugh now,
for you will mourn and weep.
Woe, when men speak well of you, for their fathers
did the same thing to the false prophets.

"But I tell you who hear: love your enemies, do good to those who hate you, bless those who curse you, and pray for those who mistreat you. To him who strikes you on the cheek, offer also the other; and from him who takes away your cloak, don't withhold your coat also. Give to everyone who asks you, and don't ask him who takes away your goods to give them back again.

"As you would like people to do to you, do exactly so to them. If you love those who love you, what credit is that to you? For even sinners love those who love them. If you do good to those who do good to you, what credit is that to you? For even sinners do the same. If you lend to those from whom you hope to receive, what credit is that to you? Even sinners lend to sinners, to receive back as much. But love your enemies, and do good, and lend, expecting nothing back; and your reward will be great, and you will be children of the Most High; for he is kind toward the unthankful and evil.

"Therefore be merciful,
even as your Father is also merciful.
Don't judge, and you won't be judged.
Don't condemn, and you won't be condemned.
Set free, and you will be set free.

"Give, and it will be given to you: good measure, pressed down, shaken together, and running over, will be given to you. For with the same measure you measure it will be measured back to you."

He spoke a parable to them. "Can the blind guide the blind? Won't they both fall into a pit? A disciple is not above his teacher, but everyone when he is fully trained will be like his teacher.

"Why do you see the speck of chaff that is in your brother's eye, but don't consider the beam that is in your own eye? Or how can you tell your brother, 'Brother, let me remove the speck of chaff that is in your eye,' when you yourself don't see the beam that is in your own eye? You hypocrite! First remove the beam from your own eye, and

77

then you can see clearly to remove the speck of chaff that is in your brother's eye.

"For there is no good tree that produces rotten fruit; nor again a rotten tree that produces good fruit. For each tree is known by its own fruit. For people don't gather figs from thorns, nor do they gather grapes from a bramble bush. The good man out of the good treasure of his heart brings out that which is good, and the evil man out of the evil treasure of his heart brings out that which is evil, for out of the abundance of the heart, his mouth speaks.

"Why do you call me, 'Lord, Lord,' and don't do the things which I say? Everyone who comes to me, and hears my words, and does them, I will show you who he is like. He is like a man building a house, who dug and went deep, and laid a foundation on the rock. When a flood arose, the stream broke against that house, and could not shake it, because it was founded on the rock. But he who hears, and doesn't do, is like a man who built a house on the earth without a foundation, against which the stream broke, and immediately it fell, and the ruin of that house was great."

*(Luke 6.20-49)*

### Jesus Heals the Centurion's Servant

After he had finished speaking in the hearing of the people, he entered into Capernaum. A certain centurion's servant, who was dear to him, was sick: paralyzed, grievously tormented and at the point of death. When he heard about Jesus, he sent to him elders of the Jews, asking him to come and save his servant.

When they came to Jesus, they begged him earnestly, saying, "He is worthy for you to do this for him, for he loves our nation, and he built our synagogue for us." Jesus said, "I will come and heal him," and went with them.

When he was now not far from the house, the centurion sent friends to him, saying to him, "Lord, don't trouble yourself, for I am not worthy for you to come under my roof. Therefore I didn't even think myself worthy to come to you; but just say the word, and my servant will be healed.

78

For I also am a man placed under authority, having under myself soldiers. I tell this one, 'Go!' and he goes; and to another, 'Come!' and he comes; and to my servant, 'Do this,' and he does it."

When Jesus heard these things, he marveled at him, and turned and said to the multitude who followed him, "I tell you, I have not found such great faith, no, not in Israel. Many will come from the east and the west, and will sit down with Abraham, Isaac, and Jacob in the Kingdom of Heaven, but the children of the Kingdom will be thrown out into the outer darkness. There will be weeping and gnashing of teeth."

Jesus said to those who were sent, "Go your way. Let it be done for him as he has believed." His servant was healed in that hour. They returned to the house and found that the servant who had been sick was well.

*(Matthew 8.5-13; Luke 7.1-10)*

## Jesus Raises the Widow's Son

Soon afterwards, he went to a city called Nain. Many of his disciples, along with a great multitude, went with him. Now when he came near to the gate of the city, behold, one who was dead was carried out, the only son of his mother, and she was a widow. Many people of the city were with her.

When the Lord saw her, he had compassion on her, and said to her, "Don't cry." He came near and touched the coffin, and the bearers stood still. He said, "Young man, I tell you, arise!" He who was dead sat up, and began to speak. And he gave him to his mother.

Fear took hold of all, and they glorified God, saying, "A great prophet has arisen among us!" and, "God has visited his people!" This report went out concerning him in the whole of Judea, and in all the surrounding region.

*(Luke 7.11-17)*

## *Jesus Answers John's Concerns*

The disciples of John (who was in prison) told him about all these things, the works of Christ. John, calling to himself two of his disciples, sent them to Jesus, saying, "Are you the one who is coming, or should we look for another?" When the men had come to him, they said, "John the Baptizer has sent us to you, saying, 'Are you he who comes, or should we look for another?'"

In that hour Jesus cured many of diseases and plagues and evil spirits; and to many who were blind he gave sight. Jesus answered them, "Go and tell John the things which you have seen and heard: that the blind receive their sight, the lame walk, the lepers are cleansed, the deaf hear, the dead are raised up, and the poor have good news preached to them. Blessed is he who finds no occasion for stumbling in me."

*(Matthew 11.2-6; Luke 7.18-23)*

## *Jesus Talks about his Cousin John*

When John's messengers had departed, Jesus began to tell the multitudes about John. He said, "What did you go out into the wilderness to see? A reed shaken by the wind? But what did you go out to see? A man clothed in soft clothing? Behold, those who are gorgeously dressed, and live delicately, are in kings' courts. But why did you go out? What did you go out to see? A prophet? Yes, I tell you, and much more than a prophet. This is he of whom it is written,

> *'Behold, I send my messenger before your face,*
> *who will prepare your way before you.' (Malachi 3.1)*

"For I tell you, among those who are born of women there is not a greater prophet than John the Baptizer, yet he who is least in God's Kingdom is greater than he. From the days of John the Baptizer until now, the Kingdom of Heaven suffers violence, and the violent take it by force. For all the prophets and the law prophesied until John. If you are willing to receive it, this is Elijah, who is to come. He who has ears to hear, let him hear."

When all the people and the tax collectors heard this, they declared God to be just, having been baptized with John's baptism. But the Pharisees and the lawyers rejected the counsel of God, not being baptized by him themselves.

But the Lord said, "To what then will I compare the people of this generation? What are they like? They are like children who sit in the marketplace, and call to their companions, saying, 'We played the flute and piped to you, and you didn't dance. We mourned for you, and you didn't weep or lament.' For John the Baptizer came neither eating bread nor drinking wine, and you say, 'He has a demon.' The Son of Man has come eating and drinking, and you say, 'Behold, a gluttonous man, and a drunkard; a friend of tax collectors and sinners!' Wisdom is justified by all her children."

*(Matthew 11.7-19; Luke 7.24-35)*

## Jesus Denounces the Cities

Then he began to denounce the cities in which most of his mighty works had been done, because they didn't repent. "Woe to you, Chorazin! Woe to you, Bethsaida! For if the mighty works had been done in Tyre and Sidon which were done in you, they would have repented long ago in sackcloth and ashes. But I tell you, it will be more tolerable for Tyre and Sidon on the day of judgment than for you. You, Capernaum, who are exalted to heaven, you will go down to Hades. For if the mighty works had been done in Sodom which were done in you, it would have remained until today. But I tell you that it will be more tolerable for the land of Sodom, on the day of judgment, than for you."

At that time, Jesus answered, "I thank you, Father, Lord of heaven and earth, that you hid these things from the wise and understanding, and revealed them to infants. Yes, Father, for so it was well-pleasing in your sight. All things have been delivered to me by my Father. No one knows the Son, except the Father; neither does anyone know the Father,

81

except the Son, and he to whom the Son desires to reveal him.

"Come to me, all you who labor and are heavily burdened, and I will give you rest. Take my yoke upon you, and learn from me, for I am gentle and humble in heart; and you will find rest for your souls. For my yoke is easy, and my burden is light."

*(Matthew 11.20-30)*

## Dinner at Simon's: A Woman Forgiven

One of the Pharisees invited him to eat with him. He entered into the Pharisee's house, and sat at the table. Behold, a woman in the city who was a sinner, when she knew that he was reclining in the Pharisee's house, she brought an alabaster jar of ointment. Standing behind at his feet weeping, she began to wet his feet with her tears, and she wiped them with the hair of her head, kissed his feet, and anointed them with the ointment.

Now when the Pharisee who had invited him saw it, he said to himself, "This man, if he were a prophet, would have perceived who and what kind of woman this is who touches him, that she is a sinner."

Jesus answered him, "Simon, I have something to tell you."

He said, "Teacher, say on."

"A certain lender had two debtors. The one owed five hundred denarii, and the other fifty. When they couldn't pay, he forgave them both. Which of them therefore will love him more?"

Simon answered, "He, I suppose, to whom he forgave the most."

He said to him, "You have judged correctly." Turning to the woman, he said to Simon, "Do you see this woman? I entered into your house, and you gave me no water for my feet, but she has wet my feet with her tears, and wiped them with the hair of her head. You gave me no kiss, but she, since the time I came in, has not ceased to kiss my feet. You didn't anoint my head with oil, but she has anointed my feet with ointment. Therefore I tell you, her sins, which are many, are forgiven, for she loved much. But to whom little is forgiven, the same loves little."

He said to her, "Your sins are forgiven."

Those who sat at the table with him began to say to themselves, "Who is this who even forgives sins?"

He said to the woman, "Your faith has saved you. Go in peace."

*(Luke 7.36-50)*

## Jesus Travels with the Twelve and Certain Women

Soon afterwards, he went about through cities and villages, preaching and bringing the good news of God's Kingdom. With him were the twelve, and certain women who had been healed of evil spirits and infirmities: Mary who was called Magdalene, from whom seven demons had gone out; and Joanna, the wife of Chuzas, Herod's steward; Susanna; and many others; who served them from their possessions.

*(Luke 8.1-3)*

## Jesus Casts out a Demon and is Confronted by Pharisees

Then one who was demonized, blind and mute, was brought to him and he healed him, so that the blind and mute man both spoke and saw. All the multitudes were amazed, and said, "Can this be the son of David?"

Jesus came into a house. The multitude came together again, so that they could not so much as eat bread. When his friends heard it, they went out to seize him: for they said, "He is insane."

But when the Pharisees and scribes who had come down from Jerusalem heard about the blind and mute man who Jesus healed, they said, "He has Beelzebul. This man does not cast out demons, except by Beelzebul, the prince of the demons."

Knowing their thoughts, Jesus summoned them, and said to them in parables, "How can Satan cast out Satan? Every kingdom divided against itself is brought to desolation, and every city or house divided against itself will not stand. If Satan has risen up against himself, and is divided, he can't stand, but has an end. How then will his kingdom stand? If I by Beelzebul cast out demons, by whom do your children cast them out? Therefore they will be your judges.

But if I, by the Spirit of God, cast out demons, then God's Kingdom has come upon you. Or how can one enter into the house of the strong man, and plunder his goods, unless he first bind the strong man? Then he will plunder his house.

"He who is not with me is against me, and he who doesn't gather with me, scatters. Therefore I tell you, every sin and blasphemy of the descendants of man will be forgiven, but the blasphemy against the Spirit will not be forgiven them. Whoever speaks a word against the Son of Man, it will be forgiven him; but whoever speaks against the Holy Spirit, it will not be forgiven him, neither in this age, nor in that which is to come, but he is subject to eternal condemnation." This was because they said, "He has an unclean spirit."

"Either make the tree good, and its fruit good, or make the tree corrupt, and its fruit corrupt; for the tree is known by its fruit. You offspring of vipers, how can you, being evil, speak good things? For out of the abundance of the heart, the mouth speaks. The good man out of his good treasure brings out good things, and the evil man out of his evil treasure brings out evil things. I tell you that every idle word that men speak, they will give account of it in the day of judgment. For by your words you will be justified, and by your words you will be condemned."

*(Matthew 12.22-37; Mark 3.19b-30;)*

84

## The Sign of Jonah the Prophet

Then certain of the scribes and Pharisees answered, "Teacher, we want to see a sign from you."

But he answered them, "An evil and adulterous generation seeks after a sign, but no sign will be given it but the sign of Jonah the prophet. For as Jonah was three days and three nights in the belly of the whale, so will the Son of Man be three days and three nights in the heart of the earth. The men of Nineveh will stand up in the judgment with this generation, and will condemn it, for they repented at the preaching of Jonah; and behold, someone greater than Jonah is here. The queen of the south will rise up in the judgment with this generation, and will condemn it, for she came from the ends of the earth to hear the wisdom of Solomon; and behold, someone greater than Solomon is here.

When an unclean spirit has gone out of a man, he passes through waterless places, seeking rest, and doesn't find it. Then he says, 'I will return into my house from which I came out,' and when he has come back, he finds it empty, swept, and put in order. Then he goes, and takes with himself seven other spirits more evil than he is, and they enter in and dwell there. The last state of that man becomes worse than the first. Even so will it be also to this evil generation."

*(Matthew 12.38-45)*

## Who is My Family?

While he was yet speaking to the multitudes, behold, his mother and his brothers came to him and stood outside because they could not come near him for the crowd. A multitude was sitting around him. They sent to him and called him, seeking to speak to him. One said to him, "Behold, your mother and your brothers  are standing outside, desiring to see you and to speak to you."

But he answered him who spoke to him, "Who is my mother? Who are my brothers?"  Looking at those who sat around him, Jesus stretched out his hand towards his

85

disciples, and said, "Behold, my mother and my brothers! For whoever does the will of God, my Father who is in heaven--whoever hears the word of God and does it-- the same is my brother, and sister, and mother."

*(Matthew 12.46-50; Mark 3.31-35; Luke 8.19-21)*

## The Parable of the Farmer

On that day Jesus went out of the house, and sat by the seaside. Great multitudes gathered to him, so that he entered into a boat in the sea, and sat down. And all the multitude stood on the beach, the land by the sea.

He spoke to them and taught them many things in parables, saying, "Listen! Behold, a farmer went out to sow. As he sowed, some seeds fell by the roadside. The seeds were trampled under foot, and the birds of the sky came and devoured them. Others fell on rocky ground, where they didn't have much soil, and immediately they sprang up, because they had no depth of earth. When the sun had risen, they were scorched. Because they had no root and moisture, they withered away. Others fell among the thorns. The thorns grew up and choked them and they yielded no fruit. Others fell on good soil, and yielded fruit, growing up and increasing. Some produced one hundred times as much, some sixty, and some thirty. He who has ears to hear, let him hear!"

*(Matthew 13.1-9; Mark 4.1-9; Luke 8.4-8)*

## Private Explanation of the Parable

When he was alone, those who were around him with the twelve came and asked him about the parables. They said to him, "Why do you speak to them in parables? What does this parable mean?"

He answered them, "To you it is given to know the mysteries of God's Kingdom, the Kingdom of Heaven, but it is not given to those who are outside. For whoever has, to him will be given, and he will have abundance, but whoever doesn't have, from him will be taken away even that which he has. Therefore I speak all things to them in parables, because seeing they don't see, and hearing, they don't hear, neither do they understand; lest perhaps they should turn again, and their sins should be forgiven them. In them the prophecy of Isaiah is fulfilled, which says,

> 'By hearing you will hear, and will
> in no way understand.
> Seeing you will see, and will in no way perceive.
> For this people's heart has grown callous,
> their ears are dull of hearing,
> they have closed their eyes;
> or else perhaps they might perceive with their eyes,
> hear with their ears,
> understand with their heart,
> and would turn again;
> and I would heal them.' (Isaiah 6.9-10)

"But blessed are your eyes, for they see; and your ears, for they hear. For most certainly I tell you that many prophets and righteous men desired to see the things which you see, and didn't see them; and to hear the things which you hear, and didn't hear them."

He said to them, "Don't you understand this parable? How will you understand all of the parables? Hear, then, the parable of the farmer. The farmer sows the seed which is the word of God. When anyone hears the word of the Kingdom, and doesn't understand it, Satan, the evil one, the devil comes, and snatches away the word which has been sown in his heart, that he may not believe and be saved. This is what was sown by the roadside.

"What was sown on the rocky places, this is he who hears the word, and receives it immediately with joy; yet he has no root in himself, but endures for a while and is short-lived. When oppression or persecution arises because of the word, immediately he stumbles and falls away in time of temptation.

"What was sown among the thorns, this is he who hears the word, but the cares of this age, the deceitfulness of riches, the lusts of other things, and the pleasures of life enter in and choke the word, and he becomes unfruitful, bringing no fruit to maturity.

"What was sown on the good ground, this is he who hears the word with an honest and good heart, accepts it, understands it, holds it tightly and produces fruit with patience. He most certainly bears fruit, and produces, some one hundred times as much, some sixty, and some thirty."

He said to them, "Is the lamp brought to be put under a basket, covered with a container or put under a bed? Isn't it put on a stand, that those who enter in may see the light? For there is nothing hidden, except that it should be revealed and made known; neither was anything made secret, but that it should come to light. If any man has ears to hear, let him hear."

He said to them, "Take heed what you hear; be careful, therefore, how you hear. With whatever measure you measure, it will be measured to you, and more will be given to you who hear. For whoever has, to him will more be given, and he who doesn't have, even that which he thinks he has will be taken away from him."

*(Matthew 13.10-23; Mark 4.10-25;*
*Luke 8.9-18)*

## Jesus Tells Other Parables

He set another parable before them, saying, "The Kingdom of Heaven is like a man who sowed good seed in his field, but while people slept, his enemy came and sowed darnel weeds also among the wheat, and went away. But when the blade sprang up and produced fruit, then the darnel weeds appeared also. The servants of the householder came and said to him, 'Sir, didn't you sow good seed in your field? Where did these darnel weeds come from?'

"He said to them, 'An enemy has done this.'

"The servants asked him, 'Do you want us to go and gather them up?'

88

"But he said, 'No, lest perhaps while you gather up the darnel weeds, you root up the wheat with them. Let both grow together until the harvest, and in the harvest time I will tell the reapers, "First, gather up the darnel weeds, and bind them in bundles to burn them; but gather the wheat into my barn.""""

He set another parable before them, saying, "How will we liken God's Kingdom? Or with what parable will we illustrate it? The Kingdom of Heaven is like a grain of mustard seed, which, when it is sown in the earth, though it is less than all the seeds that are on the earth, yet when it is sown, grows up, and becomes greater than all the herbs, and puts out great branches and becomes a tree, so that the birds of the sky/air can lodge in its branches under its shadow."

He spoke another parable to them. "The Kingdom of Heaven is like yeast, which a woman took, and hid in three measures of meal, until it was all leavened."

Jesus said, "God's Kingdom is as if a man should cast seed on the earth, and should sleep and rise night and day, and the seed should spring up and grow, he doesn't know how. For the earth bears fruit: first the blade, then the ear, then the full grain in the ear. But when the fruit is ripe, immediately he puts in the sickle, because the harvest has come."

With many such parables he spoke the word to them, as they were able to hear it. Jesus spoke all these things in parables to the multitudes; and without a parable, he didn't speak to them, that it might be fulfilled which was spoken through the prophet, saying:

> *"I will open my mouth in parables;*
> *I will utter things hidden*
> *from the foundation of the world." (Psalm 78.2)*

But privately, to his own disciples, he explained everything.

*(Matthew 13.24-35; Mark 4.26-34)*

## A Parable Explained and Others Told

Then Jesus sent the multitudes away, and went into the house. His disciples came to him, saying, "Explain to us the parable of the darnel weeds of the field."

He answered them, "He who sows the good seed is the Son of Man, the field is the world; and the good seed, these are the children of the Kingdom; and the darnel weeds are the children of the evil one. The enemy who sowed them is the devil. The harvest is the end of the age, and the reapers are angels. As therefore the darnel weeds are gathered up and burned with fire; so will it be at the end of this age. The Son of Man will send out his angels, and they will gather out of his Kingdom all things that cause stumbling, and those who do iniquity, and will cast them into the furnace of fire. There will be weeping and the gnashing of teeth. Then the righteous will shine like the sun in the Kingdom of their Father. He who has ears to hear, let him hear.

"Again, the Kingdom of Heaven is like a treasure hidden in the field, which a man found, and hid. In his joy, he goes and sells all that he has, and buys that field.

"Again, the Kingdom of Heaven is like a man who is a merchant seeking fine pearls, who having found one pearl of great price, he went and sold all that he had, and bought it.

"Again, the Kingdom of Heaven is like a dragnet, that was cast into the sea, and gathered some fish of every kind, which, when it was filled, they drew up on the beach. They sat down, and gathered the good into containers, but the bad they threw away. So will it be in the end of the world. The angels will come and separate the wicked from among the righteous, and will cast them into the furnace of fire. There will be the weeping and the gnashing of teeth." Jesus said to them, "Have you understood all these things?"

They answered him, "Yes, Lord."

He said to them, "Therefore every scribe who has been

made a disciple in the Kingdom of Heaven is like a man who is a householder, who brings out of his treasure new and old things."

*(Matthew 13.36-52)*

## Jesus Calms the Storm

When Jesus had finished these parables, he departed from there. Now when Jesus saw great multitudes around him, he gave the order to depart to the other side. Then a scribe came, and said to him, "Teacher, I will follow you wherever you go."

Jesus said to him, "The foxes have holes, and the birds of the sky have nests, but the Son of Man has nowhere to lay his head."

Another of his disciples said to him, "Lord, allow me first to go and bury my father." But Jesus said to him, "Follow me, and leave the dead to bury their own dead."

On that day, when evening had come, Jesus entered into a boat, himself and his disciples. He said to them, "Let's go over to the other side." Leaving the multitude, they took him with them, even as he was, in the boat and launched out. His disciples followed him in other small boats that were also with him. But as they sailed, Jesus fell asleep.

A big wind storm arose and came down on the lake, and the waves beat into the boat, so much that the boat was covered with the waves and taking on dangerous amounts of water. The boat was already filled. He himself was in the stern, asleep on the cushion. They came to him, woke him up, and told him, "Teacher! Master! Save us, Lord! Don't you care that we are dying?"

He awoke and said to them, "Why are you fearful, O you of little faith?" He rebuked the wind and the raging of the water, and said to the sea, "Peace! Be still!" The wind ceased, and there was a great calm. He said to them, "Why are you so afraid? How is it that you have no faith?"

They were greatly afraid. The men marveled and said to one another, "Who is this, what kind of man is he, then, that he commands even the winds, the water and the sea, and they obey him?"

*(Matthew 13.53; 8.18-27; Mark 5.35-41;*
*Luke 8.22-25)*

## The Gerasene Demoniacs

They came to the other side of the sea and arrived at the country of the Gadarenes, which is opposite Galilee.

When Jesus stepped ashore, immediately a certain man (2) out of the city who had demons for a long time met him. He wore no clothes, and didn't live in a house, but in the tombs. The unclean spirit had often seized the man, and he had been kept under guard. Nobody could bind him any more, not even with chains, because he had been often bound with fetters and chains, and the chains had been torn apart by him, and the fetters broken in pieces. Nobody had the strength to tame him. Breaking the bands apart, he was driven by the demons into the desert. Always, night and day, in the tombs and in the mountains, he was crying out, and cutting himself with stones. The man was so exceedingly fierce that nobody could pass that way.

When he saw Jesus from afar, he ran and bowed down to him, and crying out with a loud voice, he said, "What have I to do with you, Jesus, Son of the Most High God? Have you come here to torment us before the time? I adjure you by God, don't torment me." For Jesus was commanding the unclean spirit to come out of the man, saying to him, "Come out of the man, you unclean spirit!"

Jesus asked him, "What is your name?"

He said, "My name is Legion, for we are many," for many demons had entered into him. They begged him that he would not command them to go out of the country and into the abyss.

Now far away from them, on the mountainside, there was a great herd of pigs feeding. All the demons begged him, saying, "If you cast us out, send us into the pigs, that we may enter into them." At once Jesus gave them permission, and

92

said to them, "Go!" The demons came out of the man, and entered into the pigs. The herd of about two thousand pigs rushed down the steep bank into the lake, and were drowned in the water. When those who fed the pigs saw what had happened, they fled, and told it in the city and in the country.

Behold, all the people of the city came out to meet Jesus and to see what had happened. They came to Jesus, and found the man from whom the demons had gone out, sitting at Jesus' feet, clothed and in his right mind, even him who had the legion; and they were afraid. Those who saw what had happened told the others how he who had been demonized was healed, and they told them about the pigs. All the people of the surrounding country of the Gadarenes asked him to depart from the borders of their region, for they were very much afraid.

As Jesus was entering the boat to return, the man from whom the demons had gone out begged him that he might go with him. Jesus didn't allow him, but sent him away, saying, "Return to your house, and declare what great things the Lord, God has done for you, and how he had mercy on you." He went his way, proclaiming throughout the whole city and the Decapolis how Jesus had done great things for him. And everyone marveled.

*(Matthew 8.28-34; Mark 5.1-20;*
*Luke 8.26-39)*

## Jesus Crosses the Lake Again

When Jesus had crossed back over in the boat and returned to the other side of the lake, a great multitude was gathered to him; they welcomed him, for they were all waiting for him. And he was by the sea.

*(Mark 5.21; Luke 8.40)*

## *Jairus' Daughter and*
## *The Woman with the Issue of Blood*

Behold, one of the rulers of the synagogue, Jairus by name, came; and seeing Jesus, he fell at his feet, worshiped him and begged him much, saying, "My little daughter is at the point of death. Please come and lay your hands on her, that she may be made healthy, and live." She was his only daughter, about twelve years of age, and she was dying.

Jesus went with him, as did his disciples. And a great multitude followed him, and they pressed upon him on all sides. A certain woman, who had an issue/flow of blood for twelve years, had suffered many things by many physicians. She had spent all that she had, and was no better, but rather grew worse. She could not be healed by any. Having heard the things concerning Jesus, she came up behind him in the crowd, and touched his garment, the tassel of his cloak. For she said, "If I just touch his garment, I will be made well." Immediately the flow of her blood stopped and was dried up, and she felt in her body that she was healed of her affliction.

Immediately Jesus, perceiving in himself that the power had gone out from him, turned around in the crowd, and asked, "Who touched me? Who touched my clothes?"

When all denied it, Peter and his other disciples who were with him said to him, "Master, you see the multitude pressing against you and jostling you, and you say, 'Who touched me?'"

But Jesus said, "Someone did touch me, for I perceived that power has gone out of me." He looked around to see her who had done this thing. But the woman, when she saw that she was not hidden, was afraid and trembled. Knowing what had been done to her, she came and fell down before him, and told him all the truth. She declared to him in the presence of all the people the reason why she had touched him, and how she was healed immediately.

Jesus said to her, "Daughter, cheer up; your faith has made you well. Go in peace, and be cured of your disease." And the woman was made well from that hour.

While he was still speaking, people came from the synagogue ruler's house saying, "Your daughter is dead. Why bother the Teacher any more?"

But Jesus, when he heard the message spoken, immediately said to the ruler of the synagogue, "Don't be afraid, only believe, and she will be healed" He allowed no one to follow him, except Peter, James, and John the brother of James. He came to the synagogue ruler's house, and he saw an uproar: weeping, great wailing, the flute players, and the crowd in noisy disorder. When he had entered in, he said to them, "Why do you make an uproar? Don't weep. Make room, because the girl isn't dead, but sleeping."

They ridiculed him because they knew that she was dead. But he, having put them all out, took the father of the child, her mother, and those who were with him, and went in where the child was lying. Taking the child by the hand, he called to her saying, "Talitha cumi!" which means, being interpreted, "Girl, I tell you, get up!" Her spirit returned and immediately the girl rose up and walked, for she was twelve years old. He commanded that something be given to her to eat. Her parents were amazed with great amazement, but he commanded them to tell no one what had been done.

The report of this went out into all that land.

*(Matthew 9.18-26; Mark 5.22-43;*
*Luke 8.41-56)*

### Jesus Heals Two Blind Men

As Jesus passed by from there, two blind men followed him, calling out and saying, "Have mercy on us, son of David!" When he had come into the house, the blind men came to him. Jesus said to them, "Do you believe that I am able to do this?"

They told him, "Yes, Lord."

95

Then he touched their eyes, saying, "According to your faith be it done to you." Their eyes were opened. Jesus strictly commanded them, saying, "See that no one knows about this." But they went out and spread abroad his fame in all that land.

*(Matthew 9.27-31)*

## Jesus Heals a Man who is Mute

As they went out, behold, a mute man who was demonized was brought to him. When the demon was cast out, the mute man spoke. The multitudes marveled, saying, "Nothing like this has ever been seen in Israel!"

But the Pharisees said, "By the prince of the demons, he casts out demons."

*(Matthew 9.32-34)*

## Jesus is Rejected in Nazareth Again

Jesus went out from there into his own country, and his disciples followed him. When the Sabbath had come, he began teaching them in their synagogue, so that many were astonished, and said, "Where did this man get these things?" and, "What is the wisdom that is given to this man, that such mighty works come about by his hands? Isn't this the carpenter's son? Isn't this the carpenter? Isn't his mother called Mary, and his brothers, James, Joses, Simon, and Judas? Aren't all of his sisters here with us? Where then did this man get all of these things?" They were offended by him.

But Jesus said to them, "A prophet is not without honor, except in his own country, and among his own relatives, and in his own house." He could do no mighty work there--because of their unbelief-- except that he laid his hands on a few sick people, and healed them. Jesus marveled because of their unbelief.

*(Matthew 13.54-58; Mark 6.1-6a)*

## *Jesus Travels: Teaching, Preaching and Healing*

Jesus went about all the cities and the villages, teaching in their synagogues, and preaching the Good News of the Kingdom, and healing every disease and every sickness among the people. But when he saw the multitudes, he was moved with compassion for them, because they were harassed, weary and scattered, like sheep without a shepherd. Then he said to his disciples, "The harvest indeed is plentiful, but the laborers are few. Pray therefore that the Lord of the harvest will send out laborers into his harvest."

*(Matthew 9.35-38; Mark 6.6b)*

## *Jesus Sends Out the Twelve*

He called to himself his twelve disciples, and gave them power and authority over unclean spirits, to cast them out, and to heal every disease and every sickness. Jesus sent these twelve out two by two to preach God's Kingdom and to heal the sick.

He commanded them, saying, "Don't go among the Gentiles, and don't enter into any city of the Samaritans. Rather, go to the lost sheep of the house of Israel. As you go, preach, saying, 'The Kingdom of Heaven is at hand!' Heal the sick, cleanse the lepers, raise the dead and cast out demons. Freely you received, so freely give.

Don't take any gold, silver, or brass in your money belts. Take no bag for your journey, neither two coats, nor shoes, nor staff: for the laborer is worthy of his food. Into whatever city or village you enter, find out who in it is worthy; and stay there until you go on. As you enter into the household, greet it. If the household is worthy, let your peace come on it, but if it isn't worthy, let your peace return to you. Whoever doesn't receive you, nor hear your words, as you go out of that house or that city, shake off the dust from your feet for a testimony against them. Most certainly I tell you, it will be more tolerable for the land of Sodom and Gomorrah in the day of judgment than for that city.

"Behold, I send you out as sheep among wolves. Therefore be wise as serpents, and harmless as doves. But beware of men: for they will deliver you up to councils, and in their synagogues they will scourge you. Yes, and you will be brought before governors and kings for my sake, for a testimony to them and to the nations. But when they deliver you up, don't be anxious how or what you will say, for it will be given you in that hour what you will say. For it is not you who speak, but the Spirit of your Father who speaks in you.

"Brother will deliver up brother to death, and the father his child. Children will rise up against parents, and cause them to be put to death. You will be hated by all men for my name's sake, but he who endures to the end will be saved. But when they persecute you in this city, flee into the next, for most certainly I tell you, you will not have gone through the cities of Israel, until the Son of Man has come.

"A disciple is not above his teacher, nor a servant above his lord. It is enough for the disciple that he be like his teacher, and the servant like his lord. If they have called the master of the house Beelzebul, Lord of the Flies and the devil, how much more those of his household! Therefore don't be afraid of them, for there is nothing covered that will not be revealed; and hidden that will not be known. What I tell you in the darkness, speak in the light; and what you hear whispered in the ear, proclaim on the housetops. Don't be afraid of those who kill the body, but are not able to kill the soul. Rather, fear him who is able to destroy both soul and body in Gehenna.

"Aren't two sparrows sold for an assarion coin, worth half an hour's wages? Not one of them falls on the ground apart from your Father's will, but the very hairs of your head are all numbered. Therefore don't be afraid. You are of more value than many sparrows. Everyone therefore who confesses me before men, him I will also confess before my Father who is in heaven. But whoever denies me before men, him I will also deny before my Father who is in heaven.

"Don't think that I came to send peace on the earth. I didn't come to send peace, but a sword. For I came to set a man at odds against his father, and a daughter against her mother, and a daughter-in-law against her mother-in-law. A

98

man's foes will be those of his own household. He who loves father or mother more than me is not worthy of me; and he who loves son or daughter more than me isn't worthy of me. He who doesn't take his cross and follow after me, isn't worthy of me. He who seeks his life will lose it; and he who loses his life for my sake will find it.

"He who receives you receives me, and he who receives me receives him who sent me. He who receives a prophet in the name of a prophet will receive a prophet's reward. He who receives a righteous man in the name of a righteous man will receive a righteous man's reward. Whoever gives one of these little ones just a cup of cold water to drink in the name of a disciple, most certainly I tell you he will in no way lose his reward."

When Jesus had finished directing his twelve disciples, he departed from there to teach and preach in their cities.

The twelve departed and went throughout the villages, preaching the Good News and that people should repent. They cast out many demons, and anointed many with oil who were sick, and healed them everywhere.

*(Matthew 10.1,5-11.1; Mark 6.7-13;*
*Luke 9.1-6)*

# SEPTEMBER
# 27 CE

## Herod's Paranoia and
## Jesus Learns of John's Execution

At that time, Herod the tetrarch heard the report concerning Jesus, for his name had become known. Herod said to his servants, "This is John the Baptizer. He is risen from the dead. That is why these powers are at work in him." But others said, "He is Elijah." Others said, "He is a prophet, or like one of the prophets." But Herod, when he heard this, said, "This is John, whom I beheaded. He has risen from the dead." Herod said, "John I beheaded, but who is this, about whom I hear such things?" Herod sought to see Jesus.

For Herod himself had sent out, laid hold of and arrested John. He bound him, and put him in prison for the sake of Herodias, his brother Philip's wife, for he had married her. For John said to him, "It is not lawful for you to have your brother's wife." When Herod would have put John to death, he feared the multitude, because they counted him as a prophet. Herodias set herself against John, and desired to kill him, but she couldn't, for Herod feared John, knowing that he was a righteous and holy man. So Herod kept him safe. When he heard him, he did many things, and he heard him gladly.

Then a convenient day came, that Herod on his birthday made a supper for his nobles, the high officers, and the chief men of Galilee. When the daughter of Herodias herself came in and danced, she pleased Herod and those sitting with him. The king said to the young lady, "Ask me

103

whatever you want, and I will give it to you." He swore with an oath to her, "Whatever you shall ask of me, I will give you, up to half of my kingdom."

She went out, and said to her mother, "What shall I ask?"

Herodias said, "The head of John the Baptizer."

She came in immediately with haste to the king, and asked, "I want you to give me right now the head of John the Baptizer on a platter."

The king was exceedingly sorry and grieved, but for the sake of his oaths, and because of his dinner guests who sat at the table with him, he didn't wish to refuse her. Immediately the king sent out a soldier of his guard, and commanded him to bring John's head. He went and beheaded John in the prison, and brought his head on a platter, and gave it to the young lady; and the young lady gave it to her mother.

When his disciples heard this, they came and took up his corpse, and buried it, laying it in a tomb; and they went and told Jesus.

*(Matthew 14.1-12; Mark 6.14-29;*
*Luke 9.7-9)*

## A Failed Attempt to Rest and Grieve

The apostles gathered themselves together to Jesus, and they told him all things, whatever they had done, and whatever they had taught. He said to them, "You come apart into a deserted place, and rest awhile." For there were many coming and going, and they had no leisure so much as to eat.

When the apostles had returned and Jesus had heard the news about John's death, they all went away in the boat to the other side of the sea of Galilee, which is also called the Sea of Tiberias. Jesus took them, and withdrew apart to a deserted place of a city called Bethsaida.

The multitudes saw them going, and many recognized him and ran there on foot from all the cities. They followed him because they saw his signs which he did on those who were sick. They arrived before them and came together to him. Jesus came out, saw the great multitude, and he had compassion on them, because they were like sheep without a shepherd. Jesus went up into the mountain, and he sat there with his disciples.

Jesus welcomed them, taught them many things, spoke to them of God's Kingdom, and he cured those who needed healing.

Now the Passover, the feast of the Jews, was at hand. *(3)*

*(Matthew 14.13-14; Mark 6.30-34;*
*Luke 9.10-11; John 6.1-4)*

## Feeding the Five Thousand

Jesus therefore lifting up his eyes, and seeing that a great multitude was coming to him, said to Philip, "Where are we to buy bread, that these may eat?" This he said to test him, for he himself knew what he would do.

Philip answered him, "Two hundred denarii, seven month's wages, worth of bread is not sufficient for them, that everyone of them may receive a little."

One of his disciples, Andrew, Simon Peter's brother, said to him, "There is a boy here who has five barley loaves and two fish, but what are these among so many?"

The day began to wear away, and when it was late in the day, his disciples came to him, and said, "This place is deserted, and it is late in the day. Send them away, that they may go into the surrounding country, villages and farms, and buy themselves bread and get food, for they have nothing to eat."

But he answered them, "They don't need to go away. You give them something to eat."

They asked him, "Shall we go and buy two hundred denarii, seven month's wages, worth of bread, and give them something to eat?"

He said to them, "How many loaves do you have? Go see."

When they knew, they said, "We only have here five loaves and two fish."

He said, "Bring them here to me." He commanded them that everyone should sit down in groups for there was much green grass in that place. So the men sat down--in number about five thousand--in ranks, by hundreds and by fifties. He took the five loaves and the two fish, and looking up to heaven (the sky), having given thanks, he blessed and broke the loaves. He distributed to the disciples, and the disciples gave to those who were sitting down  And likewise, he divided the two fish among them all.

They all ate as much as they desired. When they were filled, he said to his disciples, "Gather up the broken pieces which are left over, that nothing be lost." So they gathered them up, and filled twelve baskets with broken pieces from the five barley loaves, which were left over by those who had eaten, also of the fish. Those who ate the loaves were about five thousand men, besides women and children.

When therefore the people saw the sign which Jesus did, they said, "This is truly the prophet who comes into the world." Jesus therefore, perceiving that they were about to come and take him by force, to make him king, immediately made the disciples get into the boat, and go ahead of him to the other side, to Capernaum *(4)*, while he sent the multitudes away. After he had sent the multitudes away, he withdrew up into the mountain by himself to pray. When evening came he was there alone.

*(Matthew 14.15-23; Mark 6.35-46;*
*Luke 9.12-17; John 6.5-17a)*

## Jesus Walks on the Water

But the boat was now in the middle of the sea, and Jesus was alone on the land. It was now dark, and Jesus had not come to them. The sea was tossed by a great wind blowing, and they had rowed about twenty-five or thirty stadia (5-6 km). Seeing them distressed in rowing by the waves-- for the wind was contrary-- in the fourth watch of the night (between 3:00 and sunrise), Jesus came to them, walking on the sea.

He would have passed by them, but when all the disciples saw him walking on the sea, they were troubled, supposing that it was a ghost, and cried out for fear. Immediately Jesus spoke to them, saying "Cheer up! It is I! Don't be afraid."

Peter answered him and said, "Lord, if it is you, command me to come to you on the waters."

He said, "Come!"

Peter stepped down from the boat, and walked on the waters to come to Jesus. But when he saw that the wind was strong, he was afraid, and beginning to sink, he cried out, saying, "Lord, save me!"

Immediately Jesus stretched out his hand, took hold of him, and said to him, "You of little faith, why did you doubt?"

When they got up into the boat, the wind ceased. Those who were in the boat came and worshiped him, saying, "You are truly the Son of God!" They were very amazed among themselves, and marveled; for they hadn't understood about the loaves, but their hearts were hardened.

*(Matthew 14.24-33; Mark 6.47-52;*
*John 6.17b-21a)*

## Great Healings in Gennesaret

When they had crossed over, they came to land at Gennesaret, and moored to the shore. When they had come out of the boat, immediately the people recognized him, and ran around that whole region, and began to bring all those who were sick, on their mats, to where they heard he was. Wherever he entered, into villages, or into cities, or into the country, they laid the sick in the marketplaces, and begged him that they might touch just the tassel of his garment; and as many as touched him were made well and whole.

*(Matthew 14.34-36; Mark 6.53-56)*

## A Seeking Multitude Finds Jesus in Capernaum

The day after Jesus fed the five thousand, the multitude that stood on the other side of the sea saw that there was no other boat there, except the one in which his disciples had embarked, and that Jesus hadn't entered with his disciples into the boat, but his disciples had gone away alone. However boats from Tiberias came near to the place where they ate the bread after the Lord had given thanks. When the multitude therefore saw that Jesus wasn't there, nor his disciples, they themselves got into the boats, and came to Capernaum, seeking Jesus.

*(John 6.22-24)*

## I am the Bread of Life

When they found him on the other side of the sea, they asked him, "Rabbi, when did you come here?"

Jesus answered them, "Most certainly I tell you, you seek me, not because you saw signs, but because you ate of the loaves, and were filled. Don't work for the food which perishes, but for the food which remains to eternal life, which the Son of Man will give to you. For God the Father has sealed him."

They said therefore to him, "What must we do, that we may work the works of God?"

Jesus answered them, "This is the work of God, that you believe in him whom he has sent."

They said therefore to him, "What then do you do for a sign, that we may see, and believe you? What work do you do? Our fathers ate the manna in the wilderness. As it is written, 'He gave them bread out of heaven to eat.'"

Jesus therefore said to them, "Most certainly, I tell you, it wasn't Moses who gave you the bread out of heaven, but my Father gives you the true bread out of heaven. For the bread of God is that which comes down out of heaven, and gives life to the world."

They said therefore to him, "Lord, always give us this bread."

Jesus said to them, "I am the bread of life. He who comes to me will not be hungry, and he who believes in me will never be thirsty. But I told you that you have seen me, and yet you don't believe. All those whom the Father gives me will come to me. He who comes to me I will in no way throw out. For I have come down from heaven, not to do my own will, but the will of him who sent me. This is the will of my Father who sent me, that of all he has given to me I should lose nothing, but should raise him up at the last day. This is the will of the one who sent me, that everyone who sees the Son, and believes in him, should have eternal life; and I will raise him up at the last day."

The Jews therefore murmured concerning him, because he said, "I am the bread which came down out of heaven." They said, "Isn't this Jesus, the son of Joseph, whose father and mother we know? How then does he say, 'I have come down out of heaven?'"

Therefore Jesus answered them, "Don't murmur among yourselves. No one can come to me unless the Father who sent me draws him, and I will raise him up in the last day. It is written in the prophets, *'They will all be taught by God.'* *(Isaiah 54.13)* Therefore everyone who hears from the Father, and has learned, comes to me. Not that anyone has seen the Father, except he who is from God. He has seen the Father. Most certainly, I tell you, he who believes in me has eternal life. I am the bread of life. Your fathers ate the manna in the wilderness, and they died. This is the bread which comes down out of heaven, that anyone may eat of it and not die. I am the living bread which came down out of heaven. If anyone eats of this bread, he will live forever. Yes, the bread which I will give for the life of the world is my flesh."

The Jews therefore contended with one another, saying, "How can this man give us his flesh to eat?"

Jesus therefore said to them, "Most certainly I tell you, unless you eat the flesh of the Son of Man and drink his blood, you don't have life in yourselves. He who eats my flesh and drinks my blood has eternal life, and I will raise him up at the last day. For my flesh is food indeed, and my blood is drink indeed. He who eats my flesh and drinks my blood lives in me, and I in him. As the living Father sent me, and I live because of the Father; so he who feeds on me, he will also live because of me. This is the bread which came down out of heaven—not as our fathers ate the manna, and died. He who eats this bread will live forever."

He said these things in the synagogue, as he taught in Capernaum. Therefore many of his disciples, when they heard this, said, "This is a hard saying! Who can listen to it?"

But Jesus knowing in himself that his disciples murmured at this, said to them, "Does this cause you to stumble? Then what if you would see the Son of Man ascending to where he was before? It is the spirit who gives life. The flesh profits nothing. The words that I speak to you are spirit, and are life. But there are some of you who don't believe." For Jesus knew from the beginning who they were who didn't believe, and who it was who would betray him. He said, "For this cause have I said to you that no one can come to me, unless it is given to him by my Father."

*(John 6.23-65)*

### Offended Disciples Walk Away

At this, many of his disciples went back, and walked no more with him. Jesus said therefore to the twelve, "You don't also want to go away, do you?"

Simon Peter answered him, "Lord, to whom would we go? You have the words of eternal life. We have come to believe and know that you are the Christ, the Son of the living God."

Jesus answered them, "Didn't I choose you, the twelve, and one of you is a devil?" Now he spoke of Judas, the son of Simon Iscariot, for it was he who would betray him, being one of the twelve.

After these things, Jesus was walking in Galilee, for he wouldn't walk in Judea, because the Jews sought to kill him.

*(John 6.66-7.1)*

## What Truly Defiles People

Then Pharisees and some of the scribes came to Jesus from Jerusalem. Now when they saw some of his disciples eating bread with defiled, that is unwashed, hands, they found fault. (For the Pharisees and all the Jews, don't eat unless they wash their hands and forearms, holding to the tradition of the elders. They don't eat when they come from the marketplace unless they bathe themselves, and there are many other things, which they have received to hold to: washings of cups, pitchers, bronze vessels, and couches.)

The Pharisees and the scribes asked him, "Why don't your disciples obey the tradition of the elders and walk according to them? For they don't wash their hands when they eat bread."

He answered them, "Why do you set aside and disobey the commandment of God because you hold tightly to the tradition of men—the washing of pitchers and cups, and many other such things? Full well do you reject the commandment of God, that you may keep your tradition.

For God, through Moses commanded, *'Honor your father and your mother,'* *(Exodus 20.12)* and, *'He who speaks evil of father or mother, let him be put to death.'* *(Exodus 21.17)* But you say, 'Whoever may tell his father or his mother, "Whatever help and profit you might otherwise have received from me is Corban, a gift devoted to God," he shall not honor his father or mother.' You have made the commandment of God void because of your tradition which you have handed down. You do many things like this. You hypocrites! Well did Isaiah prophesy of you, saying:

111

*'These people draw near to me with their mouth,*
*and honor me with their lips;*
*but their heart is far from me.*
*And in vain do they worship me,*
*teaching as doctrine rules*
*made by men.'" (Isaiah 29.13)*

He summoned the multitude, and said to them, "Hear me all of you, and understand. There is nothing from outside of the man, that going into him can defile him; but the things which proceed out of the man are those that defile the man. That which enters into the mouth doesn't defile the man; but that which proceeds out of the mouth, this defiles the man. If anyone has ears to hear, let him hear!"

When he had entered into a house away from the multitude, his disciples came, and said to him, "Do you know that the Pharisees were offended, when they heard this saying?"

But he answered, "Every plant which my heavenly Father didn't plant will be uprooted. Leave them alone. They are blind guides of the blind. If the blind guide the blind, both will fall into a pit."

Peter answered him, "Explain the parable to us."

So Jesus said, "Do you also still not understand? Don't you understand and perceive that whatever goes into the man's mouth from outside can't defile him because it doesn't go into his heart, but passes into the belly, and then out of the body into the latrine?" Thus he declared all foods clean.

"But the things which proceed out of the man's mouth come out of the heart, and they defile the man. For from within, out of the hearts of men, proceeds evil thoughts, murders, adulteries, sexual sins, thefts, covetings, wickedness, deceit, lustful desires, an evil eye, pride, false testimony, foolishness and blasphemies. All these evil things come from within, and defile the man; but to eat with unwashed hands doesn't defile the man."

*(Matthew 15.1-20; Mark 7.1-23)*

## Jesus Heals the Syrophoenician Woman's Daughter

Jesus went out from there, and withdrew into the region of Tyre and Sidon. He entered into a house, and didn't want anyone to know it, but he couldn't escape notice. For a woman, whose little daughter had an unclean spirit, having heard of Jesus, came and fell down at his feet. Now the woman was a Greek, a Canaanite, a Syrophoenician by race. She begged him that he would cast the demon out of her daughter. She cried, saying, "Have mercy on me, Lord, you son of David! My daughter is severely demonized!"

But he answered her not a word. His disciples came and begged him, saying, "Send her away; for she cries after us."

But he answered, "I wasn't sent to anyone but the lost sheep of the house of Israel."

But she came and worshiped him, saying, "Lord, help me."

But Jesus answered her, "Let the children be filled first, for it is not appropriate to take the children's bread and throw it to the dogs."

But she said, "Yes, Lord, but even the dogs under the table eat the children's crumbs which fall from their masters' table."

Then Jesus answered her, "Woman, great is your faith! Be it done to you even as you desire. For this saying, go your way. The demon has gone out of your daughter." And her daughter was healed from that hour.

*(Matthew 15.21-28; Mark 7.24-30)*

## Jesus Heals a Deaf Man and Others

Again he departed from the borders of Tyre and Sidon, and came near to the sea of Galilee, through the middle of the region of Decapolis. They brought to him one who was deaf and had an impediment in his speech. They begged him to lay his hand on him.

113

He took him aside from the multitude, privately, and put his fingers into his ears, and he spat, and touched his tongue. Looking up to heaven, he sighed, and said to him, "Ephphatha!" that is, "Be opened!" Immediately his ears were opened, and the impediment of his tongue was released, and he spoke clearly.

He commanded them that they should tell no one, but the more he commanded them, so much the more widely they proclaimed it. They were astonished beyond measure, saying, "He has done all things well. He makes even the deaf hear, and the mute speak!"

Jesus went up into the mountain, and sat there. Great multitudes came to him, having with them the lame, blind, mute, maimed, and many others, and they put them down at his feet. He healed them, so that the multitude wondered when they saw the mute speaking, injured whole, lame walking, and blind seeing—and they glorified the God of Israel.

*(Matthew 15.29-31; Mark 7.31-37)*

## Feeding the Four Thousand

In those days, when there was a very great multitude, and they had nothing to eat, Jesus called his disciples to himself, and said to them, "I have compassion on the multitude, because they have stayed with me now three days, and have nothing to eat. If I send them away fasting to their home, they will faint on the way, for some of them have come a long way."

His disciples answered him, "Where should we get so many loaves in a deserted place as to satisfy so great a multitude?"

He asked them, "How many loaves do you have?"

They said, "Seven, and a few small fish."

He commanded the multitude to sit down on the ground, and he took the seven loaves. Having given thanks, he broke them, and gave them to his disciples to serve, and they served the multitude. He took the few small fish.

114

Having blessed them, he said to serve these also. They all ate, and were filled. They took up seven baskets full of broken pieces that were left over. Those who had eaten were about four thousand, besides women and children. Then he sent the multitudes away.

*(Matthew 15.32-39a; Mark 8.1-9)*

## No Sign at Dalmanutha, Magdala

Immediately he entered into the boat with his disciples, and came into the region of Dalmanutha, into the borders of Magdala. The Pharisees and Sadducees came, questioning and testing him. They asked him to show them a sign from heaven.

Jesus sighed deeply in his spirit, and answered them, "When it is evening, you say, 'It will be fair weather, for the sky is red.' In the morning, 'It will be foul weather today, for the sky is red and threatening.' Hypocrites! You know how to discern the appearance of the sky, but you can't discern the signs of the times! Why does this generation seek a sign? An evil and adulterous generation seeks after a sign, and there will be no sign given to it, except the sign of the prophet Jonah."

He left them, and again entering into the boat, departed to the other side.

*(Matthew 15.39b-16.4; Mark 8.10-13)*

## Beware of the Yeast

The disciples came to the other side and had forgotten to take bread; they didn't have more than one loaf in the boat with them. Jesus warned them, saying, "Take heed and beware of the yeast of the Pharisees and Sadducees and the yeast of Herod."

They reasoned with one another, saying, "It's because we brought no bread."

Jesus, perceiving it, said to them, "Why do you reason among yourselves, you of little faith, that it's because you

115

brought no bread? Don't you perceive yet, neither understand? Is your heart still hardened? Having eyes, don't you see? Having ears, don't you hear? Don't you remember? When I broke the five loaves among the five thousand, how many baskets full of broken pieces did you take up?"

They told him, "Twelve."

"When the seven loaves fed the four thousand, how many baskets full of broken pieces did you take up?"

They told him, "Seven."

He asked them, "Don't you understand, yet? How is it that you don't perceive that I didn't speak to you concerning bread? But beware of the yeast of the Pharisees and Sadducees."

Then they understood that he didn't tell them to beware of the yeast of bread, but of the teaching of the Pharisees and Sadducees."

*(Matthew 16.5-12; Mark 8.14-21)*

## Blind Man at Bethsaida

Jesus came to Bethsaida. They brought a blind man to him, and begged him to touch him. He took hold of the blind man by the hand, and brought him out of the village. When he had spit on his eyes, and laid his hands on him, he asked him if he saw anything.

He looked up, and said, "I see men; for I see them like trees walking."

Then again he laid his hands on his eyes. He looked intently, and was restored, and saw everyone clearly. He sent him away to his house, saying, "Don't enter into the village, nor tell anyone in the village."

*(Mark 8.24-26)*

## Who Do People Say I Am?

Jesus went out, with his disciples, into the villages of Caesarea Philippi. On the way, he was praying alone, and he asked his disciples, saying, "Who do the multitudes say that I, the Son of Man, am?"

They said, "Some say John the Baptizer, some, Elijah, and others, Jeremiah, or one of the old prophets that is risen again."

He said to them, "But who do you say that I am?"

Simon Peter answered, "You are the Christ of God, the Son of the living God."

Jesus answered him, "Blessed are you, Simon Bar Jonah, for flesh and blood has not revealed this to you, but my Father who is in heaven. I also tell you that you are Peter, and on this rock I will build my assembly, and the gates of Hades will not prevail against it. I will give to you the keys of the Kingdom of Heaven, and whatever you bind on earth will have been bound in heaven; and whatever you release on earth will have been released in heaven."

Then he warned them and commanded the disciples that they should tell no one that he was Jesus the Christ. From that time, Jesus began to teach and show his disciples that he, the Son of Man, must go to Jerusalem and suffer many things from and be rejected by the elders, chief priests, and scribes, and be killed. And after three days, the third day, be raised up again. He spoke to them openly.

Peter took him aside, and began to rebuke him, saying, "Far be it from you, Lord! This will never be done to you."

But Jesus turned around, and seeing his disciples, rebuked Peter, and said to him, "Get behind me, Satan! You are a stumbling block to me, for you are not setting your mind on the things of God, but on the things of men."

Then Jesus called the multitude to himself with his disciples and said, "If anyone desires to come after me, let him deny himself, and take up his cross daily, and follow me.

117

For whoever desires to save his life will lose it, and whoever will lose his life for my sake and the sake of the Good News, will find and save it. For what will it profit a man, if he gains the whole world, and loses or forfeits his life, his own self? Or what will a man give in exchange for his life? For whoever will be ashamed of me and of my words in this adulterous and sinful generation, the Son of Man also will be ashamed of him, when he comes in his glory and his Father's glory, with the holy angels. For the Son of Man will then render to everyone according to his deeds.

"Most certainly I tell you, there are some standing here who will in no way taste of death, until they see the Son of Man coming in his Kingdom; until they see God's Kingdom come with power."

*(Matthew 16.13-28; Mark 8.27-9.1;*
*Luke 9.18-27)*

### The Transfiguration

After six days, Jesus took with him Peter, James, and John his brother, and brought them up into a high mountain privately by themselves to pray. As he was praying, Jesus was transfigured; he changed into another form in front of them. The appearance of his face was altered and it shone like the sun. His clothing became dazzling and glistening, exceedingly white as light, like snow, such as no launderer on earth can whiten them.

Behold, two men, Moses and Elijah, appeared to them in glory. They were talking with Jesus about his departure, his exodus, which he was about to accomplish at Jerusalem.

Now Peter and those who were with him were heavy with sleep, but when they were fully awake, they saw his glory, and the two men who stood with him. As they were parting from him, Peter said to Jesus, "Rabbi. Lord. Master. It is good for us to be here. If you want, let's make three tents here: one for you, one for Moses, and one for Elijah." For he didn't know what to say or what he was saying, for they were very afraid.

While he was still speaking, behold, a bright cloud came and overshadowed them and they were afraid as they entered into the cloud. Behold, a voice came out of the cloud, saying, "This is my beloved Son, in whom I am well pleased. Listen to him."

When the disciples heard it, they fell on their faces, and were very afraid. Jesus came and touched them and said, "Get up, and don't be afraid." Lifting up their eyes and looking around, they saw no one with them, except only Jesus alone.

As they were coming down from the mountain, he · commanded them that they should tell no one what things they had seen, until after the Son of Man had risen from the dead. They were silent and kept this saying to themselves, and told no one in those days any of the things which they had seen. But they were questioning what the "rising from the dead" meant.

*(Matthew 17.1-9; Mark 9.2-10;*
*Luke 9.28-36)*

## Elijah and John

They asked him, saying, "Why do the scribes say that Elijah must come first?"

He said to them, "Elijah indeed comes first, and will restore all things. How is it written about the Son of Man, that he should suffer many things and be despised? But I tell you that Elijah has come, and they didn't recognize him, but have also done to him whatever they wanted to, even as it is written about him."

Then the disciples understood that he spoke to them of John the Baptizer.

*(Matthew 17.10-13; Mark 9.11-13)*

119

# OCTOBER
## 27 CE

## Jesus Heals an Epileptic Boy

On the next day, when they had come down from the mountain, they came to the disciples, and he saw a great multitude around them, and scribes questioning them. Immediately all the multitude, when they saw him, were greatly amazed, and running to him greeted him. He asked the scribes, "What are you asking them?"

One man from the multitude, kneeling down to Jesus, answered, "Lord, have mercy on my son, for he is epileptic, has a mute spirit and suffers grievously. Behold, a spirit takes him, he suddenly cries out, and it convulses him so that he foams at the mouth, grinds his teeth, and wastes away. It hardly departs from him, bruising him severely. So, Teacher, I brought my only child to you. I asked your disciples to cast it out, but they weren't able to cure him."

He answered him, "Unbelieving, faithless and perverse generation, how long shall I be with you? How long shall I bear with you? Bring him to me."

They brought the boy to Jesus, and when he saw him, immediately the spirit convulsed him violently, and he fell on the ground, wallowing and foaming at the mouth.

He asked his father, "How long has it been since this has come to him?

He said, "From childhood. Often it has cast him both into the fire and into the water, to destroy him. But if you can do anything, have compassion on us, and help us."

123

Jesus said to him, "'If you can?' All things are possible to him who believes." Immediately the father of the child cried out with tears, "I believe. Help my unbelief!"

When Jesus saw that a multitude came running together, he rebuked the unclean spirit, saying to him, "You mute and deaf spirit, I command you, come out of him, and never enter him again!"

Having cried out, and convulsed greatly, it came out of him. The boy became like one dead; so much so that most of them said, "He is dead." But Jesus took him by the hand, and raised him up; and he arose. And the boy was cured from that hour. Jesus healed the boy and gave him back to his father. They were all astonished at the majesty of God.

When he had come into the house, his disciples asked him privately, "Why weren't we able to cast it out?"

He said to them, "Because of your unbelief. For most certainly I tell you, if you have faith as a grain of mustard seed, you will tell this mountain, 'Move from here to there,' and it will move; and nothing will be impossible for you. But this kind can come out by nothing, except by prayer and fasting."

*(Matthew 17.14-21; Mark 9.14-29;*
*Luke 9.37-43a)*

## *Jesus Speaks of His Death and Resurrection*

But while all were marveling at all the things which Jesus did, they went out from there, and passed through Galilee. He didn't want anyone to know it. For Jesus was teaching his disciples and saying to them, "Let these words sink into your ears, for the Son of Man is about to be delivered up and handed over to the hands of men. They will kill him, and the third day he will be raised up."

They were exceedingly sorry, but they didn't

understand this saying. It was concealed from them, that they should not perceive it, and they were afraid to ask him about this saying.

*(Matthew 17.22-23; Mark 9.30-32;*
*Luke 9.43b-45)*

## Peter, Temple Taxes and a Fish

When they had come to Capernaum, those who collected the didrachma coins for the temple tax came to Peter, and said, "Doesn't your teacher pay the didrachma?" He said, "Yes."

When he came into the house, Jesus anticipated him, saying, "What do you think, Simon? From whom do the kings of the earth receive toll or tribute? From their children, or from strangers?"

Peter said to him, "From strangers."

Jesus said to him, "Therefore the children are exempt. But, lest we cause them to stumble, go to the sea, cast a hook, and take up the first fish that comes up. When you have opened its mouth, you will find a stater coin. Take that, and give it to them for me and you."

*(Matthew 17.24-27)*

## The Greatest in the Kingdom

He came to Capernaum, and when he was in the house he asked them, "What were you arguing about among yourselves on the way?" But they were silent, for they had disputed one with another on the way about who was the greatest in the Kingdom of Heaven.

He sat down, and called the twelve; and he said to them, "If any man wants to be first, he shall be last of all, and servant of all."

Jesus, perceiving the reasoning of their hearts, took a little child, and set him by his side, in the middle of them. Taking him in his arms, he said to them, "Most certainly I tell you, unless you turn, and become as little children, you

125

will in no way enter into the Kingdom of Heaven. Whoever therefore humbles himself as this little child, the same is the greatest in the Kingdom of Heaven. Whoever receives one such little child in my name, receives me, and whoever receives me, doesn't receive me, but him who sent me. For whoever is least among you all, this one will be great."

John said to him, "Master, Teacher, we saw someone who doesn't follow us casting out demons in your name; and we forbade him, because he doesn't follow us."

But Jesus said, "Don't forbid him, for there is no one who will do a mighty work in my name, and be able quickly to speak evil of me. For whoever is not against us is for us and on our side. For whoever will give you a cup of water to drink in my name, because you are Christ's, most certainly I tell you, he will in no way lose his reward.

But whoever causes one of these little ones who believe in me to stumble, it would be better for him that a huge millstone should be hung around his neck, and that he should be sunk in the depths of the sea. Woe to the world because of occasions of stumbling! For it must be that the occasions come, but woe to that person through whom the occasion comes!

"If your hand causes you to stumble, cut it off. It is better for you to enter into life maimed, rather than having your two hands to go into Gehenna, into the eternal, unquenchable fire, 'where their worm doesn't die, and the fire is not quenched.' (Isaiah 66.24) If your foot causes you to stumble, cut it off. It is better for you to enter into life lame and crippled, rather than having your two feet to be cast into Gehenna, into the eternal fire that will never be quenched— 'where their worm doesn't die, and the fire is not quenched.' If your eye causes you to stumble, pluck it out and cast it from you. It is better for you to enter into God's Kingdom with one eye, rather than having two eyes to be cast into the Gehenna of fire, 'where their worm doesn't die, and the fire is not quenched.'

"See that you don't despise one of these little ones, for I tell you that in heaven their angels always see the face of my Father who is in heaven. For the Son of Man came to save that which was lost. What do you think? If a man has one hundred sheep, and one of them goes astray, doesn't he leave the ninety-nine, go to the mountains, and seek that which has gone astray? If he finds it, most certainly I tell you, he rejoices over it more than over the ninety-nine which have not gone astray. Even so it is not the will of your Father who is in heaven that one of these little ones should perish.

For everyone will be salted with fire, and every sacrifice will be seasoned with salt. Salt is good, but if the salt has lost its saltiness, with what will you season it? Have salt in yourselves, and be at peace with one another."

*(Matthew 18.1-14; Mark 9.33-50;*
*Luke 9.46-50)*

## If Someone Sins Against You

"If your brother sins against you, go, show him his fault between you and him alone. If he listens to you, you have gained back your brother. But if he doesn't listen, take one or two more with you, that at the mouth of two or three witnesses every word may be established. (Deuteronomy 19.15) If he refuses to listen to them, tell it to the assembly. If he refuses to hear the assembly also, let him be to you as a Gentile or a tax collector. Most certainly I tell you, whatever things you bind on earth will have been bound in heaven, and whatever things you release on earth will have been released in heaven. Again, assuredly I tell you, that if two of you will agree on earth concerning anything that they will ask, it will be done for them by my Father who is in heaven. For where two or three are gathered together in my name, there I am in the middle of them."

*(Matthew 18.15-19)*

## Parable of the Unforgiving Servant

Then Peter came and said to him, "Lord, how often shall my brother sin against me, and I forgive him? Until seven times?"

Jesus said to him, "I don't tell you until seven times, but, until seventy times seven. Therefore the Kingdom of Heaven is like a certain king, who wanted to reconcile accounts with his servants. When he had begun to reconcile, one was brought to him who owed him ten thousand talents (sixty million days worth of wages). But because he couldn't pay, his lord commanded him to be sold, with his wife, his children, and all that he had, and payment to be made. The servant therefore fell down and knelt before him, saying, 'Lord, have patience with me, and I will repay you all!' The lord of that servant, being moved with compassion, released him, and forgave him the debt.

"But that servant went out, and found one of his fellow servants, who owed him one hundred denarii (one hundred days worth of wages), and he grabbed him, and took him by the throat, saying, 'Pay me what you owe!'

"So his fellow servant fell down at his feet and begged him, saying, 'Have patience with me, and I will repay you!' He would not, but went and cast him into prison, until he should pay back that which was due.

"So when his fellow servants saw what was done, they were exceedingly sorry, and came and told to their lord all that was done. Then his lord called him in, and said to him, 'You wicked servant! I forgave you all that debt, because you begged me. Shouldn't you also have had mercy on your fellow servant, even as I had mercy on you?' His lord was angry, and delivered him to the tormentors, until he should pay all that was due to him. So my heavenly Father will also do to you, if you don't each forgive your brother from your hearts for his misdeeds."

*(Matthew 18.20-35)*

## A Disagreement between Jesus and His Brothers

Jesus was still walking in Galilee, for he wouldn't walk in Judea, because the Jews sought to kill him.

Now the feast of the Jews, the Feast of Booths, was at hand. His brothers therefore said to him, "Depart from here, and go into Judea, that your disciples also may see your works which you do. For no one does anything in secret, and himself seeks to be known openly. If you do these things, reveal yourself to the world." For even his brothers didn't believe in him.

Jesus therefore said to them, "My time has not yet come, but your time is always ready. The world can't hate you, but it hates me, because I testify about it, that its works are evil. You go up to the feast. I am not yet going up to this feast, because my time is not yet fulfilled."

Having said these things to them, he stayed in Galilee.

*(John 7.1-9)*

### *Jesus Travels Secretly to Jerusalem*

But when his brothers had gone up to the feast, then he also went up, not publicly, but as it were in secret. And it came to pass, when the days were near that he should be taken up, he intently set his face to go to Jerusalem, and sent messengers before his face. They went, and entered into a village of the Samaritans, so as to prepare for him. They didn't receive him, because he was traveling with his face set towards Jerusalem.

When his disciples, James and John, saw this, they said, "Lord, do you want us to command fire to come down from the sky, and destroy them, just as Elijah did?"

But he turned and rebuked them, "You don't know of what kind of spirit you are. For the Son of Man didn't come to destroy men's lives, but to save them."

They went to another village. As they went on the way, a certain man said to him, "I want to follow you wherever you go, Lord."

Jesus said to him, "The foxes have holes, and the birds of the sky have nests, but the Son of Man has no place to lay his head."

He said to another, "Follow me!"

129

But he said, "Lord, allow me first to go and bury my father."

But Jesus said to him, "Leave the dead to bury their own dead, but you go and announce God's Kingdom."

Another also said, "I want to follow you, Lord, but first allow me to say good-bye to those who are at my house."

But Jesus said to him, "No one, having put his hand to the plow, and looking back, is fit for God's Kingdom."

*(Luke 9.51-62; John 7.10)*

# Part 5

# The Beginning of Sukkot Until the Beginning of Hanukkah

**(October - December, 27 CE)**

# OCTOBER
# 27 CE

## Jesus Teaches in the Temple

The Jews therefore sought him at the feast, and said, "Where is he?" There was much murmuring among the multitudes concerning him. Some said, "He is a good man." Others said, "Not so, but he leads the multitude astray." Yet no one spoke openly of him for fear of the Jews.

But when it was now the middle of the feast, Jesus went up into the temple and taught. The Jews therefore marveled, saying, "How does this man know so much, having never been educated?"

Jesus therefore answered them, "My teaching is not mine, but his who sent me. If anyone desires to do his will, he will know about the teaching, whether it is from God, or if I am speaking from myself. He who speaks from himself seeks his own glory, but he who seeks the glory of him who sent him is true, and no unrighteousness is in him. Didn't Moses give you the law, and yet none of you keeps the law? Why do you seek to kill me?"

The multitude answered, "You have a demon! Who seeks to kill you?"

Jesus answered them, "I did one work, and you all marvel because of it. Moses has given you circumcision (not that it is of Moses, but of the fathers), and on the Sabbath you circumcise a boy. If a boy receives circumcision on the Sabbath, that the law of Moses may not be broken, are you angry with me, because I made a man completely healthy on

135

the Sabbath? Don't judge according to appearance, but judge righteous judgment."

Therefore some of them of Jerusalem said, "Isn't this he whom they seek to kill? Behold, he speaks openly, and they say nothing to him. Can it be that the rulers indeed know that this is truly the Christ? However we know where this man comes from, but when the Christ comes, no one will know where he comes from."

Jesus therefore cried out in the temple, teaching and saying, "You both know me, and know where I am from. I have not come of myself, but he who sent me is true, whom you don't know. I know him, because I am from him, and he sent me."

They sought therefore to take him; but no one laid a hand on him, because his hour had not yet come. But of the multitude, many believed in him. They said, "When the Christ comes, he won't do more signs than those which this man has done, will he?"

The Pharisees heard the multitude murmuring these things concerning him, and the chief priests and the Pharisees sent officers to arrest him.

Then Jesus said, "I will be with you a little while longer, then I go to him who sent me. You will seek me, and won't find me; and where I am, you can't come."

The Jews therefore said among themselves, "Where will this man go that we won't find him? Will he go to the Dispersion among the Greeks, and teach the Greeks? What is this word that he said, 'You will seek me, and won't find me; and where I am, you can't come'?"

*(John 7.11-36)*

### Is Anyone Thirsty?

Now on the last and greatest day of the feast, Jesus stood and cried out, "If anyone is thirsty, let him come to me and drink! He who believes in me, as the Scripture has said, from within him will flow rivers of living water." But he said this about the Spirit, which those believing in him were to

136

receive. For the Holy Spirit was not yet given, because Jesus wasn't yet glorified.

Many of the multitude therefore, when they heard these words, said, "This is truly the prophet." Others said, "This is the Christ." But some said, "What, does the Christ come out of Galilee? Hasn't the Scripture said that the Christ comes of the offspring of David, and from Bethlehem, the village where David was?" So there arose a division in the multitude because of him. Some of them would have arrested him, but no one laid hands on him.

The officers therefore came to the chief priests and Pharisees, and they said to them, "Why didn't you bring him?"

The officers answered, "No man ever spoke like this man!"

The Pharisees therefore answered them, "You aren't also led astray, are you? Have any of the rulers believed in him, or of the Pharisees? But this multitude that doesn't know the law is accursed."

Nicodemus (he who came to him by night, being one of them) said to them, "Does our law judge a man, unless it first hears from him personally and knows what he does?"

They answered him, "Are you also from Galilee? Search, and see that no prophet has arisen out of Galilee."

Everyone went to his own house, but Jesus went to the Mount of Olives.

*(John 7.37-8.1)*

### The Woman Caught in Adultery (5)

Now very early in the morning, he came again into the temple, and all the people came to him. He sat down, and taught them. The scribes and the Pharisees brought a woman taken in adultery. Having set her in the middle, they told him, "Teacher, we found this woman in adultery, in the very act. Now in our law, Moses commanded us to stone such women. What then do you say about her?" They said

137

this testing him, that they might have something to accuse him of.

But Jesus stooped down, and wrote on the ground with his finger. But when they continued asking him, he looked up and said to them, "He who is without sin among you, let him throw the first stone at her." Again he stooped down, and with his finger wrote on the ground.

They, when they heard it, being convicted by their conscience, went out one by one, beginning from the oldest, even to the last. Jesus was left alone with the woman where she was, in the middle. Jesus, standing up, saw her and said, "Woman, where are your accusers? Did no one condemn you?"

She said, "No one, Lord."

Jesus said, "Neither do I condemn you. Go your way. From now on, sin no more."

*(John 8.2-11)*

## The Light of the World

Again, therefore, Jesus spoke to them, saying, "I am the light of the world. He who follows me will not walk in the darkness, but will have the light of life."

The Pharisees therefore said to him, "You testify about yourself. Your testimony is not valid."

Jesus answered them, "Even if I testify about myself, my testimony is true, for I know where I came from, and where I am going; but you don't know where I came from, or where I am going. You judge according to the flesh. I judge no one. Even if I do judge, my judgment is true, for I am not alone, but I am with the Father who sent me. It's also written in your law that the testimony of two people is valid. I am one who testifies about myself, and the Father who sent me testifies about me."

They said therefore to him, "Where is your Father?"

Jesus answered, "You know neither me, nor my Father. If you knew me, you would know my Father also."

138

Jesus spoke these words in the treasury, as he taught in the temple. Yet no one arrested him, because his hour had not yet come.

*(John 8.12-20)*

## I Am From Above

Jesus said therefore again to them, "I am going away, and you will seek me, and you will die in your sins. Where I go, you can't come."

The Jews therefore said, "Will he kill himself, that he says, 'Where I am going, you can't come'?"

He said to them, "You are from beneath. I am from above. You are of this world. I am not of this world. I said therefore to you that you will die in your sins; for unless you believe that I am he, you will die in your sins."

They said therefore to him, "Who are you?"

Jesus said to them, "Just what I have been saying to you from the beginning. I have many things to speak and to judge concerning you. However he who sent me is true; and the things which I heard from him, these I say to the world."

They didn't understand that he spoke to them about the Father. Jesus therefore said to them, "When you have lifted up the Son of Man, then you will know that I am he, and I do nothing of myself, but as my Father taught me, I say these things. He who sent me is with me. The Father hasn't left me alone, for I always do the things that are pleasing to him."

*(John 8.21-29)*

## Your Father is the Devil

As he spoke these things, many believed in him. Jesus therefore said to those Jews who had believed him, "If you remain in my word, then you are truly my disciples. You will know the truth, and the truth will make you free."

They answered him, "We are Abraham's offspring, and have never been in bondage to anyone. How do you say, 'You will be made free'?"

Jesus answered them, "Most certainly I tell you, everyone who commits sin is the bondservant of sin. A bondservant doesn't live in the house forever. A son remains forever. If therefore the Son makes you free, you will be free indeed. I know that you are Abraham's offspring, yet you seek to kill me, because my word finds no place in you. I say the things which I have seen with my Father; and you also do the things which you have seen with your father."

They answered him, "Our father is Abraham."

Jesus said to them, "If you were Abraham's children, you would do the works of Abraham. But now you seek to kill me, a man who has told you the truth, which I heard from God. Abraham didn't do this. You do the works of your father."

They said to him, "We were not born of sexual immorality. We have one Father, God."

Therefore Jesus said to them, "If God were your father, you would love me, for I came out and have come from God. For I haven't come of myself, but he sent me. Why don't you understand my speech? Because you can't hear my word. You are of your father, the devil, and you want to do the desires of your father. He was a murderer from the beginning, and doesn't stand in the truth, because there is no truth in him. When he speaks a lie, he speaks on his own; for he is a liar, and its father. But because I tell the truth, you don't believe me. Which of you convicts me of sin? If I tell the truth, why do you not believe me? He who is of God hears the words of God. For this cause you don't hear, because you are not of God."

Then the Jews answered him, "Don't we say well that you are a Samaritan, and have a demon?"

Jesus answered, "I don't have a demon, but I honor my Father, and you dishonor me. But I don't seek my own glory. There is one who seeks and judges. Most certainly, I tell you, if a person keeps my word, he will never see death."

140

Then the Jews said to him, "Now we know that you have a demon. Abraham died, and the prophets; and you say, 'If a man keeps my word, he will never taste of death.' Are you greater than our father, Abraham, who died? The prophets died. Who do you make yourself out to be?"

Jesus answered, "If I glorify myself, my glory is nothing. It is my Father who glorifies me, of whom you say that he is our God. You have not known him, but I know him. If I said, 'I don't know him,' I would be like you, a liar. But I know him, and keep his word. Your father Abraham rejoiced to see my day. He saw it, and was glad."

The Jews therefore said to him, "You are not yet fifty years old, and have you seen Abraham?"

Jesus said to them, "Most certainly, I tell you, before Abraham came into existence, I AM."

Therefore they took up stones to throw at him, but Jesus was hidden, and went out of the temple, having gone through the middle of them, and so passed by.

*(John 8.30-59)*

## The Seventy Sent Out

Now after these things, the Lord also appointed seventy others, and sent them two by two ahead of him into every city and place, where he was about to come. Then he said to them, "The harvest is indeed plentiful, but the laborers are few. Pray therefore to the Lord of the harvest, that he may send out laborers into his harvest. Go your ways. Behold, I send you out as lambs among wolves. Carry no purse, nor wallet, nor sandals. Greet no one on the way.

Into whatever house you enter, first say, 'Peace be to this house.' If a son of peace is there, your peace will rest on him; but if not, it will return to you. Remain in that same house, eating and drinking the things they give, for the laborer is worthy of his wages. Don't go from house to house. Into whatever city you enter, and they receive you, eat the things that are set before you.

141

Heal the sick who are therein, and tell them, 'God's Kingdom has come near to you.' But into whatever city you enter, and they don't receive you, go out into its streets and say, 'Even the dust from your city that clings to us, we wipe off against you. Nevertheless know this, that God's Kingdom has come near to you.' I tell you, it will be more tolerable in that day for Sodom than for that city.

"Woe to you, Chorazin! Woe to you, Bethsaida! For if the mighty works had been done in Tyre and Sidon which were done in you, they would have repented long ago, sitting in sackcloth and ashes. But it will be more tolerable for Tyre and Sidon in the judgment than for you. You, Capernaum, who are exalted to heaven, will be brought down to Hades. Whoever listens to you listens to me, and whoever rejects you rejects me. Whoever rejects me rejects him who sent me."

*(Luke 10.1-16)*

## The Seventy Return Rejoicing

The seventy returned with joy, saying, "Lord, even the demons are subject to us in your name!"

He said to them, "I saw Satan having fallen like lightning from heaven. Behold, I give you authority to tread on serpents and scorpions, and over all the power of the enemy. Nothing will in any way hurt you. Nevertheless, don't rejoice in this, that the spirits are subject to you, but rejoice that your names are written in heaven."

In that same hour Jesus rejoiced in the Holy Spirit, and said, "I thank you, O Father, Lord of heaven and earth, that you have hidden these things from the wise and understanding, and revealed them to little children. Yes, Father, for so it was well-pleasing in your sight."

Turning to the disciples, he said, "All things have been delivered to me by my Father. No one knows who the Son is, except the Father, and who the Father is, except the Son, and he to whomever the Son desires to reveal him."

Turning to the disciples, he said privately, "Blessed are the eyes which see the things that you see, for I tell you that many prophets and kings desired to see the things which you see, and didn't see them, and to hear the things which you hear, and didn't hear them."

*(Luke 10.17-24)*

## Parable of the Good Samaritan

Behold, a certain lawyer stood up and tested him, saying, "Teacher, what shall I do to inherit eternal life?"

He said to him, "What is written in the law? How do you read it?"

He answered, "You shall love the Lord your God with all your heart, with all your soul, with all your strength, and with all your mind; and your neighbor as yourself."

He said to him, "You have answered correctly. Do this, and you will live."

But he, desiring to justify himself, asked Jesus, "Who is my neighbor?"

Jesus answered, "A certain man was going down from Jerusalem to Jericho, and he fell among robbers, who both stripped him and beat him, and departed, leaving him half dead. By chance a certain priest was going down that way. When he saw him, he passed by on the other side. In the same way a Levite also, when he came to the place, and saw him, passed by on the other side.

"But a certain Samaritan, as he traveled, came where he was. When he saw him, he was moved with compassion, came to him, and bound up his wounds, pouring on oil and wine. He set him on his own animal, and brought him to an inn, and took care of him.

"On the next day, when he departed, he took out two denarii, and gave them to the host, and said to him, 'Take care of him. Whatever you spend beyond that, I will repay you when I return.' Now which of these three do you think seemed to be a neighbor to him who fell among the robbers?"

He said, "He who showed mercy on him."

Then Jesus said to him, "Go and do likewise."

*(Luke 10.25-37)*

## Jesus Visits Mary and Martha

As they went on their way, he entered into a certain village, and a certain woman named Martha received him into her house. She had a sister called Mary, who also sat at Jesus' feet, and heard his word. But Martha was distracted with much serving, and she came up to him, and said, "Lord, don't you care that my sister left me to serve alone? Ask her therefore to help me."

Jesus answered her, "Martha, Martha, you are anxious and troubled about many things, but one thing is needed. Mary has chosen the good part, which will not be taken away from her."

*(Luke 10.38-42)*

# OCTOBER & NOVEMBER
## 27 CE

## *Teaching on Prayer*

When he finished praying in a certain place, one of his disciples said to him, "Lord, teach us to pray, just as John also taught his disciples."

He said to them, "When you pray, say:

'Our Father in heaven, may your name be kept holy.
May your Kingdom come.
May your will be done on earth, as it is in heaven.
Give us day by day our daily bread.
Forgive us our sins,
for we ourselves also forgive everyone
who is indebted to us.
Bring us not into temptation,
but deliver us from the evil one.'"

He said to them, "Which of you, if you go to a friend at midnight, and tell him, 'Friend, lend me three loaves of bread, for a friend of mine has come to me from a journey, and I have nothing to set before him,' and he from within will answer and say, 'Don't bother me. The door is now shut, and my children are with me in bed. I can't get up and give it to you'? I tell you, although he will not rise and give it to him because he is his friend, yet because of his persistence, he will get up and give him as many as he needs.

"I tell you, keep asking, and it will be given you. Keep seeking, and you will find. Keep knocking, and it will be opened to you.  For everyone who asks receives. He who seeks finds. To him who knocks it will be opened.

"Which of you fathers, if your son asks for bread, will give him a stone?  Or if he asks for a fish, he won't give him a snake instead of a fish, will he?  Or if he asks for an egg, he won't give him a scorpion, will he?  If you then, being evil, know how to give good gifts to your children, how much more will your heavenly Father give the Holy Spirit to those who ask him?"

*(Luke 11.1-13)*

## Jesus Casts Out a Mute Demon

He was casting out a demon, and it was mute. When the demon had gone out, the mute man spoke; and the multitudes marveled.  But some of them said, "He casts out demons by Beelzebul, the prince of the demons."  Others, testing him, sought from him a sign from heaven.  But he, knowing their thoughts, said to them, "Every kingdom divided against itself is brought to desolation. A house divided against itself falls.  If Satan also is divided against himself, how will his kingdom stand? For you say that I cast out demons by Beelzebul.  But if I cast out demons by Beelzebul, by whom do your children cast them out?  Therefore will they be your judges.  But if I by God's finger cast out demons, then God's Kingdom has come to you.

"When the strong man, fully armed, guards his own dwelling, his goods are safe.  But when someone stronger attacks him and overcomes him, he takes from him his whole armor in which he trusted, and divides his plunder.

"He that is not with me is against me. He who doesn't gather with me scatters.  The unclean spirit, when he has gone out of the man, passes through dry places, seeking rest, and finding none, he says, 'I will turn back to my house from which I came out.'  When he returns, he finds it swept and put in order.  Then he goes, and takes seven other spirits more evil than himself, and they enter in and dwell there. The last state of that man becomes worse than the first."

*(Luke 11.14-26)*

## Who is Truly Blessed?

It came to pass, as he said these things, a certain woman out of the multitude lifted up her voice, and said to him, "Blessed is the womb that bore you, and the breasts which nursed you!"

But he said, "On the contrary, blessed are those who hear the word of God, and keep it."

*(Luke 11.27-28)*

## This is an Evil Generation

When the multitudes were gathering together to him, he began to say, "This is an evil generation. It seeks after a sign. No sign will be given to it but the sign of Jonah, the prophet. For even as Jonah became a sign to the Ninevites, so will also the Son of Man be to this generation. The Queen of the South will rise up in the judgment with the men of this generation, and will condemn them: for she came from the ends of the earth to hear the wisdom of Solomon; and behold, one greater than Solomon is here. The men of Nineveh will stand up in the judgment with this generation, and will condemn it: for they repented at the preaching of Jonah, and behold, one greater than Jonah is here.

"No one, when he has lit a lamp, puts it in a cellar or under a basket, but on a stand, that those who come in may see the light. The lamp of the body is the eye. Therefore when your eye is good, your whole body is also full of light; but when it is evil, your body also is full of darkness. Therefore see whether the light that is in you isn't darkness. If therefore your whole body is full of light, having no part dark, it will be wholly full of light, as when the lamp with its bright shining gives you light."

*(Luke 11.29-36)*

## Jesus Offends the Pharisees at Supper

Now as he spoke, a certain Pharisee asked him to dine with him. He went in, and sat at the table. When the

149

Pharisee saw it, he marveled that he had not first washed himself before dinner.

The Lord said to him, "Now you Pharisees cleanse the outside of the cup and of the platter, but your inward part is full of extortion and wickedness. You foolish ones, didn't he who made the outside make the inside also? But give for gifts to the needy those things which are within, and behold, all things will be clean to you. But woe to you Pharisees! For you tithe mint and rue and every herb, but you bypass justice and the love of God. You ought to have done these, and not to have left the other undone. Woe to you Pharisees! For you love the best seats in the synagogues, and the greetings in the marketplaces. Woe to you, scribes and Pharisees, hypocrites! For you are like hidden graves, and the men who walk over them don't know it."

One of the lawyers answered him, "Teacher, in saying this you insult us also."

He said, "Woe to you lawyers also! For you load men with burdens that are difficult to carry, and you yourselves won't even lift one finger to help carry those burdens. Woe to you! For you build the tombs of the prophets, and your fathers killed them. So you testify and consent to the works of your fathers. For they killed them, and you build their tombs.

"Therefore also the wisdom of God said, 'I will send to them prophets and apostles; and some of them they will kill and persecute, that the blood of all the prophets, which was shed from the foundation of the world, may be required of this generation; from the blood of Abel to the blood of Zachariah, who perished between the altar and the sanctuary.' Yes, I tell you, it will be required of this generation. Woe to you lawyers! For you took away the key of knowledge. You didn't enter in yourselves, and those who were entering in, you hindered."

As he said these things to them, the scribes and the Pharisees began to be terribly angry, and to draw many things out of him; lying in wait for him, and seeking to catch him in something he might say, that they might accuse him.

*(Luke 11.37-54)*

150

## Jesus Warns of Persecution Again

Meanwhile, when a multitude of many thousands had gathered together, so much so that they trampled on each other, he began to tell his disciples first of all, "Beware of the yeast of the Pharisees, which is hypocrisy. But there is nothing covered up, that will not be revealed, nor hidden, that will not be known. Therefore whatever you have said in the darkness will be heard in the light. What you have spoken in the ear in the inner rooms will be proclaimed on the housetops.

"I tell you, my friends, don't be afraid of those who kill the body, and after that have no more that they can do. But I will warn you whom you should fear. Fear him, who after he has killed, has power to cast into Gehenna. Yes, I tell you, fear him.

"Aren't five sparrows sold for two assaria coins, two hours' worth of wages? Not one of them is forgotten by God. But the very hairs of your head are all numbered. Therefore don't be afraid. You are of more value than many sparrows.

"I tell you, everyone who confesses me before men, him will the Son of Man also confess before the angels of God; but he who denies me in the presence of men will be denied in the presence of the angels of God. Everyone who speaks a word against the Son of Man will be forgiven, but those who blaspheme against the Holy Spirit will not be forgiven. When they bring you before the synagogues, the rulers, and the authorities, don't be anxious how or what you will answer, or what you will say; for the Holy Spirit will teach you in that same hour what you must say."

*(Luke 12.1-12)*

## Parable of the Foolish Rich Man

One of the multitude said to him, "Teacher, tell my brother to divide the inheritance with me."

But he said to him, "Man, who made me a judge or an arbitrator over you?" He said to them, "Beware!  Keep

151

yourselves from covetousness, for a man's life doesn't consist of the abundance of the things which he possesses."

He spoke a parable to them, saying, "The ground of a certain rich man produced abundantly. He reasoned within himself, saying, 'What will I do, because I don't have room to store my crops?' He said, 'This is what I will do. I will pull down my barns, and build bigger ones, and there I will store all my grain and my goods. I will tell my soul, "Soul, you have many goods laid up for many years. Take your ease, eat, drink, be merry."'

"But God said to him, 'You foolish one, tonight your soul is required of you. The things which you have prepared—whose will they be?' So is he who lays up treasure for himself, and is not rich toward God."

*(Luke 12.13-21)*

## Do Not Be Afraid, Little Flock

He said to his disciples, "Therefore I tell you, don't be anxious for your life, what you will eat, nor yet for your body, what you will wear. Life is more than food, and the body is more than clothing. Consider the ravens: they don't sow, they don't reap, they have no warehouse or barn, and God feeds them. How much more valuable are you than birds!

"Which of you by being anxious can add a cubit to his height? If then you aren't able to do even the least things, why are you anxious about the rest? Consider the lilies, how they grow. They don't toil, neither do they spin; yet I tell you, even Solomon in all his glory was not arrayed like one of these. But if this is how God clothes the grass in the field, which today exists, and tomorrow is cast into the oven, how much more will he clothe you, O you of little faith?

"Don't seek what you will eat or what you will drink; neither be anxious. For the nations of the world seek after all of these things, but your Father knows that you need these things. But seek God's Kingdom, and all these things will be added to you.

"Don't be afraid, little flock, for it is your Father's good pleasure to give you the Kingdom.  Sell that which you have, and give gifts to the needy.  Make for yourselves purses which don't grow old, a treasure in the heavens that doesn't fail, where no thief approaches, neither moth destroys.  For where your treasure is, there will your heart be also.

*(Luke 12.22-34)*

## *Parables About Being Ready*

"Let your waist be dressed and your lamps burning.  Be like men watching for their lord, when he returns from the marriage feast; that, when he comes and knocks, they may immediately open to him.  Blessed are those servants, whom the lord will find watching when he comes.  Most certainly I tell you, that he will dress himself, and make them recline, and will come and serve them.  They will be blessed if he comes in the second or third watch, and finds them so.

But know this, that if the master of the house had known in what hour the thief was coming, he would have watched, and not allowed his house to be broken into.  Therefore be ready also, for the Son of Man is coming in an hour that you don't expect him."

Peter said to him, "Lord, are you telling this parable to us, or to everybody?"

The Lord said, "Who then is the faithful and wise steward, whom his lord will set over his household, to give them their portion of food at the right times?  Blessed is that servant whom his lord will find doing so when he comes.  Truly I tell you, that he will set him over all that he has.  But if that servant says in his heart, 'My lord delays his coming,' and begins to beat the menservants and the maidservants, and to eat and drink, and to be drunken, then the lord of that servant will come in a day when he isn't expecting him, and in an hour that he doesn't know, and will cut him in two, and place his portion with the unfaithful.  That servant, who knew his lord's will, and didn't prepare, nor do what he wanted, will be beaten with many stripes, but he who didn't know, and did things worthy of stripes, will be beaten with

153

few stripes. To whomever much is given, of him will much be required; and to whom much was entrusted, of him more will be asked.

*(Luke 12.35-48)*

## Warning about Family Conflict

"I came to throw fire on the earth. I wish it were already kindled. But I have a baptism to be baptized with, and how distressed I am until it is accomplished! Do you think that I have come to give peace in the earth? I tell you, no, but rather division. For from now on, there will be five in one house divided, three against two, and two against three. They will be divided, father against son, and son against father; mother against daughter, and daughter against her mother; mother-in-law against her daughter-in-law, and daughter-in-law against her mother-in-law."

*(Luke 12.49-53)*

## Interpret the Times

He said to the multitudes also, "When you see a cloud rising from the west, immediately you say, 'A shower is coming,' and so it happens. When a south wind blows, you say, 'There will be a scorching heat,' and it happens. You hypocrites! You know how to interpret the appearance of the earth and the sky, but how is it that you don't interpret this time? Why don't you judge for yourselves what is right? For when you are going with your adversary before the magistrate, try diligently on the way to be released from him, lest perhaps he drag you to the judge, and the judge deliver you to the officer, and the officer throw you into prison. I tell you, you will by no means get out of there, until you have paid the very last penny.

*(Luke 12.54-59)*

## *The Galileans and the Fig Tree*

Now there were some present at the same time who told him about the Galileans, whose blood Pilate had mixed with their sacrifices. Jesus answered them, "Do you think that these Galileans were worse sinners than all the other Galileans, because they suffered such things? I tell you, no, but unless you repent, you will all perish in the same way.

"Or those eighteen, on whom the tower in Siloam fell, and killed them; do you think that they were worse offenders than all the men who dwell in Jerusalem? I tell you, no, but, unless you repent, you will all perish in the same way."

He spoke this parable. "A certain man had a fig tree planted in his vineyard, and he came seeking fruit on it, and found none. He said to the vine dresser, 'Behold, these three years I have come looking for fruit on this fig tree, and found none. Cut it down. Why does it waste the soil?' He answered, 'Lord, leave it alone this year also, until I dig around it, and fertilize it. If it bears fruit, fine; but if not, after that, you can cut it down.'"

*(Luke 13.1-9)*

155

# DECEMBER
## 27 CE

## *Jesus Heals the Bent Over Woman*

He was teaching in one of the synagogues on the Sabbath day. Behold, there was a woman who had a spirit of infirmity eighteen years, and she was bent over, and could in no way straighten herself up. When Jesus saw her, he called her, and said to her, "Woman, you are freed from your infirmity." He laid his hands on her, and immediately she stood up straight, and glorified God.

The ruler of the synagogue, being indignant because Jesus had healed on the Sabbath, said to the multitude, "There are six days in which men ought to work. Therefore come on those days and be healed, and not on the Sabbath day!"

Therefore the Lord answered him, "You hypocrites! Doesn't each one of you free his ox or his donkey from the stall on the Sabbath, and lead him away to water? Ought not this woman, being a daughter of Abraham, whom Satan had bound eighteen long years, be freed from this bondage on the Sabbath day?"

As he said these things, all his adversaries were disappointed, and all the multitude rejoiced for all the glorious things that were done by him.

*(Luke 13.10-17)*

## *Parables of the Mustard Seed and the Yeast*

He said, "What is God's Kingdom like? To what shall I compare it? It is like a grain of mustard seed, which a man took, and put in his own garden. It grew, and became a large tree, and the birds of the sky live in its branches."

Again he said, "To what shall I compare God's Kingdom? It is like yeast, which a woman took and hid in three measures of flour, until it was all leavened."

*(Luke 13.18-21)*

## *The Narrow Door*

He went on his way through cities and villages, teaching, and traveling on to Jerusalem. One said to him, "Lord, are they few who are saved?"

He said to them, "Strive to enter in by the narrow door, for many, I tell you, will seek to enter in, and will not be able. When once the master of the house has risen up, and has shut the door, and you begin to stand outside, and to knock at the door, saying, 'Lord, Lord, open to us!' then he will answer and tell you, 'I don't know you or where you come from.' Then you will begin to say, 'We ate and drank in your presence, and you taught in our streets.' He will say, 'I tell you, I don't know where you come from. Depart from me, all you workers of iniquity.'

"There will be weeping and gnashing of teeth, when you see Abraham, Isaac, Jacob, and all the prophets, in God's Kingdom, and yourselves being thrown outside. They will come from the east, west, north, and south, and will sit down in God's Kingdom. Behold, there are some who are last who will be first, and there are some who are first who will be last."

*(Luke 13.22-30)*

160

# Part 6:

# The Beginning of Hanukkah Until the Approach of Passover

**(December, 27 CE - April, 28 CE)**

# DECEMBER
# 27 CE

## *Jesus Heals the Man Born Blind*

As he passed by, he saw a man blind from birth. His disciples asked him, "Rabbi, who sinned, this man or his parents, that he was born blind?"

Jesus answered, "Neither did this man sin, nor his parents; but, that the works of God might be revealed in him. I must work the works of him who sent me, while it is day. The night is coming, when no one can work. While I am in the world, I am the light of the world."

When he had said this, he spat on the ground, made mud with the saliva, anointed the blind man's eyes with the mud, and said to him, "Go, wash in the pool of Siloam" (which means "Sent"). So he went away, washed, and came back seeing.

The neighbors therefore, and those who saw that he was blind before, said, "Isn't this he who sat and begged?" Others were saying, "It is he." Still others were saying, "He looks like him." He said, "I am he." They therefore were asking him, "How were your eyes opened?"

He answered, "A man called Jesus made mud, anointed my eyes, and said to me, 'Go to the pool of Siloam, and wash.' So I went away and washed, and I received sight."

Then they asked him, "Where is he?"

He said, "I don't know."

They brought him who had been blind to the Pharisees. It was a Sabbath when Jesus made the mud and opened his eyes. Again therefore the Pharisees also asked him how he received his sight. He said to them, "He put mud on my eyes, I washed, and I see."

Some therefore of the Pharisees said, "This man is not from God, because he doesn't keep the Sabbath." Others said, "How can a man who is a sinner do such signs?" There was division among them. Therefore they asked the blind man again, "What do you say about him, because he opened your eyes?"

The man said, "He is a prophet."

The Jews therefore did not believe concerning him, that he had been blind, and had received his sight, until they called the parents of him who had received his sight, and asked them, "Is this your son, whom you say was born blind? How then does he now see?"

His parents answered them, "We know that this is our son, and that he was born blind; but how he now sees, we don't know; or who opened his eyes, we don't know. He is of age. Ask him. He will speak for himself." His parents said these things because they feared the Jews; for the Jews had already agreed that if any man would confess him as Christ, he would be put out of the synagogue. Therefore his parents said, "He is of age. Ask him."

So they called the man who was blind a second time, and said to him, "Give glory to God. We know that this man is a sinner."

He therefore answered, "I don't know if he is a sinner. One thing I do know: that though I was blind, now I see."

They said to him again, "What did he do to you? How did he open your eyes?"

He answered them, "I told you already, and you didn't listen. Why do you want to hear it again? You don't also want to become his disciples, do you?"

They insulted him and said, "You are his disciple, but we are disciples of Moses. We know that God has spoken to

Moses. But as for this man, we don't know where he comes from."

The man answered them, "How amazing! You don't know where he comes from, yet he opened my eyes. We know that God doesn't listen to sinners, but if anyone is a worshiper of God, and does his will, he listens to him. Since the world began it has never been heard of that anyone opened the eyes of someone born blind. If this man were not from God, he could do nothing."

They answered him, "You were altogether born in sins, and do you teach us?" They threw him out.

Jesus heard that they had thrown him out, and finding him, he said, "Do you believe in the Son of God?"

He answered, "Who is he, Lord, that I may believe in him?"

Jesus said to him, "You have both seen him, and it is he who speaks with you."

He said, "Lord, I believe!" and he worshiped him.

Jesus said, "I came into this world for judgment, that those who don't see may see; and that those who see may become blind."

Those of the Pharisees who were with him heard these things, and said to him, "Are we also blind?"

Jesus said to them, "If you were blind, you would have no sin; but now you say, 'We see.' Therefore your sin remains.

*(John 9.1-41)*

## The Good Shepherd

"Most certainly, I tell you, one who doesn't enter by the door into the sheep fold, but climbs up some other way, the same is a thief and a robber. But one who enters in by the door is the shepherd of the sheep. The gatekeeper opens the gate for him, and the sheep listen to his voice. He calls his own sheep by name, and leads them out. Whenever he brings out his own sheep, he goes before them, and the sheep follow him, for they know his voice. They will by no means follow a stranger, but will flee from him; for they don't know the voice of strangers."

Jesus spoke this parable to them, but they didn't understand what he was telling them.

Jesus therefore said to them again, "Most certainly, I tell you, I am the sheep's door. All who came before me are thieves and robbers, but the sheep didn't listen to them. I am the door. If anyone enters in by me, he will be saved, and will go in and go out, and will find pasture. The thief only comes to steal, kill, and destroy. I came that they may have life, and may have it abundantly.

"I am the good shepherd. The good shepherd lays down his life for the sheep. He who is a hired hand, and not a shepherd, who doesn't own the sheep, sees the wolf coming, leaves the sheep, and flees. The wolf snatches the sheep, and scatters them. The hired hand flees because he is a hired hand, and doesn't care for the sheep. I am the good shepherd. I know my own, and I'm known by my own; even as the Father knows me, and I know the Father. I lay down my life for the sheep.

"I have other sheep, which are not of this fold. I must bring them also, and they will hear my voice. They will become one flock with one shepherd. Therefore the Father loves me, because I lay down my life, that I may take it again. No one takes it away from me, but I lay it down by myself. I have power to lay it down, and I have power to take it again. I received this commandment from my Father."

*(John 10.1-18)*

### The Jews Confront Jesus and Try to Kill Him

Therefore a division arose again among the Jews because of these words. Many of them said, "He has a demon, and is insane! Why do you listen to him?" Others said, "These are not the sayings of one who is demonized. It isn't possible for a demon to open the eyes of the blind, is it?"

168

It was Hanukkah, the Feast of the Dedication, at Jerusalem. It was winter, and Jesus was walking in the temple, in Solomon's porch. The Jews therefore came around him and said to him, "How long will you hold us in suspense? If you are the Christ, tell us plainly."

Jesus answered them, "I told you, and you don't believe. The works that I do in my Father's name, these testify about me. But you don't believe, because you are not of my sheep, as I told you. My sheep hear my voice, and I know them, and they follow me. I give eternal life to them. They will never perish, and no one will snatch them out of my hand. My Father, who has given them to me, is greater than all. No one is able to snatch them out of my Father's hand. I and the Father are one."

Therefore Jews took up stones again to stone him. Jesus answered them, "I have shown you many good works from my Father. For which of those works do you stone me?"

The Jews answered him, "We don't stone you for a good work, but for blasphemy: because you, being a man, make yourself God."

Jesus answered them, "Isn't it written in your law, 'I said, you are gods?' (Psalm 82.6) If he called them gods, to whom the word of God came (and the Scripture can't be broken), do you say of him whom the Father sanctified and sent into the world, 'You blaspheme,' because I said, 'I am the Son of God?' If I don't do the works of my Father, don't believe me. But if I do them, though you don't believe me, believe the works; that you may know and believe that the Father is in me, and I in the Father."

They sought again to seize him, and he went out of their hand.

*(John 10.19-39)*

### *Pharisees Warn Jesus About Herod*

On that same day, some Pharisees came, saying to him, "Get out of here, and go away, for Herod wants to kill you."

169

He said to them, "Go and tell that fox, 'Behold, I cast out demons and perform cures today and tomorrow, and the third day I complete my mission. Nevertheless I must go on my way today and tomorrow and the next day, for it can't be that a prophet perish outside of Jerusalem.'

"Jerusalem, Jerusalem, that kills the prophets, and stones those who are sent to her! How often I wanted to gather your children together, like a hen gathers her own brood under her wings, and you refused! Behold, your house is left to you desolate. I tell you, you will not see me, until you say, 'Blessed is he who comes in the name of the Lord!'"

*(Luke 13.31-35)*

## *Jesus Leaves Jerusalem and Goes Beyond the Jordan*

He went away again beyond the Jordan into the place where John was baptizing at first, and there he stayed. Many came to him. They said, "John indeed did no sign, but everything that John said about this man is true." Many believed in him there.

*(John 10.40-42)*

# JANUARY & FEBRUARY
## 28 CE

## Jesus Heals a Swollen Man

When he went into the house of one of the rulers of the Pharisees on a Sabbath to eat bread, they were watching him. Behold, a certain man who had dropsy, severe swelling of the joints, was in front of him. Jesus, answering, spoke to the lawyers and Pharisees, saying, "Is it lawful to heal on the Sabbath?"

But they were silent.

Jesus took him, and healed him, and let him go. He answered them, "Which of you, if your son or an ox fell into a well, wouldn't immediately pull him out on a Sabbath day?"

They couldn't answer him regarding these things.

*(Luke 14.1-6)*

## Parable of the Lowest Place

He spoke a parable to those who were invited, when he noticed how they chose the best seats, and said to them, "When you are invited by anyone to a marriage feast, don't sit in the best seat, since perhaps someone more honorable than you might be invited by him, and he who invited both of you would come and tell you, 'Make room for this person.' Then you would begin, with shame, to take the lowest place. But when you are invited, go and sit in the lowest place, so that when he who invited you comes, he may tell you, 'Friend, move up higher.' Then you will be honored in the presence of all who sit at the table with you. For everyone who exalts

173

himself will be humbled, and whoever humbles himself will be exalted."

*(Luke 14.7-11)*

## Parable of the Great Supper

He also said to the one who had invited him, "When you make a dinner or a supper, don't call your friends, nor your brothers, nor your kinsmen, nor rich neighbors, or perhaps they might also return the favor, and pay you back. But when you make a feast, ask the poor, the maimed, the lame, or the blind; and you will be blessed, because they don't have the resources to repay you. For you will be repaid in the resurrection of the righteous."

When one of those who sat at the table with him heard these things, he said to him, "Blessed is he who will feast in God's Kingdom!"

But he said to him, "A certain man made a great supper, and he invited many people. He sent out his servant at supper time to tell those who were invited, 'Come, for everything is ready now.' They all as one began to make excuses.

"The first said to him, 'I have bought a field, and I must go and see it. Please have me excused.'

"Another said, 'I have bought five yoke of oxen, and I must go try them out. Please have me excused.'

"Another said, 'I have married a wife, and therefore I can't come.'

"That servant came, and told his lord these things. Then the master of the house, being angry, said to his servant, 'Go out quickly into the streets and lanes of the city, and bring in the poor, maimed, blind, and lame.'

"The servant said, 'Lord, it is done as you commanded, and there is still room.'

"The lord said to the servant, 'Go out into the highways and hedges, and compel them to come in, that my

174

house may be filled. For I tell you that none of those men who were invited will taste of my supper.'"

*(Luke 14.12-24)*

## Count the Cost Before Following

Now great multitudes were going with him. He turned and said to them, "If anyone comes to me, and doesn't disregard and hate his own father, mother, wife, children, brothers, and sisters, yes, and his own life also, he can't be my disciple. Whoever doesn't bear his own cross, and come after me, can't be my disciple.

"For which of you, desiring to build a tower, doesn't first sit down and count the cost, to see if he has enough to complete it? Or perhaps, when he has laid a foundation, and is not able to finish, everyone who sees begins to mock him, saying, 'This man began to build, and wasn't able to finish.'

Or what king, as he goes to encounter another king in war, will not sit down first and consider whether he is able with ten thousand to meet him who comes against him with twenty thousand? Or else, while the other is yet a great way off, he sends an envoy, and asks for conditions of peace. So therefore whoever of you who doesn't renounce all that he has, he can't be my disciple.

Salt is good, but if the salt becomes flat and tasteless, with what do you season it? It is fit neither for the soil nor for the manure pile. It is thrown out. He who has ears to hear, let him hear."

*(Luke 14.25-35)*

## Parables of the Lost: Sheep, Coins and Sons

Now all the tax collectors and sinners were coming close to him to hear him. The Pharisees and the scribes murmured, saying, "This man welcomes sinners, and eats with them."

Jesus told them this parable. "Which of you men, if you had one hundred sheep, and lost one of them, wouldn't

175

leave the ninety-nine in the wilderness, and go after the one that was lost, until he found it? When he has found it, he carries it on his shoulders, rejoicing. When he comes home, he calls together his friends and his neighbors, saying to them, 'Rejoice with me, for I have found my sheep which was lost!' I tell you that even so there will be more joy in heaven over one sinner who repents, than over ninety-nine righteous people who need no repentance.

Or what woman, if she had ten drachma coins (worth two days wages each), if she lost one drachma coin, wouldn't light a lamp, sweep the house, and seek diligently until she found it? When she has found it, she calls together her friends and neighbors, saying, 'Rejoice with me, for I have found the drachma which I had lost.' Even so, I tell you, there is joy in the presence of the angels of God over one sinner repenting."

He said, "A certain man had two sons. The younger of them said to his father, 'Father, give me my share of your property.' He divided his livelihood between them. Not many days after, the younger son gathered all of this together and traveled into a far country.

"There he wasted his property with riotous living. When he had spent all of it, there arose a severe famine in that country, and he began to be in need. He went and joined himself to one of the citizens of that country, and he sent him into his fields to feed pigs. He wanted to fill his belly with the husks that the pigs ate, but no one gave him any.

"But when he came to himself he said, 'How many hired servants of my father's have bread enough to spare, and I'm dying with hunger! I will get up and go to my father, and will tell him, "Father, I have sinned against heaven, and in your sight. I am no more worthy to be called your son. Make me as one of your hired servants."'

"He arose, and came to his father. But while he was still far off, his father saw him, and was moved with compassion, and ran, and fell on his neck, and kissed him. The son said to him, 'Father, I have sinned against heaven,

176

and in your sight. I am no longer worthy to be called your son.'

"But the father said to his servants, 'Bring out the best robe, and put it on him. Put a ring on his hand, and shoes on his feet. Bring the fattened calf, kill it, and let us eat, and celebrate; for this, my son, was dead, and is alive again. He was lost, and is found.' They began to celebrate.

"Now his elder son was in the field. As he came near to the house, he heard music and dancing. He called one of the servants to him, and asked what was going on. He said to him, 'Your brother has come, and your father has killed the fattened calf, because he has received him back safe and healthy.'

"But he was angry, and would not go in. Therefore his father came out, and begged him. But he answered his father, 'Behold, these many years I have served you, and I never disobeyed a commandment of yours, but you never gave me a goat, that I might celebrate with my friends. But when this, your son, came, who has devoured your living with prostitutes, you killed the fattened calf for him.'

"The father said to him, 'Son, you are always with me, and all that is mine is yours. But it was appropriate to celebrate and be glad, for this, your brother, was dead, and is alive again. He was lost, and is found.'"

*(Luke 15.1-32)*

## Parable of the Dishonest Manager

He also said to his disciples, "There was a certain rich man who had a manager. An accusation was made to him that this man was wasting his possessions. He called him, and said to him, 'What is this that I hear about you? Give an accounting of your management, for you can no longer be manager.'

"The manager said within himself, 'What will I do, seeing that my lord is taking away the management position from me? I don't have strength to dig. I am ashamed to beg. I know what I will do, so that when I am removed from management, they may receive me into their houses.'

Calling each one of his lord's debtors to him, he said to the first, 'How much do you owe to my lord?' He said, 'A hundred batos (about 395 liters) of oil.' He said to him, 'Take your bill, and sit down quickly and write fifty.' Then he said to another, 'How much do you owe?' He said, 'A hundred cors (about 2100 liters) of wheat.' He said to him, 'Take your bill, and write eighty.'

"His lord commended the dishonest manager because he had done wisely, for the children of this world are, in their own generation, wiser than the children of the light. I tell you, make for yourselves friends by means of unrighteous mammon, so that when you fail, they may receive you into the eternal tents.

He who is faithful in a very little is faithful also in much. He who is dishonest in a very little is also dishonest in much. If therefore you have not been faithful in the unrighteous mammon, who will commit to your trust the true riches? If you have not been faithful in that which is another's, who will give you that which is your own? No servant can serve two masters, for either he will hate the one, and love the other; or else he will hold to one, and despise the other. You aren't able to serve God and Mammon."

The Pharisees, who were lovers of money, also heard all these things, and they scoffed at him. He said to them, "You are those who justify yourselves in the sight of men, but God knows your hearts. For that which is exalted among men is an abomination in the sight of God. The law and the prophets were until John. From that time the Good News of God's Kingdom is preached, and everyone is forcing his way into it. But it is easier for heaven and earth to pass away, than for one tiny stroke of a pen in the law to fall."

*(Luke 16.1-18)*

## Parable of the Rich Man and Lazarus

"Now there was a certain rich man, and he was clothed in purple and fine linen, living in luxury every day. A certain beggar, named Lazarus, was laid at his gate, full of sores, and desiring to be fed with the crumbs that fell from the rich man's table. Yes, even the dogs came and licked his sores. The beggar died, and he was carried away by the angels to Abraham's bosom.

The rich man also died, and was buried. In Hades, he lifted up his eyes, being in torment, and saw Abraham far off, and Lazarus at his bosom. He cried and said, 'Father Abraham, have mercy on me, and send Lazarus, that he may dip the tip of his finger in water, and cool my tongue! For I am in anguish in this flame.'

"But Abraham said, 'Son, remember that you, in your lifetime, received your good things, and Lazarus, in the same way, bad things. But now here he is comforted and you are in anguish. Besides all this, between us and you there is a great gulf fixed, that those who want to pass from here to you are not able, and that no one may cross over from there to us.'

"He said, 'I ask you therefore, father, that you would send him to my father's house; for I have five brothers, that he may testify to them, so they won't also come into this place of torment.'

"But Abraham said to him, 'They have Moses and the prophets. Let them listen to them.'

"He said, 'No, father Abraham, but if one goes to them from the dead, they will repent.'

"He said to him, 'If they don't listen to Moses and the prophets, neither will they be persuaded if one rises from the dead.'"

*(Luke 16.19-31)*

## Stumbling, Forgiveness, Faith and Responsibility

He said to the disciples, "It is impossible that no occasions of stumbling should come, but woe to him through whom they come! It would be better for him if a millstone were hung around his neck, and he were thrown into the sea,

179

rather than that he should cause one of these little ones to stumble.

Be careful. If your brother sins against you, rebuke him. If he repents, forgive him. If he sins against you seven times in the day, and seven times returns, saying, 'I repent,' you shall forgive him."

The apostles said to the Lord, "Increase our faith." The Lord said, "If you had faith like a grain of mustard seed, you would tell this sycamore tree, 'Be uprooted, and be planted in the sea,' and it would obey you.

"But who is there among you, having a servant plowing or keeping sheep, that will say, when he comes in from the field, 'Come immediately and sit down at the table,' and will not rather tell him, 'Prepare my supper, clothe yourself properly, and serve me, while I eat and drink. Afterward you shall eat and drink'? Does he thank that servant because he did the things that were commanded? I think not. Even so you also, when you have done all the things that are commanded you, say, 'We are unworthy servants. We have done our duty.'"

*(Luke 17.1-10)*

## The Death and Raising of Lazarus

Now a certain man was sick, Lazarus from Bethany, of the village of Mary and her sister, Martha. It was that Mary who had anointed the Lord with ointment, and wiped his feet with her hair, whose brother, Lazarus, was sick. The sisters therefore sent to him, saying, "Lord, behold, he for whom you have great affection is sick." But when Jesus heard it, he said, "This sickness is not to death, but for the glory of God, that God's Son may be glorified by it."

Now Jesus loved Martha, and her sister, and Lazarus. When therefore he heard that he was sick, he stayed two days in the place where he was. Then after this he said to the disciples, "Let's go into Judea again."

The disciples told him, "Rabbi, the Jews were just trying to stone you, and are you going there again?"

Jesus answered, "Aren't there twelve hours of daylight? If a man walks in the day, he doesn't stumble, because he sees the light of this world. But if a man walks in the night, he stumbles, because the light isn't in him." He said these things, and after that, he said to them, "Our friend, Lazarus, has fallen asleep, but I am going so that I may awake him out of sleep."

The disciples therefore said, "Lord, if he has fallen asleep, he will recover."

Now Jesus had spoken of his death, but they thought that he spoke of taking rest in sleep. So Jesus said to them plainly then, "Lazarus is dead. I am glad for your sakes that I was not there, so that you may believe. Nevertheless, let's go to him."

Thomas therefore, who is called Didymus, the Twin, said to his fellow disciples, "Let's go also, that we may die with him."

So when Jesus came, he found that he had been in the tomb four days already. Now Bethany was near Jerusalem, about fifteen stadia (2.8 kilometres) away. Many of the Jews had joined the women around Martha and Mary, to console them concerning their brother.

Then when Martha heard that Jesus was coming, she went and met him, but Mary stayed in the house. Therefore Martha said to Jesus, "Lord, if you would have been here, my brother wouldn't have died. Even now I know that, whatever you ask of God, God will give you."

Jesus said to her, "Your brother will rise again."

Martha said to him, "I know that he will rise again in the resurrection at the last day."

Jesus said to her, "I am the resurrection and the life. He who believes in me will still live, even if he dies. Whoever lives and believes in me will never die. Do you believe this?"

She said to him, "Yes, Lord. I have come to believe that you are the Christ, God's Son, he who comes into the world." When she had said this, she went away, and called Mary, her sister, secretly, saying, "The Teacher is here, and is

181

calling you." When she heard this, she arose quickly, and went to him.

Now Jesus had not yet come into the village, but was in the place where Martha met him. Then the Jews who were with her in the house, and were consoling her, when they saw Mary, that she rose up quickly and went out, followed her, saying, "She is going to the tomb to weep there." Therefore when Mary came to where Jesus was, and saw him, she fell down at his feet, saying to him, "Lord, if you would have been here, my brother wouldn't have died."

When Jesus therefore saw her weeping, and the Jews weeping who came with her, he groaned in the spirit, and was troubled, and said, "Where have you laid him?"

They told him, "Lord, come and see."

Jesus wept.

The Jews therefore said, "See how much affection he had for him!" Some of them said, "Couldn't this man, who opened the eyes of him who was blind, have also kept this man from dying?"

Jesus therefore, again groaning in himself, came to the tomb. Now it was a cave, and a stone lay against it. Jesus said, "Take away the stone."

Martha, the sister of him who was dead, said to him, "Lord, by this time there is a stench, for he has been dead four days."

Jesus said to her, "Didn't I tell you that if you believed, you would see God's glory?"

So they took away the stone from the place where the dead man was lying. Jesus lifted up his eyes, and said, "Father, I thank you that you listened to me. I know that you always listen to me, but because of the multitude that stands around I said this, that they may believe that you sent me." When he had said this, he cried with a loud voice, "Lazarus, come out!"

He who was dead came out, bound hand and foot with wrappings, and his face was wrapped around with a cloth. Jesus said to them, "Free him, and let him go."

Therefore many of the Jews, who came to Mary and saw what Jesus did, believed in him. But some of them went away to the Pharisees, and told them the things which Jesus had done.

The chief priests therefore and the Pharisees gathered a council, and said, "What are we doing? For this man does many signs. If we leave him alone like this, everyone will believe in him, and the Romans will come and take away both our place and our nation."

But a certain one of them, Caiaphas, being high priest that year, said to them, "You know nothing at all, nor do you consider that it is advantageous for us that one man should die for the people, and that the whole nation not perish." Now he didn't say this of himself, but being high priest that year, he prophesied that Jesus would die for the nation, and not for the nation only, but that he might also gather together into one the children of God who are scattered abroad. So from that day forward they took counsel that they might put him to death.

*(John 11.1-53)*

183

# MARCH & APRIL
## 28 CE

## *Jesus Goes to the Village of Ephraim*

Jesus therefore walked no more openly among the Jews, but departed from there into the country near the wilderness, to a city called Ephraim. He stayed there with his disciples.

*(John 11.54)*

## *Jesus Heals Ten Lepers*

As he was on his way to Jerusalem, he was passing along the borders of Samaria and Galilee. As he entered into a certain village, ten men who were lepers met him, who stood at a distance. They lifted up their voices, saying, "Jesus, Master, have mercy on us!"

When he saw them, he said to them, "Go and show yourselves to the priests." As they went, they were cleansed. One of them, when he saw that he was healed, turned back, glorifying God with a loud voice. He fell on his face at Jesus' feet, giving him thanks; and he was a Samaritan.

Jesus answered, "Weren't the ten cleansed? But where are the nine? Were there none found who returned to give glory to God, except this stranger?" Then he said to him, "Get up, and go your way. Your faith has healed you."

*(Luke 17.11-19)*

### The Days of the Son of Man

Being asked by the Pharisees when God's Kingdom would come, he answered them, "God's Kingdom doesn't come with observation; neither will they say, 'Look, here!' or, 'Look, there!' for behold, God's Kingdom is within you."

He said to the disciples, "The days will come, when you will desire to see one of the days of the Son of Man, and you will not see it. They will tell you, 'Look, here!' or 'Look, there!' Don't go away, nor follow after them, for as the lightning, when it flashes out of the one part under the sky, shines to the other part under the sky; so will the Son of Man be in his day. But first, he must suffer many things and be rejected by this generation.

As it was in the days of Noah, even so will it be also in the days of the Son of Man. They ate, they drank, they married, they were given in marriage, until the day that Noah entered into the ship, and the flood came, and destroyed them all. Likewise, even as it was in the days of Lot: they ate, they drank, they bought, they sold, they planted, they built; but in the day that Lot went out from Sodom, it rained fire and sulfur from the sky, and destroyed them all.

It will be the same way in the day that the Son of Man is revealed. In that day, he who will be on the housetop, and his goods in the house, let him not go down to take them away. Let him who is in the field likewise not turn back. Remember Lot's wife! Whoever seeks to save his life loses it, but whoever loses his life preserves it. I tell you, in that night there will be two people in one bed. The one will be taken, and the other will be left. There will be two grinding grain together. One will be taken, and the other will be left. Two will be in the field: the one taken, and the other left."

They, answering, asked him, "Where, Lord?"

He said to them, "Where the body is, there will the vultures also be gathered together."

*(Luke 17.20-37)*

## *Parable of the Unrighteous Judge*

He also spoke a parable to them that they must always pray, and not give up, saying, "There was a judge in a certain city who didn't fear God, and didn't respect man. A widow was in that city, and she often came to him, saying, 'Defend me from my adversary!' He wouldn't for a while, but afterward he said to himself, 'Though I neither fear God, nor respect man, yet because this widow bothers me, I will defend her, or else she will wear me out by her continual coming.'"

The Lord said, "Listen to what the unrighteous judge says. Won't God avenge his chosen ones, who are crying out to him day and night, and yet he exercises patience with them? I tell you that he will avenge them quickly. Nevertheless, when the Son of Man comes, will he find faith on the earth?"

*(Luke 18.1-8)*

## *Parable of Two Men Praying*

He spoke also this parable to certain people who were convinced of their own righteousness, and who despised all others. "Two men went up into the temple to pray; one was a Pharisee, and the other was a tax collector. The Pharisee stood and prayed to himself like this: 'God, I thank you, that I am not like the rest of men, extortionists, unrighteous, adulterers, or even like this tax collector. I fast twice a week. I give tithes of all that I get.' But the tax collector, standing far away, wouldn't even lift up his eyes to heaven, but beat his breast, saying, 'God, be merciful to me, a sinner!'

"I tell you, this man went down to his house justified rather than the other; for everyone who exalts himself will be humbled, but he who humbles himself will be exalted."

*(Luke 18.9-14)*

## *Teaching on Divorce*

When Jesus had finished these words, he arose from there, departed from Galilee, and came into the borders of Judea beyond the Jordan. Great multitudes followed him. As he usually did, he was again teaching them and he healed them there. Pharisees came to him, testing him, and saying, "Is it lawful for a man to divorce his wife for any reason?"

He answered, "Haven't you read what Moses said? God, who made them from the beginning of creation, made them male and female, and said, 'For this cause a man shall leave his father and mother, and shall join to his wife; and the two shall become one flesh?' (Genesis 2.24) So that they are no more two, but one flesh. What therefore God has joined together, don't let man separate and tear apart."

They asked him, "Why then did Moses command us to give her a bill of divorce, and divorce her?"

He said to them, "Because of the hardness of your hearts Moses wrote you this commandment and allowed you to divorce your wives, but from the beginning of the creation it has not been so. I tell you that whoever divorces his wife, except for sexual immorality, and marries another, commits adultery against her; and he who marries her when she is divorced commits adultery. If a woman herself divorces her husband, and marries another, she commits adultery."

In the house, his disciples asked him again about the same matter, and said to him, "If this is the case of the man with his wife, it is not expedient to marry."

But he said to them, "Not all men can receive this saying, but those to whom it is given. For there are eunuchs who were born that way from their mother's womb, and there are eunuchs who were made eunuchs by men; and there are eunuchs who made themselves eunuchs for the Kingdom of Heaven's sake. He who is able to receive it, let him receive it."

*(Matthew 19.1-12; Mark 10.1-12)*

190

## Jesus Blesses the Little Children

They were also bringing to him their little children and babies, that he should touch them, lay his hands on them and pray.  But the disciples rebuked those who were bringing them.  But when Jesus saw it, he was moved with indignation.  He summoned them and said, "Allow the little children to come to me!  Don't forbid or hinder them, for God's Kingdom, the Kingdom of Heaven, belongs to such as these.  Most certainly I tell you, whoever will not receive God's Kingdom like a little child, he will in no way enter into it."  He took them in his arms, and blessed them, laying his hands on them.  He departed from there.

*(Matthew 19.13-15; Mark 10.13-16;*
*Luke 18.15-17)*

## The Rich Young Ruler

As he was going out into the way, a certain ruler ran to him, knelt before him, and asked him, "Good Teacher, what good thing shall I do that I may inherit eternal life?"

Jesus said to him, "Why do you call me good?  No one is good except one—that is God.  But if you want to enter into life, keep the commandments."

He said to him, "Which ones?"

Jesus said, "You know the commandments: 'You shall not murder.' 'You shall not commit adultery.' 'You shall not steal.' 'You shall not offer false testimony.' 'Honor your father and mother.' (Exodus 20.12-16)  And, 'You shall love your neighbor as yourself.'"

The young man said to him, "Teacher, I have observed all these things from my youth up.  What do I still lack?"

When he heard these things, Jesus looked at him and loved him.  Jesus said to him, "You still lack one thing. If you want to be perfect, go, sell whatever you have, and distribute it to the poor, and you will have treasure in heaven; and come, follow me, taking up the cross."

191

But when he heard these things, he became very sad. His face fell at that saying, and he went away sorrowful, for he was very rich, one who had great possessions. When Jesus saw that he became very sad, he looked around, and said to his disciples, "How difficult it is for those who have riches to enter into God's Kingdom, the Kingdom of Heaven! It is easier for a camel to enter in through a needle's eye, than for a rich man to enter into God's Kingdom."

The disciples were amazed at his words. But Jesus answered again, "Children, how hard is it for those who trust in riches to enter into God's Kingdom! It is easier for a camel to go through a needle's eye than for a rich man to enter into God's Kingdom."

Those who heard this were exceedingly astonished, saying to him, "Then who can be saved?"

Jesus, looking at them, said, "With men it is impossible, but not with God, for all things are possible with God. The things which are impossible with men are possible with God."

Then Peter answered, "Behold, we have left everything, and followed you. What then will we have?"

Jesus said to them, "Most certainly I tell you that you who have followed me, in the regeneration when the Son of Man will sit on the throne of his glory, you also will sit on twelve thrones, judging the twelve tribes of Israel. Everyone who has left houses, or brothers, or sisters, or father, or mother, or wife, or children, or lands, for my name's sake, for the sake of the Good News or for God's Kingdom's sake, will receive one hundred times more now in this time, houses, brothers, sisters, mothers, children, and land, with persecution; and in the age to come will inherit eternal life. But many will be last who are first; and first who are last."

*(Matthew 19.16-30; Mark 10.16-31;*
*Luke 18.18-30)*

## *Parable of the Vineyard Laborers*

"For the Kingdom of Heaven is like a man who was the master of a household, who went out early in the morning to hire laborers for his vineyard. When he had agreed with the laborers for a denarius a day, he sent them into his vineyard.

"He went out about the third hour (9:00 a.m.), and saw others standing idle in the marketplace. He said to them, 'You also go into the vineyard, and whatever is right I will give you.' So they went their way.

"Again he went out about the sixth hour (noon) and the ninth hour (3:00 p.m.), and did likewise. About the eleventh hour (5:00 p.m.) he went out, and found others standing idle. He said to them, 'Why do you stand here all day idle?'

"They said to him, 'Because no one has hired us.'

"He said to them, 'You also go into the vineyard, and you will receive whatever is right.'

When evening had come, the lord of the vineyard said to his manager, 'Call the laborers and pay them their wages, beginning from the last to the first.'

"When those who were hired at about the eleventh hour came, they each received a denarius. When the first came, they supposed that they would receive more; and they likewise each received a denarius. When they received it, they murmured against the master of the household, saying, 'These last have spent one hour, and you have made them equal to us, who have borne the burden of the day and the scorching heat!'

"But he answered one of them, 'Friend, I am doing you no wrong. Didn't you agree with me for a denarius? Take that which is yours, and go your way. It is my desire to give to this last just as much as to you. Isn't it lawful for me to do what I want to with what I own? Or is your eye evil, because I am good?' So the last will be first, and the first last. For many are called, but few are chosen."

*(Matthew 20.1-16)*

## Jesus Explains What Awaits Him in Jerusalem

They were on the way, going up to Jerusalem; and Jesus was going in front of them, and they were amazed; and those who followed were afraid.

He again took the twelve aside, and began to tell them the things that were going to happen to him. "Behold, we are going up to Jerusalem, and all the things that are written through the prophets concerning the Son of Man will be completed. The Son of Man will be delivered to the chief priests and the scribes. They will condemn him to death, and will hand him over to the Gentiles. They will mock him, spit on him, scourge him, treat him shamefully, crucify and kill him. On the third day he will be raised up and rise again."

They understood none of these things. This saying was hidden from them, and they didn't understand the things that were said.

*(Matthew 20.17-19; Mark 10.32-34;*
*Luke 18.31-34)*

## The Sons of Zebedee Ask for Honor

Then the mother of the sons of Zebedee came to him with her sons, James and John, kneeling and asking a certain thing of him. They said to him, "Teacher, we want you to do for us whatever we will ask."

He said to them, "What do you want me to do for you?"

She said to him, "Command that these, my two sons, may sit, one on your right hand, and one on your left hand, in your Kingdom and your glory."

But Jesus answered, "You don't know what you are asking. Are you able to drink the cup that I am about to

194

drink, and be baptized with the baptism that I am baptized with?"

They said to him, "We are able."

He said to them, "You will indeed drink my cup, and be baptized with the baptism that I am baptized with, but to sit on my right hand and on my left hand is not mine to give; but it is for whom it has been prepared by my Father."

When the ten heard it, they were indignant with the two brothers, James and John. But Jesus summoned them, and said, "You know that they who are recognized as rulers over the nations lord it over them, and their great ones exercise authority over them. But it shall not be so among you, but whoever desires to become great among you shall be your servant. Whoever wants to become first among you shall be your bondservant, and the bondservant of all. For the Son of Man also came not to be served, but to serve, and to give his life as a ransom for many."

*(Matthew 20.20-28; Mark 10.35-45)*

## Jesus Heals a Blind Man near Jericho

As he came near Jericho, a certain blind man sat by the road, begging. Hearing a multitude going by, he asked what this meant. They told him that Jesus of Nazareth was passing by. He cried out, "Jesus, you son of David, have mercy on me!" Those who led the way rebuked him, that he should be quiet; but he cried out all the more, "You son of David, have mercy on me!"

Standing still, Jesus commanded him to be brought to him. When he had come near, he asked him, "What do you want me to do?"

He said, "Lord, that I may see again."

Jesus said to him, "Receive your sight. Your faith has healed you."

Immediately he received his sight, and followed him, glorifying God. All the people, when they saw it, praised God.

*(Luke 18.35-43)*

## *Jesus Dines with Zacchaeus*

They came to Jericho. He entered and was passing through Jericho. There was a man named Zacchaeus. He was a chief tax collector, and he was rich. He was trying to see who Jesus was, and couldn't because of the crowd, because he was short. He ran on ahead, and climbed up into a sycamore tree to see him, for he was going to pass that way.

When Jesus came to the place, he looked up and saw him, and said to him, "Zacchaeus, hurry and come down, for today I must stay at your house." He hurried, came down, and received him joyfully.

When they saw it, they all murmured, saying, "He has gone in to lodge with a man who is a sinner."

Zacchaeus stood and said to the Lord, "Behold, Lord, half of my goods I give to the poor. If I have wrongfully exacted anything of anyone, I restore four times as much."

Jesus said to him, "Today, salvation has come to this house, because he also is a son of Abraham. For the Son of Man came to seek and to save that which was lost."

*(Mark 10.46a; Luke 19.1-10)*

## *Parable of the Investors*

As they heard these things, he went on and told a parable, because he was near Jerusalem, and they supposed that God's Kingdom would be revealed immediately. He said therefore, "A certain nobleman went into a far country to receive for himself a kingdom, and to return. He called ten servants of his, and gave them ten mina coins (three years' worth of wages), and told them, 'Conduct business until I come.' But his citizens hated him, and sent an envoy after him, saying, 'We don't want this man to reign over us.'

"When he had come back again, having received the kingdom, he commanded these servants, to whom he had given the money, to be called to him, that he might know what they had gained by conducting business. The first

196

came before him, saying, 'Lord, your mina has made ten more minas.'

"He said to him, 'Well done, you good servant! Because you were found faithful with very little, you shall have authority over ten cities.'

"The second came, saying, 'Your mina, Lord, has made five minas.'

"So he said to him, 'And you are to be over five cities.' Another came, saying, 'Lord, behold, your mina, which I kept laid away in a handkerchief, for I feared you, because you are an exacting man. You take up that which you didn't lay down, and reap that which you didn't sow.'

"He said to him, 'Out of your own mouth will I judge you, you wicked servant! You knew that I am an exacting man, taking up that which I didn't lay down, and reaping that which I didn't sow. Then why didn't you deposit my money in the bank, and at my coming, I might have earned interest on it?' He said to those who stood by, 'Take the mina away from him, and give it to him who has the ten minas.'

"They said to him, 'Lord, he has ten minas!'

"He said, 'For I tell you that to everyone who has, will more be given; but from him who doesn't have, even that which he has will be taken away from him. But bring those enemies of mine who didn't want me to reign over them here, and kill them before me.'"

Having said these things, he went on ahead, going up to Jerusalem.

*(Luke 19.11-28)*

## Jesus Heals Two Blind Men

As he went out from Jericho with his disciples, a great multitude followed him. Behold, two blind men were sitting by the road. One of these men was the son of Timaeus, Bartimaeus, a blind beggar. When they heard that it was Jesus the Nazarene passing by, they began to cry out, and say, "Jesus, you son of David, have mercy on us!" Many in the multitude rebuked them, that they should be quiet, but they cried out much more, "You son of David, have mercy on us!"

Jesus stood still, and said, "Call them."

They called the blind men, saying to them, "Cheer up! Get up. He is calling you!" They, casting away their cloaks, sprang up, and came to Jesus.

Jesus asked them, "What do you want me to do for you?"

The blind men said to him, "Lord, that our eyes may be opened. Rabboni, Great Teacher, that we may see again."

Jesus, being moved with compassion, touched their eyes, and said to them, "Go your way. Your faith has made you well." Immediately their eyes received their sight, and they followed Jesus on the way.

*(Mark 10.46b-52)*

## Passover Approaches

Now the Passover of the Jews was at hand. Many went up from the country to Jerusalem before the Passover, to purify themselves. Then they sought for Jesus and spoke one with another, as they stood in the temple, "What do you think—that he isn't coming to the feast at all?" Now the chief priests and the Pharisees had commanded that if anyone knew where he was, he should report it, that they might seize him.

*(John 11.55-57)*

# Part 7:

## From Bethany to the Resurrection

## (April 23 - May 2, 28 CE)

# Friday
## April 23, 28 CE

## *Jesus Prepares for His Jerusalem Entry*

When they came near to Jerusalem, and came to Bethphage and Bethany, at the Mount of Olives (called Olivet), then Jesus sent two of his disciples, saying to them, "Go your way into the village that is opposite you on the other side. Immediately as you enter into it, you will find a donkey tied, and a colt with her on which no one has sat. Untie them, and bring them to me. If anyone says anything to you and asks you, 'Why are you doing this?', you shall say, 'The Lord needs them,' and immediately he will send them."

All this was done, that it might be fulfilled which was spoken through the prophet, saying:

> *"Tell the daughter of Zion,*
> *behold, your King comes to you,*
> *humble, and riding on a donkey,*
> *on a colt, the foal of a donkey." (Zechariah 9.9)*

The disciples went, and found things just as he had told them, and did just as Jesus commanded them. They found a young donkey tied at the door outside in the open street, and they untied him. The donkey's owners and some of those who stood there asked them, "What are you doing, untying the colt, the young donkey?" They said to them, 'The Lord needs it,' just as Jesus had said. And they let them go.

*(Matthew 21.1-6a; Mark 11.1-6;*
*Luke 19.29-34)*

## *Mary Anoints Jesus at Bethany*

Then six days before the Passover, Jesus came to Bethany, where Lazarus was, who had been dead, whom he raised from the dead. He was in the house of Simon, the leper. So they made him a supper there. Martha served, but Lazarus was one of those who sat at the table with him.

Mary, therefore, came to him having an alabaster jar of very expensive ointment, a pound (340 grams) of pure nard which was very precious. She broke the jar, poured it over Jesus' head as he sat at the table, and anointed his feet. She wiped his feet with her hair. The house was filled with the fragrance of the ointment.

When Judas Iscariot, Simon's son, one of his disciples, who would betray him and some of the other disciples saw this, they were indignant among themselves. They said, "Why has this ointment been wasted? Why wasn't this ointment sold for three hundred denarii (about a years worth of wages), and given to the poor?" They grumbled against her. Now Judas Iscariot said this, not because he cared for the poor, but because he was a thief, and having the money box, used to steal what was put into it.

But Jesus, knowing they grumbled, said, "Why do you trouble the woman? Leave her alone, because she has done a good work for me. For you always have the poor with you, and whenever you want to, you can do them good; but you will not always have me. She has kept this for the day of my burial. She has done what she could and poured this ointment on my body. She did it to prepare me for burial by anointing my body beforehand. Most certainly I tell you, wherever this Good News is preached in the whole world, what this woman has done will also be spoken of for a memorial of her."

A large crowd therefore of the Jews learned that he was there, and they came, not for Jesus' sake only, but that they might see Lazarus also, whom he had raised from the dead. But the chief priests conspired to put Lazarus to death also, because on account of him many of the Jews went away and believed in Jesus.

*(Matthew 26.6-13; Mark 14.3-9;*
*John 12.1-11)*

# Saturday
# April 24, 28 CE

## *The Triumphal Entry*

O n the next day, the disciples brought the donkey and the colt to Jesus, and laid their clothes on them; and he sat on their garments. Again, as it is written, *"Don't be afraid, daughter of Zion. Behold, your King comes, sitting on a donkey's colt."* (Zechariah 9.9)

A very great multitude had come to the feast. When they heard that Jesus was coming to Jerusalem, they took the branches of the palm trees, and went out to meet him. They spread their clothes on the road while others cut branches from the trees, and spread them on the road.

As he was now getting near, at the descent of the Mount of Olives, the whole multitude of the disciples who went in front of him, and those who followed, began to rejoice and praise God with a loud voice for all the mighty works which they had seen. They kept shouting, "Hosanna to the son of David! Blessed is the King who comes in the name of the Lord, the King of Israel! Blessed is the kingdom of our father David that is coming in the name of the Lord! Peace in heaven, and glory in the highest! Hosanna in the highest!"

His disciples didn't understand these things at first, but when Jesus was glorified, then they remembered that these things were written about him, and that they had done these things to him.

Some of the Pharisees from the multitude said to him, "Teacher, rebuke your disciples!"

209

He answered them, "I tell you that if these were silent, the stones would cry out."

When he came near, he saw the city and wept over it, saying, "If you, even you, had known today the things which belong to your peace! But now, they are hidden from your eyes. For the days will come on you, when your enemies will throw up a barricade against you, surround you, hem you in on every side, and will dash you and your children within you to the ground. They will not leave in you one stone on another, because you didn't know the time of your visitation."

When he had come into Jerusalem, all the city was stirred up, saying, "Who is this?" The multitudes said, "This is the prophet, Jesus, from Nazareth of Galilee." The multitude therefore that was with him when he called Lazarus out of the tomb, and raised him from the dead, was testifying about it. For this cause also the multitude went and met him, because they heard that he had done this sign. The Pharisees therefore said among themselves, "See how you accomplish nothing. Behold, the world has gone after him."

*(Matthew 21.7-11; Mark 11.7-10;*
*Luke 19.35-44; John 12.12-19)*

## Greeks and a Grain of Wheat

Now there were certain Greeks among those that went up to worship at the feast. These, therefore, came to Philip, who was from Bethsaida of Galilee, and asked him, saying, "Sir, we want to see Jesus." Philip came and told Andrew, and in turn, Andrew came with Philip, and they told Jesus.

Jesus answered them, "The time has come for the Son of Man to be glorified. Most certainly I tell you, unless a grain of wheat falls into the earth and dies, it remains by itself alone. But if it dies, it bears much fruit. He who loves his life will lose it. He who hates his life in this world will keep it to eternal life. If anyone serves me, let him follow me. Where I am, there will my servant also be. If anyone serves me, the Father will honor him.

*(John 12.20-26)*

210

## *A Voice out of the Sky*

"Now my soul is troubled. What shall I say? 'Father, save me from this time?' But for this cause I came to this time. Father, glorify your name!"

Then there came a voice out of the sky, saying, "I have both glorified it, and will glorify it again."

The multitude therefore, who stood by and heard it, said that it had thundered. Others said, "An angel has spoken to him."

Jesus answered, "This voice hasn't come for my sake, but for your sakes. Now is the judgment of this world. Now the prince of this world will be cast out. And I, if I am lifted up from the earth, will draw all people to myself." But he said this, signifying by what kind of death he should die.

The multitude answered him, "We have heard out of the law that the Christ remains forever. How do you say, 'The Son of Man must be lifted up?' Who is this Son of Man?"

Jesus therefore said to them, "Yet a little while the light is with you. Walk while you have the light, that darkness doesn't overtake you. He who walks in the darkness doesn't know where he is going. While you have the light, believe in the light, that you may become children of light."

Jesus said these things, and he departed and hid himself from them. But though he had done so many signs before them, yet they didn't believe in him, that the word of Isaiah the prophet might be fulfilled, which he spoke:

> *"Lord, who has believed our report?*
> *To whom has the arm of the Lord*
> *been revealed?" (Isaiah 53.1)*

For this cause they couldn't believe, for Isaiah said again:

> *"He has blinded their eyes and*
> *he hardened their heart,*
> *lest they should see with their eyes,*
> *and perceive with their heart,*

211

*and would turn,*
*and I would heal them." (Isaiah 6.10)*

Isaiah said these things when he saw his glory, and spoke of him.

Nevertheless even of the rulers many believed in him, but because of the Pharisees they didn't confess it, so that they wouldn't be put out of the synagogue, for they loved men's praise more than God's praise.

Jesus entered into the temple in Jerusalem. When he had looked around at everything, it being now evening, he went out to Bethany with the twelve.

*(Matthew 21.17; Mark 11.11;*
*John 12.27-43)*

# Sunday
## April 25, 28 CE

## Jesus Curses the Fig Tree

The next day in the morning, when they had come out from Bethany and were returning to the city, he was hungry. Seeing a fig tree by the road, afar off, having leaves, he came to see if perhaps he might find anything on it. When he came to it, he found nothing but leaves, for it was not the season for figs. Jesus told it, "May no one ever eat fruit from you again! Let there be no fruit from you forever!" And his disciples heard it. Immediately the fig tree withered away.

*(Matthew 21.18-19; Mark 11.12-14)*

## Jesus Cleanses the Temple

They came to Jerusalem, and Jesus entered into the temple of God, and began to throw out those who sold and those who bought in the temple, and overthrew the tables of the money changers, and the seats of those who sold the doves. He would not allow anyone to carry a container through the temple. He taught, saying to them, "Isn't it written, *'My house will be called a house of prayer for all the nations?'* (Isaiah 56.7) But you have made it a den of robbers!" (Jeremiah 7.11)

The chief priests and the scribes heard it, and sought how they might destroy him. For they feared him, because all the multitude was astonished at his teaching.

*(Matthew 21.12-13; Mark 11.15-18;*
*Luke 19.45-46)*

215

## *Jesus Teaches and Heals in the Temple*

He was teaching daily in the temple, but the chief priests and the scribes and the leading men among the people sought to destroy him. They couldn't find what they might do, for all the people hung on to every word that he said.

The blind and the lame came to him in the temple, and he healed them. But when the chief priests and the scribes saw the wonderful things that he did, and the children who were crying in the temple and saying, "Hosanna to the son of David!" they were indignant, and said to him, "Do you hear what these are saying?"

Jesus said to them, "Yes. Did you never read, *'Out of the mouth of babes and nursing babies you have perfected praise?'" (Psalm 8.2)*

When evening came, he left them and and went out of the city to Bethany, and camped there.

*(Matthew 21.14-17; Mark 11.19;*
*Luke 19.47-48)*

# Monday
# April 26, 28 CE

## The Fig Tree is Withered

As they passed by in the morning, the disciples saw the fig tree withered away from the roots, and they marveled. Peter, remembering, said to him, "Rabbi, look! The fig tree which you cursed has withered away." The disciples asked, "How did the fig tree immediately wither away?"

Jesus answered them, "Have faith in God. For most certainly I tell you, whoever may tell this mountain, 'Be taken up and cast into the sea,' and doesn't doubt in his heart, but believes that what he says is happening; he shall have whatever he says. If you have faith, and don't doubt, you will not only do what was done to the fig tree, but even if you told this mountain, 'Be taken up and cast into the sea,' it would be done. Therefore I tell you, all things whatever you pray and ask for, believe that you have received them, and you shall have them. Whenever you stand praying, forgive, if you have anything against anyone; so that your Father, who is in heaven, may also forgive you your transgressions. But if you do not forgive, neither will your Father in heaven forgive your transgressions."

*(Matthew 21.20-22; Mark 11.20-26)*

## By What Authority?

They came again to Jerusalem, and he was walking in the temple. The chief priests, and the scribes along with the elders of the people came to him as he was teaching the people in the temple and preaching the Good News. They

219

began saying to him, "By what authority do you do these things? Or who is giving you this authority to do these things?"

Jesus said to them, "I also will ask you one question, which if you tell me, I likewise will tell you by what authority I do these things. The baptism of John, where was it from? From heaven or from men? Answer me."

They reasoned with themselves, saying, "If we should say, 'From heaven;' he will ask us, 'Why then did you not believe him?' If we should say, 'From men' we fear that all the people with stone us, for they are persuaded that John was a real prophet. They answered Jesus, "We don't know."

Jesus said to them, "Neither do I tell you by what authority I do these things."

*(Matthew 21.23-27; Mark 11.27-33;*
*Luke 20.1-8)*

## Parable of the Two Sons

He began to speak to them in parables. "But what do you think? A man had two sons, and he came to the first, and said, 'Son, go work today in my vineyard.' He answered, 'I will not,' but afterward he changed his mind, and went. He came to the second, and said the same thing. He answered, 'I go, sir,' but he didn't go. Which of the two did the will of his father?"

They said to him, "The first."

Jesus said to them, "Most certainly I tell you that the tax collectors and the prostitutes are entering into God's Kingdom before you. For John came to you in the way of righteousness, and you didn't believe him, but the tax collectors and the prostitutes believed him. When you saw it, you didn't even repent afterward, that you might believe him.

*(Matthew 21.28-32; Mark 12.1a)*

220

## *Parable of the Vineyard*

"Hear another parable. There was a man who was a master of a household, who planted a vineyard, set a hedge around it, dug a pit for the wine press in it, built a tower, leased it out to farmers, and went into another country for a long time.

"When it was the proper time and the season for the fruit came near, he sent a servant to the farmers to get from them his share of the fruit of the vineyard. They took him, beat him, and sent him away empty. Again, he sent another servant to them; and they threw stones at him, wounded him in the head, and sent him away shamefully treated and empty. Again he sent another, a third; and they killed him; and many others, beating some, and killing some.

The lord of the vineyard said, 'What shall I do?' Therefore still having one, his beloved son, he sent him last to them, saying, 'I will send my beloved son. It may be that seeing him, they will respect him.' But when those farmers saw him, they reasoned among themselves, 'This is the heir. Come, let's kill him, and seize his inheritance which will be ours.' They took him, killed him, and cast him out of the vineyard. When therefore the lord of the vineyard comes, what will he do to those farmers?"

They told him, "He will miserably destroy those miserable men, and will lease out the vineyard to other farmers, who will give him the fruit in its season."

When they heard it, they said, "May it never be!"

Jesus said to them, "Did you never read in the Scriptures:

> *'The stone which the builders rejected,*
> *the same was made the head of the corner.*
> *This was from the Lord.*
> *It is marvelous in our eyes?' (Psalm 118.22-23)*

"Therefore I tell you, God's Kingdom will be taken away from you, and will be given to a nation producing its

221

fruit. He who falls on this stone will be broken to pieces, but on whomever it falls, it will scatter him as dust."

When the chief priests and the Pharisees heard his parables, they perceived that he had spoken this parable against them. They sought to lay hands on Jesus that very hour and to seize him, but they feared the multitudes, because they considered him to be a prophet. They left him, and went away.

*(Matthew 21.33-46; Mark 12.1-12;*
*Luke 20.1-8)*

### *Parable of the Marriage Feast*

Jesus answered and spoke again in parables to them, saying, "The Kingdom of Heaven is like a certain king, who made a marriage feast for his son, and sent out his servants to call those who were invited to the marriage feast, but they would not come. Again he sent out other servants, saying, 'Tell those who are invited, "Behold, I have prepared my dinner. My cattle and my fatlings are killed, and all things are ready. Come to the marriage feast!"'

"But they made light of it, and went their ways, one to his own farm, another to his merchandise, and the rest grabbed his servants, and treated them shamefully, and killed them. When the king heard that, he was angry, and sent his armies, destroyed those murderers, and burned their city.

"Then he said to his servants, 'The wedding is ready, but those who were invited weren't worthy. Go therefore to the intersections of the highways, and as many as you may find, invite to the marriage feast.' Those servants went out into the highways, and gathered together as many as they found, both bad and good. The wedding was filled with guests. But when the king came in to see the guests, he saw there a man who didn't have on wedding clothing, and he said to him, 'Friend, how did you come in here not wearing wedding clothing?' He was speechless. Then the king said to the servants, 'Bind him hand and foot, take him away, and throw him into the outer darkness; there is where the weeping and grinding of teeth will be.' For many are called, but few chosen."

*(Matthew 22.1-14)*

## Pharisees and Herodians Question Jesus: Taxes

They watched him, and sent out spies, who pretended to be righteous, that they might trap him in something he said, so as to deliver him up to the power and authority of the governor. The Pharisees went and took counsel how they might entrap him in his talk. They sent their disciples to him, along with the Herodians, saying, "Teacher, we know that you are honest, that you teach and say what is right, and that you teach the way of God in truth, no matter whom you teach, for you aren't partial and don't defer to anyone. Tell us therefore, what do you think? Is it lawful to pay taxes to Caesar, or not? Shall we give or shall we not give?"

But Jesus perceived their wickedness and craftiness, and said, "Why do you test me, you hypocrites? Show me the tax money. Bring me a denarius that I may see it."

They brought to him a denarius.

He asked them, "Whose image and inscription are on it?"

They answered him, "Caesar's."

Then he said to them, "Give therefore to Caesar the things that are Caesar's, and to God the things that are God's."

When they heard it, they marveled greatly at his answer and were silent. They weren't able to trap him in his words before the people. They left him, and went away.

*(Matthew 22.15-22; Mark 12.13-17;*
*Luke 20.20-26)*

## The Sadducees Question Jesus: Resurrection

On that day, some Sadducees (those who say that there is no resurrection) came to him. They asked him, saying, "Teacher, Moses wrote to us, 'If a man's brother dies, and leaves a wife behind him, and leaves no children, that his brother should take his wife, and raise up offspring for his brother.' There were seven brothers. The first took a wife, and dying left no offspring. The second took her, and died, leaving no children behind him. The third likewise; and the seven took her and left no children. Last of all the woman also died. In the resurrection, when they rise, whose wife will she be of them? For the seven had her as a wife."

But Jesus answered them, "Isn't this because you are mistaken, not knowing the Scriptures, nor the power of God. The children of this age marry, and are given in marriage. But those who are considered worthy to attain to that age and the resurrection from the dead, neither marry, nor are given in marriage. For they can't die any more, for they are like the angels, and are children of God, being children of the resurrection. But that the dead are raised, even Moses showed at the bush. Haven't you read in the book of Moses, about the bush, how God spoke to him and to you, saying, 'I am the God of Abraham, and the God of Isaac, and the God of Jacob?' (Exodus 3.6) God is not the God of the dead, but of the living, for all are alive to him. You are therefore badly mistaken."

When the multitudes heard it, they were astonished at his teaching. Some of the scribes answered, "Teacher, you speak well."

*(Matthew 22.23-33; Mark 12.18-27; Luke 20.27-39)*

## A Scribe Questions Jesus: Greatest Commandment

But the Pharisees, when they heard that he had silenced the Sadducees, gathered themselves together. One of them, a scribe and a lawyer, came, and heard them questioning together. Knowing that Jesus had answered them well, he asked him a question, testing him: "Which commandment is the greatest of all in the law?"

Jesus answered, "The greatest is, 'Hear, Israel, the Lord our God, the Lord is one: you shall love the Lord your

God with all your heart, and with all your soul, and with all your mind, and with all your strength.' (Deuteronomy 6.4-5) This is the first commandment. The second is like this, 'You shall love your neighbor as yourself.' (Leviticus 19.18) There is no other commandment greater than these. The whole law and the prophets depend on these two commandments."

The scribe said to him, "Truly, teacher, you have said well that he is one, and there is none other but he, and to love him with all the heart, and with all the understanding, with all the soul, and with all the strength, and to love his neighbor as himself, is more important than all whole burnt offerings and sacrifices."

When Jesus saw that he answered wisely, he said to him, "You are not far from God's Kingdom."

No one dared ask him any more question after that.

*(Matthew 22.34-40; Mark 12.28-34;*
*Luke 20.40)*

## *Jesus Asks a Question: David's Lord*

Now while the Pharisees were gathered together, Jesus asked them a question, saying, "What do you think of the Christ? Whose son is he?"

They said to him, "David's."

He said to them, "How is it that the scribes say that the Christ is the son of David? How then does David in the book of Psalms, in the Holy Spirit, call him Lord, saying:

'The Lord said to my Lord,
sit on my right hand,
until I make your enemies a footstool
for your feet?' (Psalm 110.1)

"If then David himself calls him Lord, how can he be his son?"

No one was able to answer him a word, neither did

any man dare ask him any more questions from that day forward.

*(Matthew 22.41-46; Mark 12.35-37a;*
*Luke 20.41-44)*

## Beware of the Scribes

In the hearing of all the common people who heard him gladly, Jesus said to his disciples, "Beware of the scribes, who like to walk in long robes, and love to get greetings in the marketplaces, and the best seats in the synagogues, and the best places at feasts; those who devour widows' houses, and for a pretense make long prayers. These will receive greater condemnation."

*(Mark 12.37b-40; Luke 20.45-47)*

## The Widows Mite

Jesus sat down opposite the treasury. He looked up, and saw how the multitude cast money into the treasury. Many who were rich cast in much. A poor widow came, and she cast in two small brass coins, which equal a quadrans coin (worth about 1% of a day's wage). He called his disciples to himself, and said to them, "Most certainly I tell you, this poor widow gave more than all those who are giving into the treasury, for they all gave out of their abundance, but she, out of her poverty, gave all that she had to live on."

*(Mark 12.41-44; Luke 21.1-4)*

## The Seven Woes to the Scribes and Pharisees

Then Jesus spoke to the multitudes and to his disciples, saying, "The scribes and the Pharisees sat on Moses' seat. All things therefore whatever they tell you to observe, observe and do, but don't do their works; for they say, and don't do. For they bind heavy burdens that are grievous to be borne, and lay them on men's shoulders; but they themselves will not lift a finger to help them. But all their works they do to be seen by men. They make their phylacteries broad, enlarge the tassels of their garments, and love the place of honor at feasts, the best seats in the synagogues, the salutations in the marketplaces, and to be called 'Rabbi, Rabbi' by men.

"But don't you be called 'Rabbi,' for one is your teacher, the Christ, and all of you are brothers. Call no man on the earth your father, for one is your Father, he who is in heaven. Neither be called masters, for one is your master, the Christ. But he who is greatest among you will be your servant. Whoever exalts himself will be humbled, and whoever humbles himself will be exalted.

"But woe to you, scribes and Pharisees, hypocrites! Because you shut up the Kingdom of Heaven against men; for you don't enter in yourselves, neither do you allow those who are entering in to enter.

Woe to you, scribes and Pharisees, hypocrites! For you travel around by sea and land to make one proselyte; and when he becomes one, you make him twice as much of a son of Gehenna as yourselves.

"Woe to you, you blind guides, who say, 'Whoever swears by the temple, it is nothing; but whoever swears by the gold of the temple, he is obligated.' You blind fools! For which is greater, the gold, or the temple that sanctifies the gold? 'Whoever swears by the altar, it is nothing; but whoever swears by the gift that is on it, he is obligated?' You blind fools! For which is greater, the gift, or the altar that sanctifies the gift? He therefore who swears by the altar, swears by it, and by everything on it. He who swears by the temple, swears by it, and by him who was living in it. He who swears by heaven, swears by the throne of God, and by him who sits on it.

"Woe to you, scribes and Pharisees, hypocrites! For you tithe mint, dill, and cumin, and have left undone the weightier matters of the law: justice, mercy, and faith. But you ought to have done these, and not to have left the other undone. You blind guides, who strain out a gnat, and swallow a camel!

"Woe to you, scribes and Pharisees, hypocrites! For you clean the outside of the cup and of the platter, but within they are full of extortion, self-indulgence and

227

unrighteousness. You blind Pharisee, first clean the inside of the cup and of the platter, that its outside may become clean also.

"Woe to you, scribes and Pharisees, hypocrites! For you are like whitened tombs, which outwardly appear beautiful, but inwardly are full of dead men's bones, and of all uncleanness. Even so you also outwardly appear righteous to men, but inwardly you are full of hypocrisy and iniquity.

"Woe to you, scribes and Pharisees, hypocrites! For you build the tombs of the prophets, and decorate the tombs of the righteous, and say, 'If we had lived in the days of our fathers, we wouldn't have been partakers with them in the blood of the prophets.' Therefore you testify to yourselves that you are children of those who killed the prophets. Fill up, then, the measure of your fathers.

"You serpents, you offspring of vipers, how will you escape the judgment of Gehenna? Therefore behold, I send to you prophets, wise men, and scribes. Some of them you will kill and crucify; and some of them you will scourge in your synagogues, and persecute from city to city; that on you may come all the righteous blood shed on the earth, from the blood of righteous Abel to the blood of Zachariah son of Barachiah, whom you killed between the sanctuary and the altar. Most certainly I tell you, all these things will come upon this generation.

"Jerusalem, Jerusalem, who kills the prophets, and stones those who are sent to her! How often I would have gathered your children together, even as a hen gathers her chicks under her wings, and you would not! Behold, your house is left to you desolate. For I tell you, you will not see me from now on, until you say, 'Blessed is he who comes in the name of the Lord!'"

*(Matthew 23.1-39)*

## Prophecy about Jerusalem's Destruction

As Jesus went out from the temple, and was going on his way, his disciples came to him to show him the buildings of the temple, saying, "Teacher, see what kind of stones and buildings!" They were talking about how it was decorated with beautiful stones and gifts. But he answered them, "Do you see all of these things, these great buildings? Most certainly I tell you, the days will come in which there will not be left here one stone on another, which will not be thrown down."

*(Matthew 24.1-2; Mark 13.1-12;*
*Luke 21.5-6)*

## *Beginning of Birth Pains*

As Jesus sat on the Mount of Olives opposite the temple, Peter, James, John, and Andrew asked him privately, "Tell us, when will these things be? What is the sign of your coming and the end of the age? What is the sign that these things are all about to happen and be fulfilled?"

Jesus, answering, began to tell them, "Watch out and be careful that no one leads you astray. For many will come in my name, saying, 'I am he! I am the Christ! The time is at hand!' And they will lead many astray. Therefore, don't follow them.

"When you hear of wars and rumors of wars and disturbances, don't be troubled or terrified. For those must happen, but the end is not yet and won't come immediately. For nation will rise against nation, and kingdom against kingdom. There will be great earthquakes in various places. There will be famines, plagues and troubles. There will be terrors and great signs from heaven. These things are the beginning of birth pains.

"But watch yourselves, for before all these things, they will lay their hands on you and will persecute you, delivering you up to synagogues and prisons. They will deliver you up to councils and oppression, and will kill you. You will be beaten in synagogues. You will be hated by all of the nations and you will stand before rulers, kings and governors for my name's sake. For you it will turn out as a testimony to them.

229

"When they lead you away and deliver you up, don't be anxious beforehand, or premeditate what you will say, but say whatever will be given you in that hour. For it is not you who speaks, but the Holy Spirit. Settle it therefore in your hearts not to meditate beforehand how to answer, for I will give you a mouth and wisdom which all your adversaries will not be able to withstand or to contradict.

"You will be handed over even by parents, brothers, relatives, and friends. They will cause some of you to be put to death. Brother will deliver up brother to death, and the father his child. Children will rise up against parents, and cause them to be put to death. And not a hair of your head will perish. You will be hated by all men for my name's sake, but he who endures to the end, the same will be saved. By your endurance you will win your lives.

Then many will stumble, and will deliver up one another, and will hate one another. Many false prophets will arise, and will lead many astray. Because iniquity will be multiplied, the love of many will grow cold. But he who endures to the end, the same will be saved. This Good News of the Kingdom will be preached in the whole world for a testimony to all the nations, and then the end will come.

*(Matthew 24.3-14; Mark 13.3-13;*
*Luke 21.7-19)*

## *The Abomination of Desolation*

"But when you see Jerusalem surrounded by armies, then know that its desolation is at hand. When, therefore, you see the abomination of desolation, which was spoken of through Daniel the prophet, standing, where it ought not, in the holy place (let the reader understand), then let those who are in Judea flee to the mountains. Let those who are in the middle of her depart. Let him who is on the housetop not go down to take out things that are in his house. Let him who is in the field not return back to get his clothes or cloak. For these are days of vengeance, that all things which are written may be fulfilled. But woe to those who are with child and to nursing mothers who nurse infants in those days!

"Pray that your flight will not be in the winter, nor on a Sabbath, for then there will be great oppression, such as has not been from the beginning of the world-- from the beginning of the creation which God created-- until now, no, nor ever will be. For there will be great distress in the land, and wrath to this people. They will fall by the edge of the sword, and will be led captive into all the nations. Jerusalem will be trampled down by the Gentiles, until the times of the Gentiles are fulfilled. Unless those days had been shortened by the Lord, no flesh would have been saved. But for the sake of the chosen ones, whom he picked out, those days will be shortened.

"Then if any man tells you, 'Behold, here is the Christ,' or, 'Look, there,' don't believe it. For there will arise false christs, and false prophets, and they will show great signs and wonders, so as to lead astray, if possible, even the chosen ones. But you watch.

"Behold, I have told you all things beforehand. If therefore they tell you, 'Behold, he is in the wilderness,' don't go out; 'Behold, he is in the inner rooms,' don't believe it. For as the lightning flashes from the east, and is seen even to the west, so will be the coming of the Son of Man. For wherever the carcass is, there is where the vultures (eagles) gather together.

"There will be signs in the sun, moon, and stars; and on the earth anxiety of nations, in perplexity for the roaring of the sea and the waves; men fainting for fear, and for expectation of the things which are coming on the world. Immediately after the oppression of those days, the sun will be darkened, the moon will not give its light, the stars will fall from the sky, and the powers of the heavens will be shaken; and then the sign of the Son of Man will appear in the sky. Then all the tribes of the earth will mourn, and they will see the Son of Man coming on the clouds of the sky with great power and great glory. But when these things begin to happen, look up, and lift up your heads, because your redemption is near. He will send out his angels with a great

231

sound of a trumpet, and they will gather together his chosen ones from the four winds, from the ends of the earth to the ends of the sky and from one end of the sky to the other.

*(Matthew 24.15-31; Mark 13.14-27;*
*Luke 21.20-28)*

## Parable of the Trees

"Now from the fig tree, and all the trees, learn this parable. When its branch has now become tender, and produces its leaves, and is already budding, you see it and know by your own selves that the summer is already near. Even so you also, when you see all these things, know that God's Kingdom is near, even at the doors. Most certainly I tell you, this generation will not pass away, until all these things happen and are accomplished. Heaven and earth will pass away, but my words will not pass away. But no one knows of that day and hour, not even the angels in heaven, nor the Son, but my Father only. Watch, keep alert, and pray; for you don't know when the time is.

"As the days of Noah were, so will be the coming of the Son of Man. For as in those days which were before the flood they were eating and drinking, marrying and giving in marriage, until the day that Noah entered into the ship. And they didn't know until the flood came, and took them all away. So will be the coming of the Son of Man. Then two men will be in the field: one will be taken and one will be left; two women grinding at the mill, one will be taken and one will be left. Watch therefore, for you don't know in what hour your Lord comes. But know this, that if the master of the house had known in what watch of the night the thief was coming, he would have watched, and would not have allowed his house to be broken into. Therefore also be ready, for in an hour that you don't expect, the Son of Man will come.

*(Matthew 24.32-44; Mark 13.28-33;*
*Luke 21.29-33)*

### Parable of the Wise and Foolish Servants

"Who then is the faithful and wise servant, whom his lord has set over his household, to give them their food in due season? Blessed is that servant whom his lord finds doing so when he comes. Most certainly I tell you that he will set him over all that he has. But if that evil servant should say in his heart, 'My lord is delaying his coming,' and begins to beat his fellow servants, and eat and drink with the drunkards, the lord of that servant will come in a day when he doesn't expect it, and in an hour when he doesn't know it, and will cut him in pieces, and appoint his portion with the hypocrites. There is where the weeping and grinding of teeth will be.

"It is like a man, traveling to another country, having left his house, and given authority to his servants, and to each one his work, and also commanded the doorkeeper to keep watch. Watch therefore, for you don't know when the lord of the house is coming, whether at evening, or at midnight, or when the rooster crows, or in the morning; lest coming suddenly he might find you sleeping. What I tell you, I tell all: Watch.

*(Matthew 24.45-51; Mark 13.34-37)*

### Be Watchful

"So be careful, or your hearts will be loaded down with carousing, drunkenness, and cares of this life, and that day will come on you suddenly. For it will come like a snare on all those who dwell on the surface of all the earth. Therefore be watchful all the time, praying that you may be counted worthy to escape all these things that will happen, and to stand before the Son of Man."

*(Luke 21.34-36)*

### Parable of the Ten Virgins

"Then the Kingdom of Heaven will be like ten virgins, who took their lamps, and went out to meet the bridegroom.

233

Five of them were foolish, and five were wise. Those who were foolish, when they took their lamps, took no oil with them, but the wise took oil in their vessels with their lamps.

"Now while the bridegroom delayed, they all slumbered and slept. But at midnight there was a cry, 'Behold! The bridegroom is coming! Come out to meet him!' Then all those virgins arose, and trimmed their lamps. The foolish said to the wise, 'Give us some of your oil, for our lamps are going out.' But the wise answered, saying, 'What if there isn't enough for us and you? You go rather to those who sell, and buy for yourselves.' While they went away to buy, the bridegroom came, and those who were ready went in with him to the marriage feast, and the door was shut. Afterward the other virgins also came, saying, 'Lord, Lord, open to us.' But he answered, 'Most certainly I tell you, I don't know you.' Watch therefore, for you don't know the day nor the hour in which the Son of Man is coming.

*(Matthew 25.1-13)*

## *Parable of the Talents*

"For it is like a man, going into another country, who called his own servants, and entrusted his goods to them. To one he gave five talents (150 kilograms of silver), to another two talents (60 kilograms of silver), to another one talent (30 kilograms of silver); to each according to his own ability. Then he went on his journey. Immediately he who received the five talents went and traded with them, and made another five talents. In the same way, he also who got the two gained another two. But he who received the one talent went away and dug in the earth, and hid his lord's money.

"Now after a long time the lord of those servants came, and reconciled accounts with them. He who received the five talents came and brought another five talents, saying, 'Lord, you delivered to me five talents. Behold, I have gained another five talents besides them.'

"His lord said to him, 'Well done, good and faithful servant. You have been faithful over a few things, I will set you over many things. Enter into the joy of your lord.'

234

"He also who got the two talents came and said, 'Lord, you delivered to me two talents. Behold, I have gained another two talents besides them.'

"His lord said to him, 'Well done, good and faithful servant. You have been faithful over a few things, I will set you over many things. Enter into the joy of your lord.'

"He also who had received the one talent came and said, 'Lord, I knew you that you are a hard man, reaping where you did not sow, and gathering where you did not scatter. I was afraid, and went away and hid your talent in the earth. Behold, you have what is yours.'

"But his lord answered him, 'You wicked and slothful servant. You knew that I reap where I didn't sow, and gather where I didn't scatter. You ought therefore to have deposited my money with the bankers, and at my coming I should have received back my own with interest. Take away therefore the talent from him, and give it to him who has the ten talents. For to everyone who has will be given, and he will have abundance, but from him who doesn't have, even that which he has will be taken away. Throw out the unprofitable servant into the outer darkness, where there will be weeping and gnashing of teeth.'

*(Matthew 25.14-30)*

## Parable of the Sheep and Goats

"But when the Son of Man comes in his glory, and all the holy angels with him, then he will sit on the throne of his glory. Before him all the nations will be gathered, and he will separate them one from another, as a shepherd separates the sheep from the goats. He will set the sheep on his right hand, but the goats on the left.

"Then the King will tell those on his right hand, 'Come, blessed of my Father, inherit the Kingdom prepared for you from the foundation of the world; for I was hungry, and you gave me food to eat. I was thirsty, and you gave me drink. I was a stranger, and you took me in. I was naked, and you clothed me. I was sick, and you visited me. I was in prison, and you came to me.'

235

"Then the righteous will answer him, saying, 'Lord, when did we see you hungry, and feed you; or thirsty, and give you a drink? When did we see you as a stranger, and take you in; or naked, and clothe you? When did we see you sick, or in prison, and come to you?'

"The King will answer them, 'Most certainly I tell you, because you did it to one of the least of these my brothers and sisters, you did it to me.'

"Then he will say also to those on the left hand, 'Depart from me, you cursed, into the eternal fire which is prepared for the devil and his angels; for I was hungry, and you didn't give me food to eat; I was thirsty, and you gave me no drink; I was a stranger, and you didn't take me in; naked, and you didn't clothe me; sick, and in prison, and you didn't visit me.'

"Then they will also answer, saying, 'Lord, when did we see you hungry, or thirsty, or a stranger, or naked, or sick, or in prison, and didn't help you?'

"Then he will answer them, saying, 'Most certainly I tell you, because you didn't do it to one of the least of these, you didn't do it to me.' These will go away into eternal punishment, but the righteous into eternal life."

*(Matthew 25.31-46)*

## *Jesus' Daily Routine*

Every day Jesus was teaching in the temple, and every night he would go out and spend the night on the mountain that is called Olivet. All the people came early in the morning to him in the temple to hear him.

Jesus cried out and said, "Whoever believes in me, believes not in me, but in him who sent me. He who sees me sees him who sent me. I have come as a light into the world, that whoever believes in me may not remain in the darkness. If anyone listens to my sayings, and doesn't believe, I don't judge him. For I came not to judge the world, but to save the world. He who rejects me, and doesn't receive my sayings, has one who judges him. The word that I spoke, the same will

236

judge him in the last day. For I spoke not from myself, but the Father who sent me, he gave me a commandment, what I should say, and what I should speak. I know that his commandment is eternal life. The things therefore which I speak, even as the Father has said to me, so I speak."

*(Luke 21.37-38; John 12.44-50)*

## The Conspiracy against Jesus

When Jesus had finished all these words, he said to his disciples, "You know that after two days the Passover is coming, and the Son of Man will be delivered up to be crucified."

It was now two days before the feast of unleavened bread, which is called the Passover. Then the chief priests, the scribes, and the elders of the people were gathered together in the court of the high priest, who was called Caiaphas. They took counsel together and sought how they might seize Jesus by deception and deceit, and kill him. But they said, "Not during the feast, lest a riot occur among the people."

*(Matthew 26.1-5; Mark 14.1-2;*
*Luke 22.1-2)*

# Tuesday
# April 27, 28 CE

## *Judas Agrees to Betray Jesus*

Then Satan entered into Judas, who was also called Iscariot, who was numbered as one of the twelve. He went away, and talked with the chief priests and captains about how he might deliver him to them. They were glad. Judas said, "What are you willing to give me that I should deliver him to you?" They agreed to give him money and weighed out for him thirty pieces of silver. He consented, and from that time Judas sought an opportunity to betray Jesus and how he might conveniently deliver him to them in the absence of the multitude.

*(Matthew 26.14-16; Mark 14.10-11;*
*Luke 22.3-6)*

## *Preparation for the Passover*

The first day of unleavened bread was approaching on which the Passover must be sacrificed. Jesus sent Peter and John, saying, "Go and prepare the Passover for us, that we may eat."

They said to him, "Where do you want us to prepare for you to eat the Passover?"

He said to them, "Behold, when you have entered into the city, a man carrying a pitcher of water will meet you. Follow him into the house which he enters. Tell the master of the house, 'The Teacher says to you, "My time is at hand. I will keep the Passover at your house with my disciples.

241

Where is the guest room, where I may eat the Passover with my disciples?"' He will himself show you a large, upper room that is furnished and ready. Make preparations and get ready for us there."

His disciples went out, and came into the city, and found things as he had said to them, and they prepared for the Passover.

*(Matthew 26.17-19; Mark 14.12-16;*
*Luke 22.7-13)*

## The Last Supper

Now when evening and the hour had come, he sat down and was reclining at the table with the twelve disciples (apostles). He said to them, "I have earnestly desired to eat this Passover with you before I suffer, for I tell you, I will no longer by any means eat of it until it is fulfilled in God's Kingdom." He received a cup, and when he had given thanks, he said, "Take this, and share it among yourselves, for I tell you, I will not drink at all again from the fruit of the vine, until God's Kingdom comes."

As they were eating, he said, "Behold, the hand of him who betrays me is with me on the table. Most certainly I tell you that one of you will betray me--he who eats with me." They were exceedingly sorrowful, and one by one, they each began to ask him, "It isn't me, is it, Lord?" And another, "Surely not I?"

He answered, "It is one of the twelve. He who dipped his hand with me in the dish, the same will betray me. The Son of Man goes, as it has been determined, even as it is written of him, but woe to that man through whom the Son of Man is betrayed! It would be better for that man if he had not been born."

Judas, who betrayed him, answered, "It isn't me, is it, Rabbi?"

Jesus said to him, "You said it."

They began to question among themselves, which of them it was who would do this thing.

As they were eating, Jesus took bread, blessed it and gave thanks for it, and broke it. He gave to the disciples, and said, "Take, eat; this is my body which is given for you. Do this in memory of me." Likewise, he took the cup after supper, gave thanks, and gave to all of them, saying, "All of you drink it, for this is my blood of the new covenant, which is poured out for many for the remission of sins. Most certainly I tell you that I will not drink of this fruit of the vine from now on, until that day when I drink it anew with you in God my Father's Kingdom."

There arose also a contention among them, which of them was considered to be greatest. He said to them, "The kings of the nations lord it over them, and those who have authority over them are called 'benefactors.' But not so with you. But one who is the greater among you, let him become as the younger, and one who is governing, as one who serves. For who is greater, one who sits at the table, or one who serves? Isn't it he who sits at the table? But I am among you as one who serves. But you are those who have continued with me in my trials. I confer on you a kingdom, even as my Father conferred on me, that you may eat and drink at my table in my Kingdom. You will sit on thrones, judging the twelve tribes of Israel."

*(Matthew 26.20-29; Mark 14.17-25;*
*Luke 22.14-30)*

## Jesus Washes Feet

Now before the feast of the Passover, Jesus, knowing that his time had come that he would depart from this world to the Father, having loved his own who were in the world, he loved them to the end. During supper, the devil having already put into the heart of Judas Iscariot, Simon's son, to betray him, Jesus, knowing that the Father had given all things into his hands, and that he came from God, and was going to God, arose from supper, and laid aside his outer garments. He took a towel, and wrapped a towel around his waist. Then he poured water into the basin, and began to wash the disciples' feet, and to wipe them with the towel that was wrapped around him.

243

Then he came to Simon Peter. He said to him, "Lord, do you wash my feet?"

Jesus answered him, "You don't know what I am doing now, but you will understand later."

Peter said to him, "You will never wash my feet!"

Jesus answered him, "If I don't wash you, you have no part with me."

Simon Peter said to him, "Lord, not my feet only, but also my hands and my head!"

Jesus said to him, "Someone who has bathed only needs to have his feet washed, but is completely clean. You are clean, but not all of you." For he knew him who would betray him, therefore he said, "You are not all clean."

So when he had washed their feet, put his outer garment back on, and sat down again, he said to them, "Do you know what I have done to you? You call me, 'Teacher' and 'Lord.' You say so correctly, for so I am. If I then, the Lord and the Teacher, have washed your feet, you also ought to wash one another's feet. For I have given you an example, that you also should do as I have done to you. Most certainly I tell you, a servant is not greater than his lord, neither one who is sent greater than he who sent him. If you know these things, blessed are you if you do them. I don't speak concerning all of you. I know whom I have chosen. But that the Scripture may be fulfilled, 'He who eats bread with me has lifted up his heel against me.' (Psalm 41.9) From now on, I tell you before it happens, that when it happens, you may believe that I am he. Most certainly I tell you, he who receives whomever I send, receives me; and he who receives me, receives him who sent me."

When Jesus had said this, he was troubled in spirit, and testified, "Most certainly I tell you that one of you will betray me."

The disciples looked at one another, perplexed about whom he spoke.

*(John 13.1-22)*

### Jesus Privately Exposes the Betrayer

One of his disciples, whom Jesus loved, was at the table, leaning against Jesus' breast. Simon Peter therefore beckoned to him, and said to him, "Tell us who it is of whom he speaks." He, leaning back, as he was, on Jesus' breast, asked him, "Lord, who is it?"

Jesus therefore answered, "It is he to whom I will give this piece of bread when I have dipped it." So when he had dipped the piece of bread, he gave it to Judas, the son of Simon Iscariot. After the piece of bread, then Satan entered into him.

Then Jesus said to him, "What you do, do quickly."

Now no man at the table knew why he said this to him. For some thought, because Judas had the money box, that Jesus said to him, "Buy what things we need for the feast," or that he should give something to the poor. Therefore having received that morsel, Judas went out immediately. It was night.

*(John 13.23-30)*

### A New Commandment

When Judas had gone out, Jesus said, "Now the Son of Man has been glorified, and God has been glorified in him. If God has been glorified in him, God will also glorify him in himself, and he will glorify him immediately. Little children, I will be with you a little while longer. You will seek me, and as I said to the Jews, 'Where I am going, you can't come,' so now I tell you. A new commandment I give to you, that you love one another. Just as I have loved you, you also love one another. By this everyone will know that you are my disciples, if you have love for one another."

*(John 13.31-35)*

### First Warning for Peter

Simon Peter said to him, "Lord, where are you going?"

Jesus answered, "Where I am going, you can't follow now, but you will follow afterwards."

Peter said to him, "Lord, why can't I follow you now? I will lay down my life for you."

The Lord said, "Simon, Simon, behold, Satan asked to have you, that he might sift you as wheat, but I prayed for you, that your faith wouldn't fail. You, when once you have turned again, establish your brothers and sisters."

He said to him, "Lord, I am ready to go with you both to prison and to death!"

Jesus answered him, "Will you lay down your life for me? Most certainly I tell you, Peter, the rooster will by no means crow today until you deny that you know me three times.

He said to them, "When I sent you out without purse, and wallet, and shoes, did you lack anything?"

They said, "Nothing."

Then he said to them, "But now, whoever has a purse, let him take it, and likewise a wallet. Whoever has none, let him sell his cloak, and buy a sword. For I tell you that this which is written must still be fulfilled in me: 'He was counted with transgressors.' (Isaiah 53.12) For that which concerns me has an end."

They said, "Lord, behold, here are two swords."

He said to them, "That is enough."

*(Luke 22.31-38; John 13.36-38)*

## Where are You Going?

"Don't let your heart be troubled. Believe in God. Believe also in me. In my Father's house are many dwelling places. If it weren't so, I would have told you. I am going to prepare a place for you. If I go and prepare a place for you, I will come again, and will receive you to myself; that where I am, you may be there also. Where I go, you know, and you know the way."

Thomas said to him, "Lord, we don't know where you are going. How can we know the way?"

Jesus said to him, "I am the way, the truth, and the life. No one comes to the Father, except through me. If you had known me, you would have known my Father also. From now on, you know him, and have seen him."

Philip said to him, "Lord, show us the Father, and that will be enough for us."

Jesus said to him, "Have I been with you such a long time, and do you not know me, Philip? He who has seen me has seen the Father. How do you say, 'Show us the Father?' Don't you believe that I am in the Father, and the Father in me? The words that I tell you, I speak not from myself; but the Father who lives in me does his works. Believe me that I am in the Father, and the Father in me; or else believe me for the very works' sake.

"Most certainly I tell you, he who believes in me, the works that I do, he will do also; and he will do greater works than these, because I am going to my Father. Whatever you will ask in my name, that will I do, that the Father may be glorified in the Son. If you will ask anything in my name, I will do it. If you love me, keep my commandments.

"I will pray to the Father, and he will give you another Helper, that he may be with you forever,—the Spirit of truth, whom the world can't receive; for it doesn't see him, neither knows him. You know him, for he lives with you, and will be in you. I will not leave you orphans. I will come to you. Yet a little while, and the world will see me no more; but you will see me. Because I live, you will live also. In that day you will know that I am in my Father, and you in me, and I in you. One who has my commandments, and keeps them, that person is one who loves me. One who loves me will be loved by my Father, and I will love him, and will reveal myself to him."

Judas (not Iscariot) said to him, "Lord, what has happened that you are about to reveal yourself to us, and not to the world?"

Jesus answered him, "If a man loves me, he will keep my word. My Father will love him, and we will come to him, and make our home with him. He who doesn't love me doesn't keep my words. The word which you hear isn't mine, but the Father's who sent me. I have said these things to you, while still living with you. But the Helper, the Holy Spirit, whom the Father will send in my name, he will teach you all things, and will remind you of all that I said to you.

"Peace I leave with you. My peace I give to you; not as the world gives, give I to you. Don't let your heart be troubled, neither let it be fearful. You heard how I told you, 'I go away, and I come to you.' If you loved me, you would have rejoiced, because I said 'I am going to my Father;' for the Father is greater than I. Now I have told you before it happens so that, when it happens, you may believe.

"I will no more speak much with you, for the prince of the world comes, and he has nothing in me. But that the world may know that I love the Father, and as the Father commanded me, even so I do.

"Arise, let us go from here."

When they had sung a hymn, He came out, and went, as his custom was, to the Mount of Olives. His disciples also followed him.

*(Matthew 26.30;*
*Mark 14.26; Luke 22.39; John 14.1-31)*

# Wednesday
## April 28, 28 CE

## Second Warning for Peter

Then Jesus said to them, "All of you will be made to stumble because of me tonight, for it is written, *'I will strike the shepherd, and the sheep of the flock will be scattered.'* *(Zechariah 13.7)* However, after I am raised up, I will go before you into Galilee."

But Peter answered him, "Even if all will be offended and made to stumble because of you, yet I will never be made to stumble."

Jesus said to him, "Most certainly I tell you, that you today, even this night, before the rooster crows twice, you will deny me three times."

Peter, all the more, said to him, "Even if I must die with you, I will not deny you." Likewise, all of the disciples also said the same thing.

*(Matthew 26.31-35; Mark 14.27-31)*

## I am the True Vine

"I am the true vine, and my Father is the farmer. Every branch in me that doesn't bear fruit, he takes away. Every branch that bears fruit, he prunes, that it may bear more fruit. You are already pruned clean because of the word which I have spoken to you. Remain in me, and I in you. As the branch can't bear fruit by itself, unless it remains in the vine, so neither can you, unless you remain in me.

251

"I am the vine. You are the branches. He who remains in me, and I in him, the same bears much fruit, for apart from me you can do nothing. If a man doesn't remain in me, he is thrown out as a branch, and is withered; and they gather them, throw them into the fire, and they are burned. If you remain in me, and my words remain in you, you will ask whatever you desire, and it will be done for you.

"In this is my Father glorified, that you bear much fruit; and so you will be my disciples. Even as the Father has loved me, I also have loved you. Remain in my love. If you keep my commandments, you will remain in my love; even as I have kept my Father's commandments, and remain in his love. I have spoken these things to you, that my joy may remain in you, and that your joy may be made full.

*(John 15.1-11)*

## No Longer Servants, but Friends

"This is my commandment, that you love one another, even as I have loved you. Greater love has no one than this, that someone lay down his life for his friends. You are my friends, if you do whatever I command you. No longer do I call you servants, for the servant doesn't know what his lord does. But I have called you friends, for everything that I heard from my Father, I have made known to you. You didn't choose me, but I chose you, and appointed you, that you should go and bear fruit, and that your fruit should remain; that whatever you will ask of the Father in my name, he may give it to you.

*(John 15.12-16)*

## The World Will Hate You

"I command these things to you, that you may love one another. If the world hates you, you know that it has hated me before it hated you. If you were of the world, the world would love its own. But because you are not of the world, since I chose you out of the world, therefore the world hates you. Remember the word that I said to you: 'A servant is not greater than his lord.' If they persecuted me, they will

252

also persecute you. If they kept my word, they will keep yours also.

But all these things will they do to you for my name's sake, because they don't know him who sent me. If I had not come and spoken to them, they would not have had sin; but now they have no excuse for their sin. He who hates me, hates my Father also. If I hadn't done among them the works which no one else did, they wouldn't have had sin. But now have they seen and also hated both me and my Father. But this happened so that the word may be fulfilled which was written in their law, *'They hated me without a cause.'* *(Psalm 35.19)*

"When the Helper has come, whom I will send to you from the Father, the Spirit of truth, who proceeds from the Father, he will testify about me. You will also testify, because you have been with me from the beginning.

"These things have I spoken to you, so that you wouldn't be caused to stumble. They will put you out of the synagogues. Yes, the time comes that whoever kills you will think that he offers service to God. They will do these things because they have not known the Father, nor me. But I have told you these things, so that when the time comes, you may remember that I told you about them. I didn't tell you these things from the beginning, because I was with you. But now I am going to him who sent me, and none of you asks me, 'Where are you going?' But because I have told you these things, sorrow has filled your heart.

*(John 15.17-16.6)*

## When the Helper Comes

"Nevertheless I tell you the truth: It is to your advantage that I go away, for if I don't go away, the Helper won't come to you. But if I go, I will send him to you. When he has come, he will convict the world about sin, about righteousness, and about judgment; about sin, because they don't believe in me; about righteousness, because I am going to my Father, and you won't see me any more; about judgment, because the prince of this world has been judged.

253

"I have yet many things to tell you, but you can't bear them now. However when he, the Spirit of truth, has come, he will guide you into all truth, for he will not speak from himself; but whatever he hears, he will speak. He will declare to you things that are coming. He will glorify me, for he will take from what is mine, and will declare it to you. All things whatever the Father has are mine; therefore I said that he takes of mine, and will declare it to you. A little while, and you will not see me. Again a little while, and you will see me."

*(John 16.7-16)*

## The Disciples' Confusion

Some of his disciples therefore said to one another, "What is this that he says to us, 'A little while, and you won't see me, and again a little while, and you will see me;' and, 'Because I go to the Father'?" They said therefore, "What is this that he says, 'A little while'? We don't know what he is saying."

Therefore Jesus perceived that they wanted to ask him, and he said to them, "Do you inquire among yourselves concerning this, that I said, 'A little while, and you won't see me, and again a little while, and you will see me?' Most certainly I tell you, that you will weep and lament, but the world will rejoice. You will be sorrowful, but your sorrow will be turned into joy. A woman, when she gives birth, has sorrow, because her time has come. But when she has delivered the child, she doesn't remember the anguish any more, for the joy that a human being is born into the world. Therefore you now have sorrow, but I will see you again, and your heart will rejoice, and no one will take your joy away from you.

*(John 16.17-22)*

## Ask in My Name

"In that day you will ask me no questions. Most certainly I tell you, whatever you may ask of the Father in my name, he will give it to you. Until now, you have asked nothing in my name. Ask, and you will receive, that your joy may be made full. I have spoken these things to you in figures of speech. But the time is coming when I will no more speak to you in figures of speech, but will tell you plainly about the Father. In that day you will ask in my name; and I don't say to you, that I will pray to the Father for you, for the Father himself loves you, because you have loved me, and have believed that I came from God. I came from the Father, and have come into the world. Again, I leave the world, and go to the Father."

His disciples said to him, "Behold, now you speak plainly, and speak no figures of speech. Now we know that you know all things, and don't need for anyone to question you. By this we believe that you came from God."

Jesus answered them, "Do you now believe? Behold, the time is coming, yes, and has now come, that you will be scattered, everyone to his own place, and you will leave me alone. Yet I am not alone, because the Father is with me. I have told you these things, that in me you may have peace. In the world you have oppression; but cheer up! I have overcome the world."

*(John 16.23-33)*

### The Son Talks to the Father

Jesus said these things, and lifting up his eyes to heaven, he said, "Father, the time has come. Glorify your Son, that your Son may also glorify you; even as you gave him authority over all flesh, he will give eternal life to all whom you have given him. This is eternal life, that they should know you, the only true God, and him whom you sent, Jesus Christ.

"I glorified you on the earth. I have accomplished the work which you have given me to do. Now, Father, glorify me with your own self with the glory which I had with you before the world existed. I revealed your name to the people whom you have given me out of the world. They were yours, and you have given them to me. They have kept your word. Now they have known that all things whatever you have given me are from you, for the words which you have given me I have given to them, and they received them, and knew for sure that I came from you, and they have believed that you sent me.

"I pray for them. I don't pray for the world, but for those whom you have given me, for they are yours. All things that are mine are yours, and yours are mine, and I am glorified in them. I am no more in the world, but these are in the world, and I am coming to you. Holy Father, keep them through your name which you have given me, that they may be one, even as we are. While I was with them in the world, I kept them in your name. Those whom you have given me I have kept. None of them is lost, except the son of destruction, that the Scripture might be fulfilled. But now I come to you, and I say these things in the world, that they may have my joy made full in themselves. I have given them your word.

"The world hated them, because they are not of the world, even as I am not of the world. I pray not that you would take them from the world, but that you would keep them from the evil one. They are not of the world even as I am not of the world. Sanctify them in your truth. Your word is truth. As you sent me into the world, even so I have sent them into the world. For their sakes I sanctify myself, that they themselves also may be sanctified in truth.

"Not for these only do I pray, but for those also who believe in me through their word, that they may all be one; even as you, Father, are in me, and I in you, that they also may be one in us; that the world may believe that you sent me. The glory which you have given me, I have given to them; that they may be one, even as we are one; I in them, and you in me, that they may be perfected into one; that the world may know that you sent me, and loved them, even as you loved me.

"Father, I desire that they also whom you have given me be with me where I am, that they may see my glory, which you have given me, for you loved me before the foundation of the world. Righteous Father, the world hasn't known you, but I knew you; and these knew that you sent me. I made known to them your name, and will make it known; that the love with which you loved me may be in them, and I in them."

*(John 17.1-26)*

## Jesus in Gethsemane

When Jesus had spoken these words, he went with his disciples over the brook Kidron, and came to a garden called Gethsemane, into which he and his disciples entered. Now Judas, who betrayed him, also knew the place, for Jesus often met there with his disciples. Then Jesus said to his disciples, "Sit here, while I go there and pray." He took with him Peter and James and John, the two sons of Zebedee, and began to be sorrowful and severely troubled and greatly distressed. Then he said to them, "My soul is exceedingly sorrowful, even to death. Stay here, and watch with me."

He went forward a little, withdrawing about a stone's throw. He knelt down, fell on his face, and prayed that, if it were possible, the hour might pass away from him. He said, "Abba. My Father, all things are possible to you. Please remove this cup from me. However, not my will and what I desire, but let your will and what you desire be done."

He came to the disciples, and found them sleeping, and said to Peter, "Simon, are you sleeping? What, couldn't you watch with me for one hour? Watch and pray, that you don't enter into temptation. The spirit indeed is willing, but the flesh is weak."

Again, a second time he went away, and prayed, saying, "My Father, if this cup can't pass away from me unless I drink it, your desire be done." He came again and found them sleeping, for their eyes were heavy, and they didn't know what to answer him.

He left them again, went away, and prayed a third time, saying the same words. An angel from heaven appeared to him, strengthening him. Being in agony he prayed more earnestly. His sweat became like great drops of blood falling down on the ground. Then he came to his disciples, and said to them, "Sleep on now, and take your rest. It is enough. Behold, the hour is at hand, and has come.

257

Behold, the Son of Man is betrayed into the hands of sinners. Arise, let's be going. Behold, he who betrays me is at hand."

*(Matthew 26.36-46; Mark 14.32-42; Luke 22.40-46; John 18.1-2)*

## Jesus is Arrested

Immediately, while he was still speaking, Judas, one of the twelve, came, and he was leading a great multitude with swords and clubs, from the chief priest and elders of the people. Judas had taken a detachment of soldiers and officers from the chief priests and the Pharisees, and came there with lanterns, torches, and weapons. Now he who betrayed him gave them a sign, saying, "Whomever I will kiss, that is he. Seize him, and lead him away safely." Immediately he came to Jesus, to kiss him.

Jesus said, "Judas, do you betray the Son of Man with a kiss?"

Judas said, "Hail, Rabbi!" and he kissed him.

Jesus said to him, "Friend, why are you here?"

Jesus therefore, knowing all the things that were happening to him, went out, and said to them, "Who are you looking for?"

They answered him, "Jesus of Nazareth."

Jesus said to them, "I am he."

Judas also, who betrayed him, was standing with them. When therefore he said to them, "I am he," they went backward, and fell to the ground. Again therefore he asked them, "Who are you looking for?"

They said, "Jesus of Nazareth."

Jesus answered, "I told you that I am he. If therefore you seek me, let these go their way," that the word might be fulfilled which he spoke, "Of those whom you have given me, I have lost none."

Then they came and laid hands on Jesus, and seized him. When those who were around him saw what was about

258

to happen, they said to him, "Lord, shall we strike with the sword?" Simon Peter, one of those who was standing by with Jesus, stretched out his hand. Having a sword, he drew it, and struck the high priest's servant, and cut off his right ear. The servant's name was Malchus. Then Jesus said to Peter, "Put your sword back into its sheath, for all those who take the sword will die by the sword. Or do you think that I couldn't ask my Father, and he would even now send me more than twelve legions of angels? How then would the Scriptures be fulfilled that it must be so? The cup which the Father has given me, shall I not surely drink it? Let me at least do this"—and he touched his ear, and healed him."

In that hour Jesus said to the multitudes, the chief priests, captains of the temple, and elders, who had come against him, "Have you come out as against a robber with swords and clubs to seize me? I sat daily, teaching in the temple with you, and you didn't stretch out your hand against me and arrest me. But all this has happened, that the Scriptures of the prophets might be fulfilled for this is your hour, and the power of darkness."

Then all the disciples left him, and fled. A certain young man followed him, having a linen cloth thrown around himself, over his naked body. The young men grabbed him, but he left the linen cloth, and fled from them naked.

*(Matthew 26.47-56; Mark 14.43-52;*
*Luke 22.47-53; John 18.3-12)*

## Jesus Sent to Annas

So the detachment, the commanding officer, and the officers of the Jews, seized Jesus and bound him, and led him to Annas first, for he was father-in-law to Caiaphas, who was high priest that year. Now it was Caiaphas who advised the Jews that it was expedient that one man should perish for the people.

The high priest therefore asked Jesus about his disciples, and about his teaching. Jesus answered him, "I spoke openly to the world. I always taught in synagogues, and in the temple, where the Jews always meet. I said

259

nothing in secret. Why do you ask me? Ask those who have heard me what I said to them. Behold, these know the things which I said."

When he had said this, one of the officers standing by slapped Jesus with his hand, saying, "Do you answer the high priest like that?"

Jesus answered him, "If I have spoken evil, testify of the evil; but if well, why do you beat me?"

*(John 18.13-14, 19-23)*

## Jesus Sent to Caiaphas

Annas sent him away bound. Those who had taken Jesus led him away to Caiaphas the high priest's house, where the scribes and the elders were gathered together.

But Simon Peter followed Jesus from a distance, as did another disciple, to the court of the high priest. Now that disciple was known to the high priest, and entered in with Jesus into the court of the high priest; but Peter was standing at the door outside. So the other disciple, who was known to the high priest, went out and spoke to her who kept the door, and brought in Peter. Then the maid who kept the door said to Peter, "Are you also one of this man's disciples?"

He said, "I am not." Peter entered into the courtyard, to see the end. He was sitting with the officers, and warming himself in the light of the fire.

Now the chief priests, the elders, and the whole council sought false testimony against Jesus, that they might put him to death; and they found none. Even though many false witnesses came forward, they found none. For many gave false testimony against him, and their testimony didn't agree with each other. But at last two false witnesses came forward, and said, "We heard this man say, 'I will destroy this temple that is made with hands, and in three days I will build another made without hands.'" Even so, their testimony did not agree.

The high priest stood up in the middle, and asked Jesus, "Have you no answer? What is this that these testify against you?" But Jesus held his peace, stayed quiet, and answered nothing. Again, the high priest asked him, "I adjure you by the living God, that you tell us: Are you the Christ, the Son of God, the Blessed?."

Jesus said to him, "I am. You have said it. Nevertheless, I tell you, after this you will see the Son of Man sitting at the right hand of Power, and coming on the clouds of the sky."

Then the high priest tore his clothing, saying, "He has spoken blasphemy! Why do we need any more witnesses? Behold, now you have heard his blasphemy. What do you think?" They all condemned him answering, "He is worthy of death!"

*(Matthew 26.57-66; Mark 14.53-64;*
*Luke 22.54; John 18.24)*

## Peter's Denial

When the servants and the officers had kindled a fire of coal in the middle of the courtyard below (for it was cold), and had sat down together, Peter sat among them. While Peter was standing and warming himself, they said therefore to him, "You aren't also one of his disciples, are you?" He denied it, and said, "I am not."

One of the maids of the high priest, a certain servant girl came and saw Peter as he sat in the light warming himself. And looking intently at him, she said, "This man was also with the Galilean! You were also with the Nazarene, Jesus!" But he denied it before them all, saying, "Woman, I don't know him or what you are talking about. I neither know, nor understand what you are saying." He went out on the porch, and the rooster crowed.

When he had gone out onto the porch, someone else saw him, and said to those who were there, "This is one of them. This man also was with Jesus of Nazareth. You are also one of them!" Again he denied it with an oath, "Man, I am not! I don't know the man."

261

After a little while (about an hour passed) those who stood by confidently affirmed and said to Peter, "Surely you are also one of them, for you are a Galilean, for your speech makes you known." And one of the servants of the high priest, being a relative of him whose ear Peter had cut off, said, "Didn't I see you in the garden with him?"

Peter denied it again and he began to curse and to swear, saying, "I don't know this man of whom you speak!" Immediately, while he was still speaking the rooster crowed the second time. The Lord turned and looked at Peter. Then Peter remembered the Lord's word which Jesus had said to him, "Before the rooster crows twice, you will deny me three times." When he thought about that, he went out and wept bitterly.

*(Matthew 26.69-75; Mark 14.66-72; Luke 22.55-62; John 18.15-18, 25-27)*

## The Jews Mock and Beat Jesus

The men who held Jesus mocked him and beat him. They spit in his face and beat him with their fists. They blindfolded him, and some struck and slapped him on the face, saying, "Prophesy to us, you Christ! Who hit you?" The officers struck him with the palms of their hands. They spoke many other things against him, insulting him.

*(Matthew 26.67-68; Mark 14.65; Luke 22.63-65)*

## Jesus Before the Sanhedrin

As soon as morning had come and it was day, the assembly of the elders of the people was gathered together, both chief priests and scribes, and they held a consultation and took counsel against Jesus to put him to death. They led him away into their council, saying, "If you are the Christ, tell us."

But he said to them, "If I tell you, you won't believe, and if I ask, you will in no way answer me or let me go. From now on, the Son of Man will be seated at the right hand of the power of God."

They all said, "Are you then the Son of God?"

He said to them, "You say it, because I am."

They said, "Why do we need any more witness? For we ourselves have heard from his own mouth!"

*(Matthew 27.1; Mark 15.1a;*
*Luke 22.66-71)*

### *Jesus Brought to Pontius Pilate*

The whole company of them rose up, bound Jesus and led him, therefore, from Caiaphas into the Praetorium. It was early, and they themselves didn't enter into the Praetorium, that they might not be defiled, but might eat the Passover.

Pontius Pilate, the governor, therefore went out to them, and said, "What accusation do you bring against this man?"

They answered him, "If this man weren't an evildoer, we wouldn't have delivered him up to you." They began to accuse him, saying, "We found this man perverting the nation, forbidding paying taxes to Caesar, and saying that he himself is Christ, a king."

Pilate therefore said to them, "Take him yourselves, and judge him according to your law."

Therefore the Jews said to him, "It is not lawful for us to put anyone to death." This was so that the word of Jesus might be fulfilled, which he spoke, signifying by what kind of death he should die.

Pilate therefore entered again into the Praetorium and called Jesus. Jesus stood before the governor. And the governor asked him, "Are you the King of the Jews?"

Jesus answered him, "So you say. Do you say this by yourself, or did others tell you about me?"

Pilate answered, "I'm not a Jew, am I? Your own nation and the chief priests delivered you to me. What have you done?"

Jesus answered, "My Kingdom is not of this world. If my Kingdom were of this world, then my servants would fight, that I wouldn't be delivered to the Jews. But now my Kingdom is not from here."

Pilate therefore said to him, "Are you a king then?"

Jesus answered, "You say that I am a king. For this reason I have been born, and for this reason I have come into the world, that I should testify to the truth. Everyone who is of the truth listens to my voice."

Pilate said to him, "What is truth?"

When he had said this, he went out again to the Jews, and Pilate said to the chief priests and the multitudes, "I find no basis for a charge against this man."

But they insisted, saying, "He stirs up the people, teaching throughout all Judea, beginning from Galilee even to this place." But when Pilate heard Galilee mentioned, he asked if the man was a Galilean. When he found out that he was in Herod's jurisdiction, he sent him to Herod, who was also in Jerusalem during those days.

*(Matthew 27.2,11; Mark 15.1b-2;*
*Luke 23.1-7; John 18.28-38)*

## Jesus Before Herod Antipas

Now when Herod saw Jesus, he was exceedingly glad, for he had wanted to see him for a long time, because he had heard many things about him. He hoped to see some miracle done by him. He questioned him with many words, but Jesus gave no answers. The chief priests and the scribes stood, vehemently accusing him. Herod with his soldiers humiliated him and mocked him. Dressing him in luxurious clothing, they sent him back to Pilate. Herod and Pilate became friends with each other that very day, for before that they were enemies with each other.

*(Luke 23.8-11)*

## Jesus Before Pilate and the Crowd

Pilate called together the chief priests and the rulers and the people. When Jesus was accused of many things by the chief priests and elders, he answered nothing. Then Pilate said to him, "Don't you hear how many things they testify against you?" But Jesus gave him no further answer, not even one word, so that the governor marveled greatly.

Pilate said to them, "You brought this man to me as one that perverts the people, and see, I have examined him before you, and found no basis for a charge against this man concerning those things of which you accuse him. Neither has Herod, for I sent you to him, and see, nothing worthy of death has been done by him. I will therefore punish him and release him."

Now at the feast the governor was accustomed to release to the multitude one prisoner, whom they asked for and desired. They had then a notable prisoner, called Barabbas. He had been thrown into prison, bound with his fellow insurgents, men who in the insurrection, a certain revolt in the city, had committed murder and was a robber.

The multitude, crying aloud, began to ask Pilate to do as he always did for them. Pilate answered them, saying, "You have a custom, that I should release someone to you at the Passover. Therefore do you want me to release to you the King of the Jews?" For he perceived that for envy the chief priests had delivered him up. But the chief priests stirred up the multitude, that he should release Barabbas to them instead. When therefore they were gathered together, Pilate said to them, "Whom do you want me to release to you? Barabbas, or Jesus, who is called Christ?"

While Pilate was sitting on the judgment seat, his wife sent to him, saying, "Have nothing to do with that righteous man, for I have suffered many things today in a dream because of him." Now the chief priests and the elders

265

persuaded the multitudes to ask for Barabbas, and destroy Jesus. But the governor answered them, "Which of the two do you want me to release to you?"

They said, "Away with this man! Release to us Barabbas!"

Pilate spoke again, wanting to release Jesus, saying to them, "What then shall I do to Jesus, who is called Christ, the King of the Jews?"

They all shouted and said to him, "Crucify! Crucify him! Let him be crucified!"

But the governor said to them the third time, "Why? What evil has he done? I have found no capital crime in him. I will therefore punish him and release him." But they were urgent with loud voices, asking that he might be crucified. They cried out exceedingly, saying, "Let him be crucified!"

So when Pilate saw that nothing was being gained, but rather that a disturbance was starting, he took water, and washed his hands before the multitude, saying, "I am innocent of the blood of this righteous person. You see to it."

All the people answered, "May his blood be on us, and on our children!" Their voices and the voices of the chief priests prevailed. Pilate decreed that what they asked for should be done. Wishing to please the crowd, he released to them Barabbas who had been thrown into prison for insurrection and murder, the one for whom they had asked.

*(Matthew 27.12-26a; Mark 15.3-15a;*
*Luke 23.12-25a; John 18.39-40)*

### The Gentiles Mock and Beat Jesus

So Pilate took Jesus, flogged him and then handed him over to be crucified. Then the governor's soldiers took Jesus into the court, which is the Praetorium, and gathered the whole garrison (cohort) together against him. They stripped him, and put a purple garment on him. They twisted and braided a crown of thorns and put it on his head, and put a reed in his right hand; and bowing their knees, they did homage to him. They saluted and mocked him, and

266

kept saying, "Hail, King of the Jews!" and kept slapping him. They spat on him, and took the reed and struck him on the head.

Then Pilate went out again, and said to them, "Behold, I bring him out to you, that you may know that I find no basis for a charge against him." Jesus therefore came out, wearing the crown of thorns and the purple garment. Pilate said to them, "Behold, the man!"

When therefore the chief priests and the officers saw him, they shouted, saying, "Crucify! Crucify!"

Pilate said to them, "Take him yourselves, and crucify him, for I find no basis for a charge against him."

The Jews answered him, "We have a law, and by our law he ought to die, because he made himself the Son of God." When therefore Pilate heard this saying, he was more afraid.

*(Matthew 27.26b-30; Mark 15.15b-19;*
*John 19.1-8)*

## Pilate Speaks Privately to Jesus

He entered into the Praetorium again, and said to Jesus, "Where are you from?" But Jesus gave him no answer. Pilate therefore said to him, "Aren't you speaking to me? Don't you know that I have power to release you, and have power to crucify you?"

Jesus answered, "You would have no power at all against me, unless it were given to you from above. Therefore he who delivered me to you has greater sin."

At this, Pilate was seeking to release him, but the Jews cried out, saying, "If you release this man, you aren't Caesar's friend! Everyone who makes himself a king speaks against Caesar!"

When Pilate therefore heard these words, he brought Jesus out, and sat down on the judgment seat at a place called "The Pavement", but in Hebrew, "Gabbatha." Now it was the Preparation Day of the Passover, at about the sixth hour (6:00 a.m.). He said to the Jews, "Behold, your King!"

They cried out, "Away with him! Away with him! Crucify him!"

Pilate said to them, "Shall I crucify your King?"

The chief priests answered, "We have no king but Caesar!"

So then Pilate delivered Jesus up to their will. He delivered him to them to be crucified

*(Luke 23.15b; John 19.9-16a)*

## Judas' Repentance and Suicide

Then Judas, who betrayed him, when he saw that Jesus was condemned, felt remorse, and brought back the thirty pieces of silver to the chief priests and elders, saying, "I have sinned in that I betrayed innocent blood."

But they said, "What is that to us? You see to it."

He threw down the pieces of silver in the sanctuary, and departed. He went away and hanged himself. The chief priests took the pieces of silver, and said, "It's not lawful to put them into the treasury, since it is the price of blood." They took counsel, and bought the potter's field with them, to bury strangers in. Therefore that field was called "The Field of Blood" to this day. Then that which was spoken through the prophet was fulfilled, saying:

> *"They took the thirty pieces of silver,*
> *the price of him upon whom a price had been set,*
> *whom some of the children of Israel priced,*
> *and they gave them for the potter's field,*
> *as the Lord commanded me."*

*(Matthew 27.3-10)*

## *The Way to Golgotha and the Crucifixion*

When they had mocked Jesus, they took the purple robe off of him, and put his clothes on him, and led him away, bearing his cross, to crucify him.  As they came out, they found and grabbed a man of Cyrene, Simon by name, the father of Alexander and Rufus.  He was passing by, coming from the country, and they compelled him to go with them, laid on him the cross that he might carry it after Jesus.

A great multitude of the people followed him, including women who also mourned and lamented him.  But Jesus, turning to them, said, "Daughters of Jerusalem, don't weep for me, but weep for yourselves and for your children.  For behold, the days are coming in which they will say, 'Blessed are the barren, the wombs that never bore, and the breasts that never nursed.'  Then they will begin to tell the mountains, 'Fall on us!' and tell the hills, 'Cover us.'  For if they do these things in the green tree, what will be done in the dry?"  There were also others, two criminals, led with him to be put to death.

They came to a place called Golgotha, that is being interpreted, "The place of a skull."  They gave him sour wine (vinegar) mixed with myrrh and gall to drink. When he had tasted it, he would not take it and drink.  When they had crucified him, Jesus said, "Father, forgive them, for they don't know what they are doing."  With him they crucified two criminals, robbers; one on his right hand, and one on his left, and Jesus in the middle.

Then the soldiers  took his garments and made four parts, to every soldier a part; and also the coat. Now the coat was without seam, woven from the top throughout.  Then they said to one another, "Let's not tear it, but cast lots for it to decide whose it will be,"  that the scripture and that which was spoken by the prophet might be fulfilled which say:

> *"They divided my garments among them,*
> *and for my clothing they cast lots" (Psalm 22:18)*

Therefore the soldiers did these things.

It was the third hour (9:00 a.m.), and they crucified him. They sat and watched him there. They set up over his head the superscription of the accusation against him. The title which Pilate had written and was put on the cross read, "THIS IS JESUS OF NAZARETH, THE KING OF THE JEWS." Therefore many of the Jews read this title, inscription, for the place where Jesus was crucified was near the city; and it was written in Hebrew, in Latin, and in Greek. The chief priests of the Jews therefore said to Pilate, "Don't write, 'The King of the Jews,' but, 'he said, I am King of the Jews.'"

Pilate answered, "What I have written, I have written."

*(Matthew 27.31-38; Mark 15.20-28;*
*Luke 23.26-34,38; John 19.16b-24)*

## Jesus on the Cross

The people stood watching. Those who passed by blasphemed him, wagging their heads, and saying, "Ha! You who destroy the temple, and build it in three days, save yourself! If you are the Son of God, come down from the cross!"

Likewise the chief priests also mocking among themselves, with the scribes, the Pharisees, and the elders, said, "He saved others, but he can't save himself. If he is the Christ of God, his chosen one and the King of Israel, let him come down from the cross now that we may see, and we will believe in him. He trusts in God. Let God deliver him now, if he wants him; for he said, 'I am the Son of God.'"

The robbers also who were crucified with him insulted him and cast on him the same reproach. The soldiers also mocked him, coming to him and offering him vinegar, and saying, "If you are the King of the Jews, save yourself!"

One of the criminals who was hanged was insulting him, saying, "If you are the Christ, save yourself and us!" But the other answered, and rebuking him said, "Don't you even fear God, seeing you are under the same condemnation? And we indeed justly, for we receive the due reward for our deeds, but this man has done nothing wrong." He said to

270

Jesus, "Lord, remember me when you come into your Kingdom."

Jesus said to him, "Assuredly I tell you, today you will be with me in Paradise."

Now from the sixth hour (noon) there was darkness over the whole land until the ninth hour (3:00 p.m.).

But there were standing by the cross of Jesus his mother, and his mother's sister, Mary the wife of Clopas, and Mary Magdalene. Therefore when Jesus saw his mother, and the disciple whom he loved standing there, he said to his mother, "Woman, behold your son!" Then he said to the disciple, "Behold, your mother!" From that hour, the disciple took her to his own home.

About the ninth hour (3:00 p.m.), Jesus cried with a loud voice, saying, "Eli, Eli, lima sabachthani?" which is, being interpreted, *"My God, my God, why have you forsaken me?" (Psalm 22.1)* Some of them who stood there, when they heard it, said, "Behold, this man is calling Elijah." After this, Jesus, seeing and knowing that all things were now finished, that the Scripture might be fulfilled, said, "I am thirsty." Now a vessel full of vinegar was set there. Immediately one of them ran, and took a sponge, and filled it with vinegar, and put it on a hyssop reed, held it at his mouth and gave it to him to drink. The rest said, "Let him be. Let's see whether Elijah comes to save him."

*(Matthew 27.39-49; Mark 15.29-36;*
*Luke 23.35-37,39-44; John 19.25-29)*

### Jesus Dies

When Jesus therefore had received the vinegar, he cried out with a loud voice, saying, "Father, into your hands I commit my spirit! It is finished" Having said this, he bowed his head, breathed his last and yielded up his spirit.

Behold, the sun was darkened and the veil of the temple was torn in two from the top to the bottom. The earth quaked, the rocks were split, and the tombs were opened and many bodies of the saints who had fallen asleep were raised;

271

and coming out of the tombs after his resurrection, they entered into the holy city and appeared to many.

Now the centurion who stood by opposite him, and those who were with him saw that Jesus cried out like this and breathed his last. And when they saw the earthquake, and the things that were done, they feared exceedingly and glorified God, saying, "Certainly this was a righteous man. Truly this man was the Son of God!"

All the multitudes that came together to see this, when they saw the things that were done, returned home beating their breasts. All his acquaintances stood at a distance, watching these things. Many women were also there watching from afar. These were the women who, when he was in Galilee, followed him, and served him. Among them were Mary Magdalene, Mary the mother of James the less and of Joses, Salome, the mother of the sons of Zebedee and many other women who came up with him to Jerusalem.

Therefore the Jews, because it was the Preparation Day, so that the bodies wouldn't remain on the cross on the Sabbath (for that Sabbath was a special one, a high day), asked of Pilate that their legs might be broken, and that they might be taken away. Therefore the soldiers came, and broke the legs of the first, and of the other who was crucified with him; but when they came to Jesus, and saw that he was already dead, they didn't break his legs. However one of the soldiers pierced his side with a spear, and immediately blood and water came out. He who has seen has testified, and his testimony is true. He knows that he tells the truth, that you may believe. For these things happened, that the Scripture might be fulfilled, *"A bone of him will not be broken."* *(Exodus 12.46)* Again another Scripture says, *"They will look on him whom they pierced."* *(Zechariah 12.10)*

*(Matthew 27.50-56; Mark 15.37-41;*
*Luke 23.45b-49; John 19.30-37)*

### Jesus is Buried

After these things, when evening had now come, because it was the Preparation Day, that is, the day before the Sabbath, Joseph, a rich and prominent council member who also himself was looking and waiting for God's Kingdom, came. He was from Arimathaea, a city of the Jews. He was a good and righteous man (he had not consented to their counsel and deed), and he was a disciple of Jesus, but secretly for fear of the Jews. He boldly went in to Pilate, and asked for Jesus' body, that he might take it away. Pilate marveled and wondered if Jesus were already dead; and summoning the centurion, he asked him whether he had been dead long. When he found out from the centurion, he granted permission that the body be given up to Joseph.

Joseph took Jesus down and wrapped him in the linen cloth which he had bought. Now in the place where he was crucified there was a garden. In the garden was a new tomb that belonged to Joseph of Arimathaea and in which no man had ever yet been laid. He laid Jesus in this tomb which had been cut out of a rock. He rolled a great stone against the door of the tomb and departed. It was the day of Preparation, and the Sabbath was drawing near.

The women, who had come with him out of Galilee, followed after. Mary Magdalene and the other Mary, the mother of Joses, were there sitting opposite the tomb. They saw the tomb and they saw where and how his body was laid. They returned.

Nicodemus, who at first came to Jesus by night, also came bringing a mixture of myrrh and aloes, about a hundred Roman pounds (33 kilograms). So they took Jesus' body, and bound it in linen cloths with the spices, as the custom of the Jews is to bury. Then because of the Jews' Preparation Day (for the tomb was near at hand) they laid Jesus there.

*(Matthew 27.57-61; Mark 15.42-47;*
*Luke 23.50-56a; John 19.38-42)*

# Thursday
## April 29, 28 CE

## *The Jews Request a Tomb Guard*

Now on the next day, which was the day after the Preparation Day, the chief priests and the Pharisees were gathered together to Pilate, saying, "Sir, we remember what that deceiver said while he was still alive: 'After three days I will rise again.' Command, therefore, that the tomb be made secure until the third day, lest perhaps his disciples come at night and steal him away, and tell the people, 'He is risen from the dead;' and the last deception will be worse than the first."

Pilate said to them, "You have a guard. Go, make it as secure as you can." So they went with the guard and made the tomb secure, sealing the stone.

*(Matthew 27.62-66)*

277

# Friday
# April 30, 28 CE

## *The Women Buy and Prepare Spices*

When the Sabbath was past, Mary Magdalene, and Mary the mother of James, and Salome, bought and prepared spices and ointments, that they might come and anoint him.

*(Mark 16.1; Luke 23.56a)*

# Saturday
## May 1, 28 CE

## The Women Rest on the Sabbath

On the Sabbath they rested according to the commandment.

*(Luke 23.56b)*

## An Angel Opens the Tomb

Behold, there was a great earthquake, for an angel of the Lord descended from the sky, and came and rolled away the stone from the door, and sat on it. His appearance was like lightning, and his clothing white as snow. For fear of him, the guards shook, and became like dead men.

*(Matthew 28.2-4)*

# Sunday
## May 2, 28 CE

## The Empty Tomb

Now on the first day of the week, Mary Magdalene went early, while it was still dark, to the tomb, and saw the stone taken away from the tomb. Therefore she ran and came to Simon Peter, and to the other disciple whom Jesus loved, and said to them, "They have taken away the Lord out of the tomb, and we don't know where they have laid him!"

Therefore Peter and the other disciple went out, and they went toward the tomb. They both ran together. The other disciple outran Peter, and came to the tomb first. Stooping and looking in, he saw the linen cloths lying, yet he didn't enter in. Then Simon Peter came, following him, and entered into the tomb. He saw the linen cloths lying, and the cloth that had been on his head, not lying with the linen cloths, but rolled up in a place by itself. So then the other disciple who came first to the tomb also entered in, and he saw and believed. For as yet they didn't know the Scripture, that he must rise from the dead. So the disciples went away again to their own homes.

*(John 20.1-10)*

## Jesus Appears First to Mary Magdalene

Now when he had risen early on the first day of the week, Jesus appeared first to Mary Magdalene, from whom he had cast out seven demons. Mary was standing outside at the tomb weeping. So, as she wept, she stooped and looked into the tomb, and she saw two angels in white sitting, one at the head, and one at the feet, where the body of Jesus had lain. They told her, "Woman, why are you weeping?"

She said to them, "Because they have taken away my Lord, and I don't know where they have laid him." When she had said this, she turned around and saw Jesus standing, and didn't know that it was Jesus.

Jesus said to her, "Woman, why are you weeping? Who are you looking for?"

She, supposing him to be the gardener, said to him, "Sir, if you have carried him away, tell me where you have laid him, and I will take him away."

Jesus said to her, "Mary."

She turned and said to him, "Rabboni!" which is to say, "Teacher!"

Jesus said to her, "Don't hold me, for I haven't yet ascended to my Father; but go to my brothers, and tell them, 'I am ascending to my Father and your Father, to my God and your God.'"

Mary Magdalene went and told those who had been with him, as they mourned and wept. She told the disciples that she had seen the Lord, and that he had said these things to her. When they heard that he was alive, and had been seen by her, they disbelieved.

*(Mark 16.9-11 (6); John 20.11-18)*

## Jesus Appears to Other Women

At early dawn on the first day of the week, when the sun had risen, Mary, the mother of James, Salome, Joanna and some others came to the tomb, bringing the spices which they had prepared. They were saying among themselves, "Who will roll away the stone from the door of the tomb for us?" for it was very big. Looking up, they saw that the stone was rolled back.

The angel who had rolled the stone away from the door and sat on it answered the women, "Don't be afraid, for I know that you seek Jesus, who has been crucified. He is not here, for he has risen, just like he said. Come, see the place where the Lord was lying."

Entering into the tomb, they saw a young man sitting on the right side, dressed in a white robe, but they did not find the Lord Jesus' body. And they were amazed. He said to them, "Don't be amazed. You seek Jesus, the Nazarene, who has been crucified. He has risen. He is not here. Behold, the place where they laid him!"

While they were greatly perplexed about this, behold, two men stood by them in dazzling clothing. Becoming terrified, they bowed their faces down to the earth. They said to them, "Why do you seek the living among the dead? He isn't here, but is risen. Remember what he told you when he was still in Galilee, saying that the Son of Man must be delivered up into the hands of sinful men, and be crucified, and the third day rise again?

"But go quickly and tell his disciples and Peter, 'He has risen from the dead, and behold, he goes before you into Galilee; there you will see him, as he said to you.' Behold, I have told you."

They departed quickly and fled from the tomb with fear and great joy. Trembling and astonishment had come on them, and they said nothing to anyone; for they were afraid. As they were running to tell his disciples, behold, Jesus met them, saying, "Greetings!"

They came and took hold of his feet, and worshiped him. Then Jesus said to them, "Don't be afraid. Go tell my brothers and sisters that they should go into Galilee, and there they will see me."

They remembered his words.

*(Matthew 28.1,5-10; Mark 16.2-8;*
*Luke 24.1-8)*

### The Guards are Bribed

Now while they were going, behold, some of the guards came into the city, and told the chief priests all the things that had happened. When they were assembled with

291

the elders, and had taken counsel, they gave a large amount of silver to the soldiers, saying, "Say that his disciples came by night, and stole him away while we slept. If this comes to the governor's ears, we will persuade him and keep you out of trouble and make you free of worry." So they took the money and did as they were told. This saying was spread abroad among the Jews, and continues until today.

*(Matthew 28.11-15)*

## The Women Tell the Disciples

The women returned from the tomb, and told all these things to the eleven, and to all the rest. Now it was Mary Magdalene, Joanna, and Mary the mother of James and the other women with them who told these things to the apostles. These words seemed to them to be nonsense, and they didn't believe them. But Peter got up and ran to the tomb. Stooping and looking in, he saw the strips of linen lying by themselves, and he departed to his home, wondering what had happened.

*(Luke 24.9-12)*

## On the Road to Emmaus

After these things he was revealed in another form to two of them, as they walked, on their way into the country. Behold, two of them were going that very day to a village named Emmaus, which was sixty stadia (11 kilometers) from Jerusalem. They talked with each other about all of these things which had happened. While they talked and questioned together, Jesus himself came near, and went with them. But their eyes were kept from recognizing him. He said to them, "What are you talking about as you walk?" They stood still, looking sad.

One of them, named Cleopas, answered him, "Are you the only stranger in Jerusalem who doesn't know the things which have happened there in these days?"

He said to them, "What things?"

They said to him, "The things concerning Jesus, the Nazarene, who was a prophet mighty in deed and word before

292

God and all the people; and how the chief priests and our rulers delivered him up to be condemned to death, and crucified him. But we were hoping that it was he who would redeem Israel. Yes, and besides all this, it is now the third day since these things happened. Also, certain women of our company amazed us, having arrived early at the tomb; and when they didn't find his body, they came saying that they had also seen a vision of angels, who said that he was alive. Some of us went to the tomb, and found it just like the women had said, but they didn't see him."

He said to them, "Foolish men, and slow of heart to believe in all that the prophets have spoken! Didn't the Christ have to suffer these things and to enter into his glory?" Beginning from Moses and from all the prophets, he explained to them in all the Scriptures the things concerning himself.

They came near to the village, where they were going, and he acted like he would go further. They urged him, saying, "Stay with us, for it is almost evening, and the day is almost over." He went in to stay with them.

When he had sat down at the table with them, he took the bread and gave thanks. Breaking it, he gave to them. Their eyes were opened, and they recognized him, and he vanished out of their sight. They said to one another, "Weren't our hearts burning within us, while he spoke to us along the way, and while he opened the Scriptures to us?"

They rose up that very hour, returned to Jerusalem, and found the eleven gathered together, and those who were with them, saying, "The Lord is risen indeed, and has appeared to Simon!" They related the things that happened along the way, and how he was recognized by them in the breaking of the bread. But they didn't believe them, either.

*(Mark 16.12-13; Luke 24.13-35)*

### Jesus Appears to the Disciples

Therefore it was evening, on that day, the first day of the week, and the doors were locked where the disciples were assembled, for fear of the Jews. As the two disciples from

293

Emmaus said these things, Jesus himself came and stood among them in the middle, and said to them, "Peace be to you." But they were terrified and filled with fear, and supposed that they had seen a spirit.

He said to them, "Why are you troubled? Why do doubts arise in your hearts? See my hands and my feet, that it is truly me. Touch me and see, for a spirit doesn't have flesh and bones, as you see that I have." When he had said this, he showed them his hands, feet and his side. While they still didn't believe for joy, and wondered, he said to them, "Do you have anything here to eat?"

They gave him a piece of a broiled fish and some honeycomb. He took them, and ate in front of them. He said to them, "This is what I told you, while I was still with you, that all things which are written in the law of Moses, the prophets, and the psalms, concerning me must be fulfilled."

The disciples therefore were glad when they saw the Lord and bowed down to him. Jesus therefore said to them again, "Peace be to you. As the Father has sent me, even so I send you." When he had said this, he breathed on them, and said to them, "Receive the Holy Spirit! If you forgive anyone's sins, they have been forgiven them. If you retain anyone's sins, they have been retained."

But Thomas, one of the twelve, called Didymus, wasn't with them when Jesus came. The other disciples therefore said to him, "We have seen the Lord!"

But he said to them, "Unless I see in his hands the print of the nails, and put my hand into his side, I will not believe."

But the eleven disciples went into Galilee, to the mountain where Jesus had sent them.

*(Matthew 28.16-17; Luke 24.36-44; John 20.19-25)*

# Part 8:

## After the Resurrection Until Ten Days Before Shavuot

ישוע

**(May 3 - June 10, 28 CE)**

# MAY AND JUNE
## 28 CE

## *Thomas Sees and Believes*

Eight days after Jesus had first appeared to his disciples, again they were inside, and Thomas was with them. Jesus came, the doors being locked, and stood in the middle, and said, "Peace be to you."

Then he said to Thomas, "Reach here your finger, and see my hands. Reach here your hand, and put it into my side. Don't be unbelieving, but believing."

Thomas answered him, "My Lord and my God!"

Jesus said to him, "Because you have seen me, you have believed. Blessed are those who have not seen, and have believed." Jesus rebuked them for their unbelief and hardness of heart, because they didn't believe those who had seen him after he had risen.

Therefore Jesus did many other signs in the presence of his disciples, which are not written in this book; but these are written, that you may believe that Jesus is the Christ, the Son of God, and that believing you may have life in his name.

*(Mark.16.14 (6); John 20.26-31)*

## *Jesus Appears by the Sea of Tiberias*

After these things, Jesus revealed himself again to the disciples at the sea of Tiberias. He revealed himself this way. Simon Peter, Thomas called Didymus, Nathanael of Cana in Galilee, and the sons of Zebedee, and two others of his disciples were together. Simon Peter said to them, "I'm going fishing."

They told him, "We are also coming with you." They immediately went out, and entered into the boat. That night, they caught nothing.

But when day had already come, Jesus stood on the beach, yet the disciples didn't know that it was Jesus. Jesus therefore said to them, "Children, have you anything to eat?"

They answered him, "No."

He said to them, "Cast the net on the right side of the boat, and you will find some."

They cast it therefore, and now they weren't able to draw it in for the multitude of fish. That disciple therefore whom Jesus loved said to Peter, "It's the Lord!"

So when Simon Peter heard that it was the Lord, he wrapped his coat around him (for he was naked), and threw himself into the sea. But the other disciples came in the little boat (for they were not far from the land, but about two hundred cubits, 91 meters away), dragging the net full of fish. So when they got out on the land, they saw a fire of coals there, and fish laid on it, and bread. Jesus said to them, "Bring some of the fish which you have just caught."

Simon Peter went up, and drew the net to land, full of great fish, one hundred fifty-three; and even though there were so many, the net wasn't torn.

Jesus said to them, "Come and eat breakfast." None of the disciples dared inquire of him, "Who are you?" knowing that it was the Lord.

Then Jesus came and took the bread, gave it to them, and the fish likewise. This is now the third time that Jesus was revealed to his disciples, after he had risen from the dead.

*(John 21.1-14)*

## *Jesus Questions Peter*

So when they had eaten their breakfast, Jesus said to Simon Peter, "Simon, son of Jonah, do you love me more than these?"

He said to him, "Yes, Lord; you know that I have affection for you."

Jesus said to him, "Feed my lambs." He said to him again a second time, "Simon, son of Jonah, do you love me?"

Peter said to him, "Yes, Lord; you know that I have affection for you."

He said to him, "Tend my sheep." Jesus said to him the third time, "Simon, son of Jonah, do you have affection for me?"

Peter was grieved because he asked him the third time, "Do you have affection for me?" He said to him, "Lord, you know everything. You know that I have affection for you."

Jesus said to him, "Feed my sheep. Most certainly I tell you, when you were young, you dressed yourself, and walked where you wanted to. But when you are old, you will stretch out your hands, and another will dress you, and carry you where you don't want to go."

Now he said this, signifying by what kind of death he would glorify God. When he had said this, he said to him, "Follow me."

Then Peter, turning around, saw a disciple following. This was the disciple whom Jesus loved, the one who had also leaned on Jesus' breast at the supper and asked, "Lord, who is going to betray You?" Peter seeing him, said to Jesus, "Lord, what about this man?"

Jesus said to him, "If I desire that he stay until I come, what is that to you? You follow me." This saying therefore went out among the brothers and sisters, that this disciple wouldn't die. Yet Jesus didn't say to him that he wouldn't die, but, "If I desire that he stay until I come, what is that to you?"

This is the disciple who testifies about these things, and wrote these things. We know that his witness is true.

*(John 21.15-24)*

## The Great Commission

Jesus came to them and spoke to them, saying, "All authority has been given to me in heaven and on earth. Go, therefore, and make disciples of all nations, baptizing them in the name of the Father and of the Son and of the Holy Spirit, teaching them to observe all things that I commanded you. Behold, I am with you always, even to the end of the age."

He said to them, "Go into all the world, and preach the Good News to the whole creation. He who believes and is baptized will be saved; but he who disbelieves will be condemned. These signs will accompany those who believe: in my name they will cast out demons; they will speak with new languages; they will take up serpents; and if they drink any deadly thing, it will in no way hurt them; they will lay hands on the sick, and they will recover."

*(Matthew 28.18-20a; Mark 16.15-18 **(6)**)*

## Open Minds to Understand the Scriptures

Then he opened their minds, that they might understand the Scriptures. He said to them, "Thus it is written, and thus it was necessary for the Christ to suffer and to rise from the dead the third day, and that repentance and remission of sins should be preached in his name to all the nations, beginning at Jerusalem. You are witnesses of these things. Behold, I send out the promise of my Father on you. But wait in the city of Jerusalem until you are clothed with power from on high."

*(Luke 24.45-49)*

## Jesus' Final Instructions

Jesus continued to both do and teach until the day in which he was received up, after he had given commandment through the Holy Spirit to the apostles whom he had chosen. To these he also showed himself alive after he suffered, by many proofs, appearing to them over a period of forty days, and speaking about God's Kingdom.

Being assembled together with them, he commanded them, "Don't depart from Jerusalem, but wait for the promise of the Father, which you heard from me. For John indeed baptized in water, but you will be baptized in the Holy Spirit not many days from now."

Therefore when they had come together, they asked him, "Lord, are you now restoring the kingdom to Israel?"

He said to them, "It isn't for you to know times or seasons which the Father has set within his own authority. But you will receive power when the Holy Spirit has come upon you. You will be witnesses to me in Jerusalem, in all Judea and Samaria, and to the uttermost parts of the earth."

*(Acts 1.1b-8)*

## Jesus Ascends to the Father

After he had spoken these things to them, Jesus led them out as far as Bethany, and he lifted up his hands, and blessed them. While he blessed them, he withdrew from them. As they were looking, he was taken up, carried up into heaven. A cloud received him out of their sight, and Jesus sat down at the right hand of God.

While they were looking steadfastly into the sky as he went, behold, two men stood by them in white clothing, who also said, "You men of Galilee, why do you stand looking into the sky? This Jesus, who was received up from you into the sky will come back in the same way as you saw him going into the sky."

They worshiped Jesus, and returned to Jerusalem with great joy, and were continually in the temple, praising and blessing God.

They went out, and preached everywhere, the Lord working with them, and confirming the word by the signs that followed.

*(Mark 16.15-20a (6); Luke 24.50-53;*
*Acts 1.9-11)*

## The World Could Not Contain the Books

There are also many other things which Jesus did, which if they would all be written, I suppose that even the world itself wouldn't have room for the books that would be written.

Amen.

*(Matthew 28.20b; Mark 16.20b (6);*
*Luke 24.53b; John 21.25)*

# Appendix 1:
# Scripture Reference Charts

# Part 1: The Beginning, Birth and Childhood
## (4 BCE - 10 CE)

|  | MATTHEW | MARK | LUKE | JOHN |
|---|---|---|---|---|
| Introduction  p1 |  |  | 1.1-4 |  |
| Prologue  p1 |  |  |  | 1.1-18 |
| Gabriel Visits Zacharias p2 |  |  | 1.5-25 |  |
| Gabriel Visits Mary  p3 |  |  | 1. 26-28 |  |
| An Angel in Joseph's Dream  p4 | 1.18-25 |  |  |  |
| Mary Visits Elizabeth  p5 |  |  | 1.39-56 |  |
| John's Birth  p6 |  |  | 1.57-80 |  |
| Jesus' Birth  p7 |  |  | 2.1-20 |  |
| Jesus is Circumcised  p9 |  |  | 2.21 |  |
| Jesus is Redeemed  p9 |  |  | 2.22-40 |  |
| The Magi Visit Jesus p10 | 2.1-12 |  |  |  |
| Jesus' Family Flees to Egypt  p11 | 2.13-23 |  |  |  |
| Twelve Year Old Jesus Visits the Temple  p12 |  |  | 2.41-52 |  |
| The Genealogy of Jesus Through His Mother  p13 | 1.1-17 |  |  |  |
| The Genealogy of Jesus Through His Father  p14 |  |  | 3.23b-38 |  |

## Part 2: Public Ministry of Jesus
### a. Baptism until the end of Passover
### (February - April, 27 CE)

| | MATTHEW | MARK | LUKE | JOHN |
|---|---|---|---|---|
| The Ministry of John, Son of Zacharias p19 | 3.1-12 | 1.2-8 | 3.1-17 | |
| The Baptism of Jesus p23 | 3.13-17 | 1.9-11 | 3.21, 22 | |
| Jesus is Tempted by Satan p23 | 4.1-11 | 1.12,13 | 4.1-13 | |
| John Testifies about Jesus p27 | | | 3.23a | 1.19-34 |
| Jesus' First Disciples p28 | | | | 1.35-42 |
| Into Galilee and More Disciples p29 | | | | 1.43-51 |
| The Wedding at Cana p33 | | | | 2.1-12 |
| Jesus Cleanses the Temple p34 | | | | 2.13-25 |
| Jesus Talks with Nicodemus p35 | | | | 3.1-21 |

## Part 3: Public Ministry of Jesus
## b. The end of Passover until the end of Shavuot
### (April - June, 27 CE)

|  | MATTHEW | MARK | LUKE | JOHN |
|---|---|---|---|---|
| John's Final Testimony about Jesus  p41 |  |  |  | 3.22-36 |
| Jesus Visits Samaria p42 |  |  |  | 4.1-42 |
| Jesus Heals a Nobleman's Son  p44 |  |  |  | 4.43-54 |
| John, Son of Zacharias, is Imprisoned  p45 |  |  | 3.18-20 |  |
| Jesus Heals the Man at the Pool of Bethesda p45 |  |  |  | 5.1-47 |

## Part 4: Public Ministry of Jesus
### c. The end of Shavuot until the beginning of Sukkot
### (June - October, 27 CE)

| | MATTHEW | MARK | LUKE | JOHN |
|---|---|---|---|---|
| Jesus is Rejected in Nazareth p53 | 4.12 | 1.14a | 4.14-30 | |
| Jesus Goes to Capernaum p54 | 4.13-17 | 1.14b | | |
| Jesus Calls Four Fishermen p55 | 4.18-22 | 1.16-20 | | |
| The Man with the Unclean Spirit p55 | | 1.21-28 | 4.31-37 | |
| Jesus Heals Peter's Mother-in-Law p56 | 8.14-17 | 1.29-38 | 4.38-43 | |
| Jesus Travels Throughout Galilee p57 | 4.23-25 | 1.39 | 4.44 | |
| The Call by the Sea p61 | | | 5.1-11 | |
| The Teaching on the Mountain p62 | 5.1-7.29 | | | |
| Jesus Heals a Leper p68 | 8.1-4 | 1.40-45 | 5.12-16 | |
| A Paralytic and Four Friends p68 | 9.1-7 | 2.1-12 | 5.17-26 | |
| Jesus Calls Matthew (Levi) p69 | 9.9-13 | 2.13-17 | 5.27-32 | |
| Old Garments and New Wine p70 | 9.14-17 | 2.18-22 | 5.33-39 | |
| Jesus is Lord of the Sabbath p73 | 12.1-8 | 2.23-28 | 6.1-5 | |
| Jesus Heals a Man's Withered Hand p74 | 12.9-14 | 3.1-6 | 6.6-11 | |
| Crowds Come to Jesus p74 | 12.15-21 | 3.7-12 | | |

|  | MATTHEW | MARK | LUKE | JOHN |
|---|---|---|---|---|
| Jesus Chooses the Twelve  p75 | 10.2-4 | 3.13-19 | 6.12-19 | |
| The Teaching on the Plain  p76 | | | 6.20-49 | |
| Jesus Heals the Centurion's Servant p78 | 8.5-13 | | 7.1-10 | |
| Jesus Raises the Widow's Son  p79 | | | 7.11-17 | |
| Jesus Answers John's Concerns  p80 | 11.2-6 | | 7.18-23 | |
| Jesus Talks about his Cousin John  p80 | 11.7-19 | | 7.24-35 | |
| Jesus Denounces the Cities  p81 | 11.20-30 | | | |
| Dinner at Simon's: A Woman Forgiven  p82 | | | 7.36-50 | |
| Jesus Travels with the Twelve  and Certain Women p83 | | | 8.1-3 | |
| Jesus Casts out a Demon and is Confronted  p83 | 12.22-37 | 3.19b-30 | | |
| The Sign of Jonah the Prophet  p85 | 12.38-45 | | | |
| Who is My Family?  p85 | 12.46-50 | 3.31-35 | 8.19-21 | |
| The Parable of the Farmer  p86 | 13.1-9 | 4.1-9 | 8.4-8 | |
| Private Explanation of the Parable  p86 | 13.10-23 | 4.10-25 | 8.9-18 | |
| Jesus Tells Other Parables  p88 | 13.24-35 | 4.26-34 | | |

| | MATTHEW | MARK | LUKE | JOHN |
|---|---|---|---|---|
| A Parable Explained and Others Told p90 | 13.36-52 | | | |
| Jesus Calms the Storm p91 | 13.53; 8.18-27 | 5.35-41 | 8.22-25 | |
| The Gerasene Demoniacs p92 | 8.28-34 | 5.1-20 | 8.26-39 | |
| Jesus Crosses the Lake Again p93 | | 5.21 | 8.40 | |
| Jairus' Daughter and The Woman with the Issue of Blood p94 | 9.18-26 | 5.22-43 | 8.41-56 | |
| Jesus Heals Two Blind Men p95 | 9.27-31 | | | |
| Jesus Heals a Man who is Mute p96 | 9.32-34 | | | |
| Jesus is Rejected in Nazareth Again p96 | 13.54-58 | 6.1-6a | | |
| Jesus Travels: Teaching, Preaching and Healing p97 | 9.35-38 | 6.6b | | |
| Jesus Sends Out the Twelve p97 | 10.1,5-11.1 | 6.7-13 | 9.1-6 | |
| Herod's Paranoia and Jesus Learns of John's Execution p103 | 14.1-12 | 6.14-29 | 9.7-9 | |
| A Failed Attempt to Rest and Grieve p104 | 14.13-14 | 6.30-34 | 9.10-11 | 6.1-4 |
| Feeding the Five Thousand p105 | 14.15-23 | 6.35-46 | 9.12-17 | 6.5-17a |
| Jesus Walks on the Water p106 | 14.24-33 | 6.47-52 | | 6.17b-21a |
| A Seeking Multitude Finds Jesus in Capernaum p108 | | | | 6.22-24 |

| | MATTHEW | MARK | LUKE | JOHN |
|---|---|---|---|---|
| I am the Bread of Life p108 | | | | 6.23-65 |
| Offended Disciples Walk Away p110 | | | | 6.66-7.1 |
| What Truly Defiles People p111 | 15.1-20 | 7.1-23 | | |
| Jesus Heals the Syrophonecian Woman's Daughter p113 | 15.21-28 | 7.24-30 | | |
| Jesus Heals a Deaf Man and Others p113 | 15.29-31 | 7.31-37 | | |
| Feeding the Four Thousand p114 | 15.32-39a | 8.1-9 | | |
| No Sign at Dalmanutha, Magdala p115 | 15.39b-16.4 | 8.10-13 | | |
| Beware of the Yeast p115 | 16.5-12 | 8.14-21 | | |
| Blind Man at Bethsaida p116 | | 8.24-26 | | |
| Who Do People Say I Am? p117 | 16.13-28 | 8.27-9.1 | 9.18-27 | |
| The Transfiguration p118 | 17.1-9 | 9.2-10 | 9.28-36 | |
| Elijah and John p119 | 17.10-13 | 9.11-13 | | |
| Jesus Heals an Epileptic Boy p123 | 17.14-21 | 9.14-29 | 9.37-43a | |
| Jesus Speaks of His Death and Resurrection p124 | 17.22-23 | 9.30-32 | 9.43b-45 | |
| Peter, Temple Taxes and a Fish p125 | 17.24-27 | | | |

|  | MATTHEW | MARK | LUKE | JOHN |
|---|---|---|---|---|
| The Greatest in the Kingdom  p125 | 18.1-14 | 9.33-50 | 9.46-50 | |
| If Someone Sins Against You  p127 | 18.15-19 | | | |
| Parable of the Unforgiving Servant p127 | 18.20-35 | | | |
| A Disagreement between Jesus and His Brothers  p128 | | | | 7.1-9 |
| Jesus Travels Secretly to Jerusalem  p129 | | | 9.51-62 | 7.10 |

## Part 5: Public Ministry of Jesus
## d. The beginning of Sukkot until the beginning of Hanukkah
### (October - December, 27 CE)

|  | MATTHEW | MARK | LUKE | JOHN |
|---|---|---|---|---|
| Jesus Teaches in the Temple  p135 |  |  |  | 7.11-36 |
| Is Anyone Thirsty?  p136 |  |  |  | 7.37-8.1 |
| The Woman Caught in Adultery  p137 |  |  |  | 8.2-11 |
| The Light of the World  p138 |  |  |  | 8.12-20 |
| I Am From Above  p139 |  |  |  | 8.21-29 |
| Your Father is the Devil p139 |  |  |  | 8.30-59 |
| The Seventy Sent Out  p141 |  |  | 10.1-16 |  |
| The Seventy Return Rejoicing  p142 |  |  | 10.17-24 |  |
| Parable of the Good Samaritan  p143 |  |  | 10.25-37 |  |
| Jesus Visits Mary and Martha  p144 |  |  | 10.38-42 |  |
| Teaching on Prayer  p147 |  |  | 11.1-13 |  |
| Jesus Casts Out a Mute Demon  p148 |  |  | 11.14-26 |  |
| Who is Truly Blessed? p149 |  |  | 11.27-28 |  |
| This is an Evil Generation  p149 |  |  | 11.29-36 |  |
| Jesus Offends the Pharisees at Supper  p149 |  |  | 11.37-54 |  |

| | MATTHEW | MARK | LUKE | JOHN |
|---|---|---|---|---|
| Jesus Warns of Persecution Again p151 | | | 12.1-12 | |
| Parable of the Foolish Rich Man p151 | | | 12.13-21 | |
| Do Not Be Afraid, Little Flock p152 | | | 12.22-34 | |
| Parables About Being Ready p153 | | | 12.35-48 | |
| Warning about Family Conflict p154 | | | 12.49-53 | |
| Interpret the Times p154 | | | 12.54-59 | |
| The Galileans and the Fig Tree p155 | | | 13.1-9 | |
| Jesus Heals the Bent Over Woman p159 | | | 13.10-17 | |
| Parables of the Mustard Seed and the Yeast p160 | | | 13.18-21 | |
| The Narrow Door p160 | | | 13.22-30 | |

## Part 6: Public Ministry of Jesus
### e. The Beginning of Hanukkah until the approach of Passover
### (December, 27 CE - April, 28 CE)

|  | MATTHEW | MARK | LUKE | JOHN |
|---|---|---|---|---|
| Jesus Heals the Man Born Blind  p165 |  |  |  | 9.1-41 |
| The Good Shepherd p167 |  |  |  | 10.1-18 |
| The Jews Confront Jesus and Try to Kill Him p168 |  |  |  | 10.19-39 |
| Pharisees Warn Jesus About Herod  p169 |  |  | 13.31-35 |  |
| Jesus Leaves Jerusalem and Goes Beyond the Jordan  p170 |  |  |  | 10.40-42 |
| Jesus Heals a Swollen Man  p173 |  |  | 14.1-6 |  |
| Parable of the Lowest Place  p173 |  |  | 14.7-11 |  |
| Parable of the Great Supper  p174 |  |  | 14.12-24 |  |
| Count the Cost Before Following  p175 |  |  | 14.25-35 |  |
| Parables of the Lost: Sheep, Coins and Sons  p175 |  |  | 15.1-32 |  |
| Parable of the Dishonest Manager  p177 |  |  | 16.1-18 |  |
| Parable of the Rich Man and Lazarus  p178 |  |  | 16.19-31 |  |
| Stumbling, Forgiveness, Faith and Responsibility p179 |  |  | 17.1-10 |  |

| | MATTHEW | MARK | LUKE | JOHN |
|---|---|---|---|---|
| The Death and Raising of Lazarus  p 180 | | | | 11.1-53 |
| Jesus Goes to the Village of Ephraim  p187 | | | | 11.54 |
| Jesus Heals Ten Lepers p187 | | | 17.11-19 | |
| The Days of the Son of Man  p188 | | | 17.20-37 | |
| Parable of the Unrighteous Judge  p189 | | | 18.1-8 | |
| Parable of Two Men Praying  p189 | | | 18.9-14 | |
| Teaching on Divorce  p190 | 19.1-12 | 10.1-12 | | |
| Jesus Blesses the Little Children  p191 | 19.13-15 | 10.13-16 | 18.15-17 | |
| The Rich Young Ruler  p191 | 19.16-30 | 10.16-31 | 18.18-30 | |
| Parable of the Vineyard Laborers  p193 | 20.1-16 | | | |
| Jesus Explains What Awaits Him in Jerusalem p194 | 20.17-19 | 10.32-34 | 18.31-34 | |
| The Sons of Zebedee Ask for Honor  p194 | 20.20-28 | 10.35-45 | | |
| Jesus Heals a Blind Man near Jericho  p195 | | | 18.35-43 | |
| Jesus Dines with Zacchaeus  p196 | | 10.46a | 19.1-10 | |
| Parable of the Investors p196 | | | 19.11-28 | |
| Jesus Heals Two Blind Men  p197 | | 10.46b-52 | | |
| Passover Approaches  p198 | | | | 11.55-57 |

## Part 7: The Last Week:
## From Bethany to the Resurrection
## (April 23 - May 2, 28 CE)

| | MATTHEW | MARK | LUKE | JOHN |
|---|---|---|---|---|
| **Friday, April 23, 28 CE** | | | | |
| Jesus Prepares for His Jerusalem Entry  p203 | 21.1-6a | 11.1-6 | 19.29-34 | |
| Mary Anoints Jesus at Bethany  p204 | 26.6-13 | 14.3-9 | | 12.1-11 |
| **Saturday, April 24, 28 CE** | | | | |
| The Triumphal Entry p209 | 21.7-11 | 11.7-10 | 19.35-44 | 12.12-19 |
| Greeks and a Grain of Wheat  p210 | | | | 12.20-26 |
| A Voice out of the Sky p211 | 21.17 | 11.11 | | 12.27-43 |
| **Sunday, April 25, 28 CE** | | | | |
| Jesus Curses the Fig Tree  p215 | 21.18-19 | 11.12-14 | | |
| Jesus Cleanses the Temple  p215 | 21.12-13 | 11.15-18 | 19.45-46 | |
| Jesus Teaches and Heals in the Temple  p216 | 21.14-17 | 11.19 | 19.47-48 | |
| **Monday, April 26, 28 CE** | | | | |
| The Fig Tree is Withered p219 | 21.20-22 | 11.20-26 | | |
| By What Authority? p219 | 21.23-27 | 11.27-33 | 20.1-8 | |

| | MATTHEW | MARK | LUKE | JOHN |
|---|---|---|---|---|
| Parable of the Two Sons p220 | 21.28-32 | 12.1a | | |
| Parable of the Vineyard p221 | 21.33-46 | 12.1-12 | 20.1-8 | |
| Parable of the Marriage Feast p222 | 22.1-14 | | | |
| Pharisees and Herodians Question Jesus: Taxes p223 | 22.15-22 | 12.13-17 | 20.20-26 | |
| The Sadducees Question Jesus: Resurrection p223 | 22.23-33 | 12.18-27 | 20.27-39 | |
| A Scribe Questions Jesus: Greatest Commandment p224 | 22.34-40 | 12.28-34 | 20.40 | |
| Jesus Asks a Question: David's Lord p225 | 22.41-46 | 12.35-37a | 20.41-44 | |
| Beware of the Scribes p226 | | 12.37b-40 | 20.45-47 | |
| The Widows Mite p226 | | 12.41-44 | 21.1-4 | |
| The Seven Woes to the Scribes and Pharisees p226 | 23.1-39 | | | |
| Prophecy about Jerusalem's Destruction p228 | 24.1-2 | 13.1-12 | 21.5-6 | |
| Beginning of Birth Pains p229 | 24.3-14 | 13.3-13 | 21.7-19 | |
| The Abomination of Desolation p230 | 24.15-31 | 13.14-27 | 21.20-28 | |
| Parable of the Trees p232 | 24.32-44 | 13.28-33 | 21.29-33 | |
| Parable of the Wise and Foolish Servants p233 | 24.45-51 | 13.34-37 | | |
| Be Watchful p233 | | | 21.34-36 | |
| Parable of the Ten Virgins p233 | 25.1-13 | | | |
| Parable of the Talents p234 | 25.14-30 | | | |

|  | MATTHEW | MARK | LUKE | JOHN |
|---|---|---|---|---|
| Parable of the Sheep and Goats  p235 | 25.31-46 |  |  |  |
| Jesus' Daily Routine  p236 |  |  | 21.37-38 | 12.44-50 |
| The Conspiracy against Jesus  p237 | 26.1-5 | 14.1-2 | 22.1-2 |  |
| **Tuesday, April 27, 28 CE** |  |  |  |  |
| Judas Agrees to Betray Jesus  p241 | 26.14-16 | 14.10-11 | 22.3-6 |  |
| Preparation for the Passover p241 | 26.17-19 | 14.12-16 | 22.7-13 |  |
| The Last Supper  p242 | 26.20-29 | 14.17-25 | 22.14-30 |  |
| Jesus Washes Feet p243 |  |  |  | 13.1-22 |
| Jesus Privately Exposes the Betrayer  p245 |  |  |  | 13.23-30 |
| A New Commandment  p245 |  |  |  | 13.31-35 |
| First Warning for Peter p245 |  |  | 22.31-38 | 13.36-38 |
| Where are You Going?  p246 | 26.30 | 14.26 | 22.39 | 14.1-31 |
| **Wednesday, April 28, 28 CE** |  |  |  |  |
| Second Warning for Peter  p251 | 26.31-35 | 14.27-31 |  |  |
| I am the True Vine  p251 |  |  |  | 15.1-11 |
| No Longer Servants, but Friends  p252 |  |  |  | 15.12-16 |
| The World Will Hate You p252 |  |  |  | 15.17-16.6 |
| When the Helper Comes p253 |  |  |  | 16.7-16 |
| The Disciples' Confusion p254 |  |  |  | 16.17-22 |

|  | MATTHEW | MARK | LUKE | JOHN |
|---|---|---|---|---|
| Ask in My Name 254 |  |  |  | 16.23-33 |
| The Son Talks to the Father p255 |  |  |  | 17.1-26 |
| Jesus in Gethsemane p257 | 26.36-46 | 14.32-42 | 22.40-46 | 18.1-2 |
| Jesus is Arrested p258 | 26.47-56 | 14.43-52 | 22.47-53 | 18.3-12 |
| Jesus Sent to Annas p259 |  |  |  | 18.13-14, 19-23 |
| Jesus Sent to Caiaphas p260 | 26.57-66 | 14.53-64 | 22.54 | 18.24 |
| Peter's Denial p261 | 26.69-75 | 14.66-72 | 22.55-62 | 18.15-18, 25-27 |
| The Jews Mock and Beat Jesus p262 | 26.67-68 | 14.65 | 22.63-65 |  |
| Jesus Before the Sanhedrin p262 | 27.1 | 15.1a | 22.66-71 |  |
| Jesus Brought to Pontius Pilate p263 | 27.2,11 | 15.1b-2 | 23.1-7 | 18.28-38 |
| Jesus Before Herod Antipas p264 |  |  | 23.8-11 |  |
| Jesus Before Pilate and the Crowd p265 | 27.12-26a | 15.3-15a | 23.12-25a | 18.39-40 |
| The Gentiles Mock and Beat Jesus p266 | 27.26b-30 | 15.15b-19 |  | 19.1-8 |
| Pilate Speaks Privately to Jesus p267 |  |  | 23.15b | 19.9-16a |
| Judas' Repentance and Suicide p268 | 27.3-10 |  |  |  |
| The Way to Golgotha and the Crucifixion p269 | 27.31-38 | 15.20-28 | 23.26-34,38 | 19.16b-24 |

| | MATTHEW | MARK | LUKE | JOHN |
|---|---|---|---|---|
| Jesus on the Cross  p270 | 27.39-49 | 15.29-36 | 23.35-37,39-44 | 19.25-29 |
| Jesus Dies  p271 | 27.50-56 | 15.37-41 | 23.45b-49 | 19.30-37 |
| Jesus is Buried  p272 | 27.57-61 | 15.42-47 | 23.50-56a | 19.38-42 |
| **Thursday, April 29, 28 CE** | | | | |
| The Jews Request a Tomb Guard  p277 | 27.62-66 | | | |
| **Friday, April 30, 28 CE** | | | | |
| The Women Buy and Prepare Spices  p281 | | 16.1 | 23.56a | |
| **Saturday, May 1, 28 CE** | | | | |
| The Women Rest on the Sabbath  p285 | | | 23.56b | |
| An Angel Opens the Tomb  p285 | 28.2-4 | | | |
| **Sunday, May 2, 28 CE** | | | | |
| The Empty Tomb  p289 | | | | 20.1-10 |
| Jesus Appears First to Mary Magdalene  p289 | | 16.9-11 | | 20.11-18 |
| Jesus Appears to Other Women  p290 | 28.1,5-10 | 16.2-8 | 24.1-8 | |
| The Guards are Bribed  p291 | 28.11-15 | | | |
| The Women Tell the Disciples  p292 | | | 24.9-12 | |
| On the Road to Emmaus  p292 | | 16.12-13 | 24.13-35 | |
| Jesus Appears to the Disciples  p293 | 28.16-17 | 16.14 | 24.36-44 | 20.19-25 |

323

## Part 8: After the Resurrection until Ten Days before Shavuot (May 3 – June 10, 28 CE)

|  | MATTHEW | MARK | LUKE | JOHN |
|---|---|---|---|---|
| Thomas Sees and Believes  p299 |  | 16.14 |  | 20.26-31 |
| Jesus Appears by the Sea of Tiberias  p299 |  |  |  | 21.1-14 |
| Jesus Questions Peter p301 |  |  |  | 21.15-24 |
| The Great Commission p302 | 28.18-20a | 16.15-18 |  |  |
| Open Minds to Understand the Scriptures  p302 |  |  | 24.45-49 |  |
| Jesus' Final Instructions p303 |  |  | Acts 1.1b-8 |  |
| Jesus Ascends to the Father  p303 |  | 16.15-20a | 24.50-53; Acts 1.9-11 |  |
| The World Could Not Contain the Books  p304 | 28.20b | 16.20b | 24.53b | 21.25 |

# Appendix 2:
# Jesus' Ministry Calendar

As is true with this entire volume, my hope is that this ministry calendar will help the reader to appreciate the earthly life of Jesus as a truly historic occurrence. He was a real person who journeyed through months and seasons and years just as we do.

I believe that there are very good reasons for dating many (but certainly not all) of the events as they appear below. Passionate discussion and disagreement about such things should be encouraged as long as such discourse does not lead to disunity and a breaking of fellowship. As I stated in the Introduction to this volume, I take seriously the possibility that I could be wrong.

The Jewish calendar does not follow the same month and year format as our Gregorian calendar. The new month in the Jewish year begins when the first sliver of the new moon is sighted in Jerusalem. Although I have kept the Gregorian format for the *Jesus' Ministry Calendar*, I have marked when the new moon occurred during each month with a "**(NM)**" next to the date. The dates were taken from *TorahCalendar.com*.

The page numbers for each event are listed in parenthesis. For example, "+ *Jesus Cleanses the Temple (34),*" means that you will find the text for that event on page 34.

326

## February 27 CE

| SUN | MON | TUE | WED | THU | FRI | SAT |
|---|---|---|---|---|---|---|
| | | | | | | 1 |
| 2 | 3 | 4 | 5 | 6 | 7 | 8 |
| 9 | 10 | 11 | 12 | 13 | 14 | 15 |
| 16<br>+ Jesus is Baptized (23) | 17<br>+ Jesus is in the wilderness for 40 days until March 28 | 18 | 19 | 20 | 21 | 22 |
| 23 | 24 | 25 | 26   (NM) | 27 | 28 | |

## March 27 CE

| SUN | MON | TUE | WED | THU | FRI | SAT |
|---|---|---|---|---|---|---|
| | | | | | | 1 |
| 2<br><br>+ Jesus is in the Judean wilderness during this week | 3 | 4 | 5 | 6 | 7 | 8 |
| 9<br><br>+ Jesus is in the Judean wilderness during this week | 10 | 11 | 12 | 13 | 14 | 15 |
| 16<br><br>+ Jesus is in the Judean wilderness during this week | 17 | 18 | 19 | 20 | 21 | 22 |
| 23<br><br>+ Jesus is in the Judean wilderness during this week | 24 | 25 | 26 | 27   (NM) | 28<br><br>+ John testifies about Jesus (27) | 29<br><br>+ Jesus returns from the wilderness<br><br>+ "Behold the Lamb" |
| 30<br><br>+ Jesus' First Disciples (28) | 31<br><br>+ Into Galilee and More Disciples (29) | | | | | |

## April 27 CE

| SUN | MON | TUE | WED | THU | FRI | SAT |
|---|---|---|---|---|---|---|
| | | 1<br><br>+ Wedding at Cana (33) | 2 | 3 | 4 | 5 |
| 6 | 7 | 8 | 9 | 10<br><br>+ Jesus Cleanses the Temple (34) | 11<br><br>**PESHACH (Passover)** | 12<br><br>**UNLEAVENED BREAD** begins<br><br>+ Jesus Talks with Nicodemus (35) |
| 13<br><br>**FIRST FRUITS** | 14 | 15 | 16 | 17 | 18<br><br>**UNLEAVENED BREAD** ends | 19 |
| 20<br><br>+ Jesus and His Disciple begin Baptizing in Judea | 21 | 22 | 23 | 24 | 25 | 26    **(NM)** |
| 27 | 28 | 27 | 30 | | | |

## May 27 CE

| SUN | MON | TUE | WED | THU | FRI | SAT |
|---|---|---|---|---|---|---|
| | | | | 1 | 2 | 3 |
| 4 | 5 | 6 | 7 | 8 | 9 | 10 |
| 11<br><br>+John's Final Testimony about Jesus (41) | 12 | 13 | 14 | 15 | 16 | 17 |
| 18<br><br>+ Jesus Leaves Judea | 19<br><br>+ Jesus visits Samaria (42) | 20 | 21 | 22 | 23<br><br>+ Jesus Heals a Nobleman's Son (44) | 24 |
| 25 (NM) | 26 | 27 | 28 | 29 | 30 | 31<br><br>+ Jesus Heals the Man at the Pool of Bethsaida (45) |

## June 27 CE

| SUN | MON | TUE | WED | THU | FRI | SAT |
|---|---|---|---|---|---|---|
| **1**<br><br>**SHAVUOT (Pentecost)** begins<br><br>+ Jesus teaches in the Temple | **2**<br><br>**SHAVUOT (Pentecost)** ends<br><br>+ Jesus Leaves for Galilee | **3** | **4** | **5** | **6** | **7**<br><br>+ Jesus is Rejected in Nazareth (53) |
| **8**<br><br>+ Jesus goes to Capernaum (54) | **9** | **10** | **11** | **12** | **13**<br><br>+ Jesus Calls Four Fishermen (55) | **14**<br><br>+ The Man with the Unclean Spirit (55)<br><br>+ Jesus Heals Peter's Mother-in-Law (56) |
| **15**<br><br>+ Jesus leaves Capernaum (without the fishermen)... | **16**<br><br>...He begins to proclaim the Gospel of the Kingdom around Galilee... | **17**<br><br>...using Capernaum as his home base... | **18**<br><br>This first teaching and ministry tour lasts until early July. | **19** | **20** | **21** |
| **22**<br><br>+ Jesus travels alone (?) through Galilee during this week | **23  (NM)** | **24** | **25** | **26** | **27** | **28** |
| **29**<br><br>+ Jesus travels alone (?) through Galilee during this week | **30** | | | | | |

## July 27 CE

| SUN | MON | TUE | WED | THU | FRI | SAT |
|---|---|---|---|---|---|---|
| | | **1**<br>+ Jesus travels alone (?) through Galilee during this week | **2** | **3** | **4** | **5** |
| **6** | **7**<br>+ The Call by the Sea (61) | **8**<br>+ Sermon on the Mount (62) | **9** | **10** | **11** | **12** |
| **13** | **14**<br>+ Jesus Heals a Leper (68) | **15** | **16** | **17** | **18** | **19** |
| **20** | **21**<br>+ A Paralytic and Four Friends (68) | **22** | **23 (NM)**<br>+ Jesus Calls Matthew (69) | **24** | **25** | **26** |
| **27** | **28** | **29**<br>+ Old Garments and New Wine (70) | **30** | **31** | | |

332

## August 27 CE

| SUN | MON | TUE | WED | THU | FRI | SAT |
|---|---|---|---|---|---|---|
| | | | | | **1** | **2**<br>+ Jesus is Lord of the Sabbath (73)<br>+ Jesus Heals a Man with a Withered Hand (74) |
| **3** | **4**<br>+ Crowds Come to Jesus (74) | **5**<br>+ Jesus Chooses the Twelve (75)<br>+ Sermon on the Plain (76) | **6**<br>+ Jesus Heals the Centurion's Servant (78) | **7**<br>+ Jesus Raises the Widow's Son (79)<br>+ Jesus Answers John's Concerns (80) | **8**<br>+ Dinner at Simon's: A Woman Forgiven (82) | **9** |
| **10** | **11**<br>+ Jesus Travels with the Twelve and Certain Women (83) | **12** | **13**<br>+ Jesus Cast out a Demon (83)<br>+ The Sign of Jonah the Prophet (85) | **14**<br>+ Who is My Family? (85) | **15**<br>+ Parable of the Farmer and Other Parables are Told and Explained (86) | **16** |
| **17** | **18**<br>+ Jesus Calms the Sea (91) | **19**<br>+ The Gerasene Demoniac (92) | **20**<br>+ Jairus' Daughter and the Woman with the Issue of Blood (94) | **21  (NM)**<br>+ Jesus Heals Two Blind Men (95)<br>+ Jesus Heals Mute (96) | **22** | **23**<br>+ Jesus is Rejected in Nazareth Again (96) |
| **24**<br>+ Jesus Travels (97)<br>+ Jesus Sends out the Twelve (97) | **25**<br>+ The Twelve are travelling and ministering in pairs until mid-September | **26** | **27** | **28** | **29** | **30** |
| **31**<br>+ The Twelve are travelling... | ...and ministering in pairs during this week | | | | | |

## September 27 CE

| SUN | MON | TUE | WED | THU | FRI | SAT |
|---|---|---|---|---|---|---|
| | **1**<br><br>+ The Twelve are travelling and ministering in pairs during this week | **2** | **3**<br><br>+ Herod's Paranoia (103) | **4** | **5** | **6** |
| **7**<br><br>+ The Twelve are travelling and ministering in pairs during this week | **8**<br><br>+ Jesus Learns of John's Execution (103) | **9** | **10**<br><br>+ The Twelve Return | **11**<br><br>+ A Failed Attempt to Rest and Grieve (104)<br>+ Feeding the Five Thousand (105) | **12**<br><br>+ Jesus Walks on the Water (106)<br>+ Great Healings in Gennesaret (107)<br>+ A Seeking Crowd Finds Jesus in Capernaum (108) | **13**<br><br>+ I Am the Bread of Life (108)<br>+ Offended Disciples Walk Away (110)<br>+ What Truly Defiles a Man (111) |
| **14** | **15**<br><br>+ Jesus Heals the Syrophoenician Woman's Daughter (113) | **16** | **17**<br><br>+ Jesus Heals a Deaf Man and Others (113) | **18** | **19**<br><br>+ Feeding the Four Thousand (114)<br>+ No Sign at Dalmanutha, Magdala (115) | **20**   **(NM)**<br><br>+ Beware the Yeast (115) |
| **21**<br><br>**YOM TERUAH (Day of Trumpets)** | **22**<br><br>+ Blind Man at Bethsaida (116) | **23**<br><br>+ Who do People Say I Am? (117) | **24** | **25** | **26** | **27** |
| **28** | **29** | **30**<br><br>**YOM KIPPUR (Day of Atonement)**<br><br>+ The Trans-figuration (118)<br>+ Elijah and John (119) | | | | |

# October 27 CE

| SUN | MON | TUE | WED | THU | FRI | SAT |
|---|---|---|---|---|---|---|
| | | | **1**<br>+ There are many entries for this day and are listed at the bottom of this page. * | **2**<br>+ Jesus travels secretly to Jerusalem (129) | **3** | **4** |
| **5**<br>**SUKKOT**<br>(Tabernacles)<br>begins | **6**<br>+ Jesus teaches in the Temple... | **7**<br>...during Sukkot (135) | **8** | **9** | **10** | **11** |
| **12**<br>**SUKKOT**<br>(Tabernacles)<br>ends<br><br>+ Is Anyone Thirsty? (136) | **13**<br>+ The Woman Caught in Adultery (137)<br>+ The Light of the World (138)<br>+ I Am from Above (139)<br>+ Your Father is the Devil (139) | **14**<br>+ The Seventy Sent Out (141) | **15**<br>+ The Seventy Return Rejoicing (Luke records this event as a summary of the staggered return of the Seventy that occurred between Sukkot and Hanukkah.) | **16**<br>+ The Parable of the Good Samaritan (143) | **17**<br>+ Jesus Visits Mary and Martha (144) | **18** |
| **19**  **(NM)**<br>+ During the next two months, Jesus travels and teaches (with the Twelve) to the villages where the Seventy have gone. | **20**<br>** From mid-October until December 12th (the eve of Hanukkah), there are many events and teachings without specific dates... | **21**<br>...A few take place on a Sabbath. The events and teachings have been randomly spread out, keeping the order in which Luke records them. | **22**<br>+ Teaching on Prayer (147) | **23** | **24**<br>+ Jesus Casts Out a Mute Demon (148) | **25** |
| **26**<br>+ Jesus travels to the villages where the Seventy have gone during this week | **27**<br>+ Who is Truly Blessed? (149) | **28** | **29**<br>+ This is an Evil Generation (149) | **30** | **31** | |

**\*Wednesday, October 1, 27 CE**

+ Jesus Heals an Epileptic Boy (123)
+ Jesus Speaks of His Death and Resurrection (124)
+ Peter, Temple Tax and a Fish (125)
+ The Greatest in the Kingdom (125)
+ If Someone Sins Against You (127)
+ Parable of the Unforgiving Servant (127)
+ A Disagreement Between Jesus and His Brothers (128)

## November 27 CE

| SUN | MON | TUE | WED | THU | FRI | SAT |
|-----|-----|-----|-----|-----|-----|-----|
| | | | | | | **1**<br>+ Jesus is travelling this whole month to the villages where the Seventy have been |
| **2**<br>+ Jesus continues to travel | **3**<br>+ Jesus Offends the Pharisees at Supper (149) | **4** | **5** | **6** | **7** | **8** |
| **9**<br>+ Jesus continues to travel | **10** | **11**<br>+ Jesus Warns of Persecution Again (151) | **12**<br>+ Parable of the Foolish Rich Man (151)<br><br>+ Don't be Afraid Little Flock (152) | **13** | **14** | **15** |
| **16**<br>+ Jesus continues to travel | **17** | **18** (NM)<br>+ Parables about Being Ready (153) | **19**<br>+ Warning about Family Conflict (154) | **20** | **21** | **22** |
| **23**<br>+ Jesus continues to travel<br>——<br>30 | **24** | **25** | **26**<br>+ Interpret the Times (154) | **27** | **28**<br>+ The Galileans and the Fig Tree (155) | **29** |

## December 27 CE

| SUN | MON | TUE | WED | THU | FRI | SAT |
|---|---|---|---|---|---|---|
| | **1** | **2** | **3** | **4** | **5** | **6**<br><br>+ Jesus Heals a Bent Over Woman (159) |
| **7** | **8**<br><br>+ Parable of the Mustard Seed and the Yeast (160) | **9** | **10**<br><br>+ The Narrow Door (160) | **11** | **12** | **13**<br><br>+ Jesus Heals the Man Born Blind (165) |
| **14**<br><br>**HANUKKAH (Dedication) begins**<br><br>+ The Good Shepherd (167) | **15** | **16**<br><br>+ The Jews Confront and Try to Kill Jesus (168) | **17** | **18** **(NM)**<br><br>+ The Pharisees Warn Jesus about Herod (169) | **19** | **20**<br><br>**HANUKKAH (Dedication) ends** |
| **21**<br><br>+ Jesus Leaves Jerusalem and Goes Beyond the Jordan (170) | **22**<br><br>** From late December until late February (when Lazarus dies), there are events and teachings without specific dates... | **23**<br><br>...A few take place on a Sabbath. The events and teachings have been randomly spread out, keeping the order in which Luke records them. | **24** | **25** | **26** | **27** |
| **28** | **29** | **30** | **31** | | | |

## January 28 CE

| SUN | MON | TUE | WED | THU | FRI | SAT |
|-----|-----|-----|-----|-----|-----|-----|
| | | | | 1 | 2 | 3<br><br>+ Jesus Heals a Swollen Man (173)<br>+ Parable of the Lowest Place (173)<br>+ Parable of the Great Supper (174) |
| 4 | 5 | 6 | 7<br><br>+ Count the Cost before Following (175) | 8 | 9 | 10 |
| 11<br><br>+ Parables of the Lost: Sheep, Coins and Sons (175) | 12 | 13 | 14 | 15 | 16 | 17     (NM) |
| 18 | 19 | 20 | 21 | 22 | 23 | 24 |
| 25 | 26 | 27 | 28<br><br>+ Parable of the Dishonest Manager (177) | 29 | 30 | 31 |

## February 28 CE

| SUN | MON | TUE | WED | THU | FRI | SAT |
|---|---|---|---|---|---|---|
| 1 | 2 | 3 | 4 | 5 | 6 | 7 |
| 8 | 9 | 10 | 11 | 12 | 13 | 14 |
| 15    (NM) | 16 | 17 | 18 | 19<br><br>+ Parable of the Rich Man and Lazarus (178) | 20<br><br>+ Stumbling, Forgiveness, Faith and Responsibility (179) | 21 |
| 22<br><br>+ The Death and Raising of Lazarus (180) | 23<br><br>**(The events surrounding the death and raising of Lazarus... | 24<br><br>... took place over a week and a half period of time.) | 25 | 26 | 27 | 28 |
| 29 | | | | | | |

## March 28 CE

| SUN | MON | TUE | WED | THU | FRI | SAT |
|---|---|---|---|---|---|---|
|  | 1 | 2<br><br>+ Jesus Goes to the Village of Ephraim (187) | 3 | 4 | 5 | 6 |
| 7 | 8 | 9 | 10 | 11 | 12 | 13 |
| 14 | 15 | 16    (NM) | 17 | 18<br><br>The barley is not mature enough when the NEW MOON is sighted, so there is... | 19<br><br>... an Adar Bet (13th month) before the new calendar year begins. | 20 |
| 21<br><br>** Because of the Adar Bet (13th month), Jesus now has an extra five weeks before... | 22<br><br>...he needs to go up to Jerusalem for Passover. The events and teachings during this time do not have any specific date attached to | 23<br><br>...them. They have been randomly spread out, keeping the order in which Luke records them. | 24<br><br>+ Jesus Heals Ten Lepers (187) | 25 | 26<br><br>+ The Days of the Son of Man (188)<br><br>+ Parable of the Unrighteous Judge (189) | 27 |
| 28<br><br>+ Parable of Two Men Praying (189) | 29 | 30 | 31<br><br>+ Teaching on Divorce (190) |  |  |  |

# April 28 CE

| SUN | MON | TUE | WED | THU | FRI | SAT |
|---|---|---|---|---|---|---|
| | | | | **1** | **2**<br>+ Jesus Blesses the Little Children (191) | **3** |
| **4** | **5**<br>+ The Rich Young Ruler (191)<br><br>+ Parable of the Vineyard Laborers (193) | **6** | **7** | **8**<br>+ Jesus Explains what Awaits Him in Jerusalem (194) | **9** | **10** |
| **11**<br>+ The Sons of Zebedee Ask for Honor (194) | **12** | **13**<br>+ Jesus Heals a Blind Man Near Jericho (195) | **14** (NM) | **15** | **16**<br>+ Jesus Dines with Zacchaeus (196) | **17** |
| **18**<br>+ Parable of the Investors (196) | **19** | **20** | **21**<br>+ Jesus Heals Two Blind Men (197) | **22**<br>+ Passover Approaches (198) | **23**<br>+ Jesus Prepares for His Jerusalem Entry (203)<br><br>+ Mary Anoints Jesus at Bethany (204) | **24**<br>+ The Triumphal Entry (209)<br><br>+ Greeks and a Grain of Wheat (210)<br><br>+ A Voice Out of the Sky (211) |
| **25**<br>** The events and teachings for this week are quite numerous. The following page has a calendar week just for this time period | **26**<br>**See the next page | **27**<br>**See the next page | **28**<br>**See the next page | **29**<br>**See the next page | **30**<br>**See the next page | |

## April 25 – May 1, 28 CE

| SUN | MON | TUE | WED | THU | FRI | SAT |
|---|---|---|---|---|---|---|
| 25 | 26 | 27 | 28 | 29 | 30 | 1 |
| + Jesus Curses the Fig Tree (215)<br><br>+ Jesus Cleanses the Temple (215)<br><br>+ Jesus Teaches and Heals in the Temple (216) | + The Fig Tree is Withered (219)<br><br>+ By What Authority? (219)<br><br>+ Parable of the Two Sons (220)<br><br>+ Parable of the Vineyard (221)<br><br>+ Parable of the Marriage Feast (222)<br><br>+ Pharisees and Herodians Question Jesus: Taxes (223)<br><br>+ The Sadducees Question Jesus: Resurrection (223)<br><br>+ A Scribe Questions Jesus: Greatest Commandment (224)<br><br>+ Jesus Asks a Question: David's Lord (225)<br><br>+ Beware of the Scribes (226)<br><br>+ The Widows Mite (226)<br><br>(Continued) | + Judas Agrees to Betray Jesus (241)<br><br>+ Preparation for the Passover (241)<br><br>+ The Last Supper (242)<br><br>+ Jesus Washes Feet (243)<br><br>+ Jesus Privately Exposes the Betrayer (245)<br><br>+ A New Commandment (245)<br><br>+ First Warning for Peter (245)<br><br>+ Where are You Going? (246) | + Second Warning for Peter (251)<br><br>+ I am the True Vine (251)<br><br>+ No Longer Servants, but Friends (252)<br><br>+ The World will Hate You (252)<br><br>+ When the Helper Comes (253)<br><br>+ The Disciples' Confusion (254)<br><br>+ Ask in My Name (254)<br><br>+ The Son Talks to the Father (255)<br><br>+ Jesus in Gethsemane (257)<br><br>+ Jesus is Arrested (258)<br><br>+ Jesus Sent to Anna (259)<br><br>+ Jesus Sent to Caiaphas (260)<br><br>+ Peter's Denial (261)<br><br>+ The Jews Mock and Beat Jesus (262)<br><br>+ Jesus before the Sanhedrin (262)<br><br>+ Jesus Brought to Pontius Pilate (263)<br><br>(Continued) | + The Jews Request a Tomb Guard (277) | + The Women Buy and Prepare Spices (281) | + The Women Rest on the Sabbath (285)<br><br>+ An Angel Opens the Tomb (285) |

## April 25 – May 1, 28 CE
## (continued)

| SUN | MON | TUE | WED | THU | FRI | SAT |
|---|---|---|---|---|---|---|
| 25 | 26 | 27 | 28 | 29 | 30 | 1 |
|  | + Seven Woes to the Scribes and Pharisees (226)<br><br>+ Prophecy about Jerusalem's Destruction (228)<br><br>+ Beginning of Birth Pains (229)<br><br>+ The Abomination of Desolation (230)<br><br>+ Parable of the Trees (232)<br><br>+ Parable of the Wise and Foolish Servants (233)<br><br>+ Be Watchful (233)<br><br>+ Parable of the Ten Virgins (233)<br><br>+ Parable of the Talents (234)<br><br>+ Parable of the Sheep and Goats (235)<br><br>+ Jesus' Daily Routine (236)<br><br>+ The Conspiracy against Jesus (237) |  | + Jesus Before Herod Antipas (264)<br><br>+ Jesus Before Pilate and the Crowd (265)<br><br>+ The Gentiles Mock and Beat Jesus (266)<br><br>+ Pilate Speaks Privately to Jesus (267)<br><br>+ Judas' Repentance and Suicide (268)<br><br>+ The Way to Golgotha and the Crucifixion (269)<br><br>+ Jesus on the Cross (270)<br><br>+ Jesus Dies (271)<br><br>+ Jesus is Buried (272) |  |  |  |

## May 28 CE

| SUN | MON | TUE | WED | THU | FRI | SAT |
|---|---|---|---|---|---|---|
| | | | | | | **1**<br><br>+ The Women Rest on the Sabbath (285)<br><br>+ An Angel Opens the Tomb (285) |
| **2**<br><br>+ The Empty Tomb (289)<br><br>+ Jesus Appears First to Mary Magdalene (289)<br><br>+ Jesus Appears to the Other Women (290)<br><br>+ The Guards are Bribed (291)<br><br>+ The Women Tell the Disciples (292)<br><br>+ On the Road to Emmaus (292)<br><br>+ Jesus Appears to the Disciples (293) | **3** | **4** | **5** | **6** | **7** | **8** |
| **9** | **10**<br><br>+ Thomas Sees and Believes (299) | **11** | **12** | **13** | **14 (NM)** | **15** |
| **16** | **17** | **18** | **19** | **20** | **21** | **22** |
| **23**<br><br>———<br><br>**30** | **24**<br><br>———<br><br>**31** | **25** | **26**<br><br>+ Jesus Appears by the Sea of Tiberias (299)<br><br>+ Jesus Questions Peter (301) | **27** | **28** | **29** |

## June 28 CE

| SUN | MON | TUE | WED | THU | FRI | SAT |
|---|---|---|---|---|---|---|
| | | 1 | 2 | 3 | 4 | 5 |
| 6 | 7 | 8<br><br>+ The Great Commission (302)<br><br>+ Open Minds to Understand the Scriptures (302) | 9<br><br>+ Jesus' Final Instructions (303) | 10<br><br>+ Jesus Ascends to the Father (303) | 11 | 12 (NM) |
| 13 | 14 | 15 | 16 | 17 | 18 | 19 |
| 20<br><br>**SHAVUOT (Pentecost)** begins | 21<br><br>**SHAVUOT (Pentecost)** ends | 22 | 23 | 24 | 25 | 26 |
| 27 | 28 | 29 | 30 | | | |

# ENDNOTES

(1) This volume uses "demonized" instead of "demon possessed" because the editor believes that it is a more accurate translation of the original Greek word **daimonizomenoi**. It also avoids many of the contemporary connotations and difficulties associated with the phrase "demon possessed." A fuller discussion of this topic is presented in **Power Healing** by John Wimber, pp 109-110.

(2) Matthew records that there were two demonized men who approached Jesus and were healed. Mark and Luke focus on Jesus' interaction with the man who had the Legion.

(3) John 6.4 is the main (and possibly, only) problematic text for the one year ministry theory. On the one hand, there is very little (if any) textual evidence that would give us any reason to question that John 6.4 was part of the original manuscript. On the other hand, there are significant internal problems with the idea that a Passover was at hand and Jesus did **not** go up to Jerusalem as the Torah required. Although I have left John 6.4 in the text of **A Life Worth Knowing**, I am much more comfortable explaining the tension created by this text as the result of a scribal error as opposed to being the result of Jesus behaving in a way that contradicts his mission as a Jewish Messiah.

(4) Mark records that they were heading across the lake to Bethsaida. John records that they were heading for Capernaum. The distance from Bethsaida to Capernaum is about 7 kilometers (4 miles).

(5) The story of the woman caught in adultery (John 7.53-8.11) is not found in the oldest manuscripts. Most scholars do not believe that it was part of John's original Gospel.

(6) Some of the earliest manuscripts do not include Mark 16:9–20.

# ABOUT THE COMPILER

David R. Barrett is an elementary school teacher who makes his home in Ontario, Canada with his beautiful wife and four amazing children.

*Other Titles available from*
*Fresh Ink Media*

*St. Catharines, Ontario*

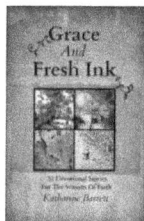

## Grace and Fresh Ink: 52 Devotional Stories for the Seasons of Faith
by Katharine Barrett

"Grace. It's in the everyday. In real life. It is under the laundry pile, and behind the desk. It's there in our sun filled days, dark sleepless nights and all of our beautiful mess. It covers us. It swirls around us, and whispers for us to stop, see, and know it. When we do, we find gratitude spilling out around us, fresh ink on the pages of our lives..."

With these words, the author invites you to walk through the seasons, sharing stories of living, loving and everyday Grace.

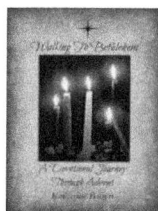

## Walking to Bethlehem: A Devotional Journey through Advent
by Katharine Barrett

It's time to journey to Bethlehem! What will our footprints look like? How will we be released from hopelessness, unrest, sorrow and loneliness; into hope, peace, joy and love?

As we journey to Bethlehem together, can we invite Emmanuel, our redeeming, compassionate God to transform our story and illuminate our lives?

Imagine... we're travelling together to Bethlehem, each carrying a light. Older ones helping the younger, in expectation of Emmanuel's coming. I'm envisioning a ribbon of light, the illumination of God's redeeming, transforming work in our lives, and I am hearing the words of Isaiah:

The people who walk in darkness will see a great light...

Join us on a four week, daily devotional journey as we celebrate the coming of Emmanuel!

*\*Included in the book is an interactive candle-lighting script for families with young children.*

\*For more information and to order e-book or print copies, visit the Fresh Ink Media web site at http://www.graceandfreshink.com/.

351